Peter Gi

PLAYS TWO

Peter Gill was born in 1939 in Cardiff and started his professional career as an actor. A director as well as a writer, he has directed over eighty productions in the UK, Europe and North America. At the Royal Court Theatre in the sixties, he was responsible for introducing D. H. Lawrence's plays to the theatre. The founding director of Riverside Studios and the Royal National Theatre Studio, Peter Gill lives in London. His plays include *The Sleepers Den* (Royal Court, London, 1965), *Over Gardens Out* (Royal Court, London, 1968), *Small Change* (Royal Court, London, 1976), *Kick for Touch* (National Theatre, London, 1983), *Cardiff East* (National Theatre, London, 1997), *Certain Young Men* (Almeida Theatre, 1999), *The York Realist* (English Touring Theatre, 2001) and *Original Sin* (Sheffield Crucible, 2002).

by the same author

PLAYS ONE
(*The Sleepers Den*, *Over Gardens Out*, *Small Change*, *Kick for Touch*, *Mean Tears*, *In the Blue*)

adaptations

A PROVINCIAL LIFE (after Chekhov)
THE CHERRY ORCHARD (by Chekhov)
AS I LAY DYING (after the novel by Faulkner)
THE SEAGULL (by Chekhov)

PETER GILL

Plays Two

Cardiff East

Certain Young Men

The York Realist

Original Sin

The Look Across the Eyes

Lovely Evening

with an introduction by
Nicholas Wright

faber and faber

This collection first published in 2008
by Faber and Faber Limited
3 Queen Square London WC1N 3AU

Typeset by Country Setting, Kingsdown, Kent CT14 8ES
Printed in England by CPI Bookmarque, Croydon, Surrey

A CIP record for this book is available from the British Library

0-571-24539-0

2 4 6 8 10 9 7 5 3 1

Contents

Introduction

I first heard of Peter Gill in 1959 through a friend of mine at Drama School, Harriet Devine. Her father, George Devine, had recently left home and, in the wake of this, her mother, Sophie, had taken Peter on as a lodger: he was then a young actor whom Harriet had befriended when they were both dressers at the Lyric, Hammersmith.

Sophie would encourage her daughter to ask her friends around on Sunday afternoons to her beautiful, shabby eighteenth-century house on the bank of the Thames in Hammersmith for those loose, warm gatherings of young people that lonely parents enjoy. Sophie would bake a cake, serve tea and do the washing up. This last task took her most of the afternoon, and nobody could ever quite work out where she got her seemingly endless supply of dirty crockery from: it seemed to come from nowhere and end up nowhere, to the point where we suspected her of washing the same plates many times over.

Peter was twenty. He was thin, wiry, black-haired and bright-eyed, very attractive both because of his looks and because of the packed electric energy that emanated from him. Very talkative, highly opinionated, very good at organising complicated parlour games. Politically he was combative. As a colonial boy, I was baffled and excited by his assaults on private education, or his outrage at some media slur on a trade union. He was a radical who could never have joined a movement: that, in a way, is the most basic thing you need to know about him.

Sophie adored him. In the twenties, she, her sister Percy and a friend had formed the theatre design group Motley, which had introduced simplicity and a kind of unforced elegance into the theatre of their day, and she was still a working designer. A lot of what I will say about Peter will point up the contradictions in him, and this is one: he was a theatrical subversive who nevertheless had a love of the theatre that Sophie had helped to create – the (by then) unfashionable art theatre of Michel St Denis, Komisarjevsky and John Gielgud. 'Oh what shall I do?' she would say on a Sunday evening. The designs for something or other were due the next morning and she couldn't think of a thing. 'Don't worry, Sophie,' Peter might say. 'What about an ankle-length white dress with a pink rosebud in her buttonhole and a straw boater, like you did for Angela Baddeley in 1937?' Sophie would lick her brush and draw.

He was an extremely good actor, but often out of work. The RSC took him on in its first days at the Aldwych. But as a mouthy, non-Cambridge intellectual, derisive of theory of any kind, the RSC wasn't his natural home. In fact, acting at all wasn't really the job for anyone so controlling.

His connections at the Royal Court were excellent: there was Sophie, there was Tony Richardson, living at the top of the house in an extravagant flat populated by iguanas and toucans. And Peter's best friend was Bill Gaskill, a major figure at the Court, and later to run it. Clearly Peter would end up there in some form or another: the only question was how and what as. Offers were slow in forthcoming until, for a very short period, he became the Royal Court's press officer, a job for whose emollient demands he was spectacularly unsuited.

For quite a while, he was simply a figure at the Court, someone who didn't demand to be paid except when doing some specific job: assisting on a main-house show, or doing a Sunday night production without decor. (If this sounds vague, I ought to explain that in those days it was often quite difficult to know whether you were actually working at the Royal Court or not. You obviously couldn't ask, for fear of getting the wrong answer, so you had to go to the accountant's office on Friday morning, ask for your pay-packet and see if you got one.) Employed or not, Peter clearly belonged there.

I joined the Court as Casting Director in 1967, in time to work on Peter's revival of D. H. Lawrence's *The Daughter-in-Law*, along with *A Collier's Friday Night* and *The Widowing of Mrs Holroyd*, making up the Court's Lawrence trilogy. I'd not seen him for a while and never worked with him, and found him very different. Although very ambitious, he had held off from directing until he felt he was ready to roll. Now, with only a handful of shows behind him, he was obsessed. Reports came in from the rehearsal room of his maniacal attention to detail, of his springing onto the set to adjust the angle of an actor's hand, the disposition of a prop, the weight of an inflection. What strikes me as odd, after all these years, is that everyone connected with the productions knew exactly what he was doing: he was transforming the dead tradition of kitchen-sink naturalism into a poetic form, one that gave a classic nobility to working-class life.

My memories of the Lawrence trilogy include a run-through onstage of *The Widowing of Mrs Holroyd* at which, when the dead miner was washed by his widow and mother, both Bill Gaskill and I blubbed like babies; a particular moment in *A Collier's Friday Night*, still one of the half-dozen best productions I've ever seen, when a marvellous, long-forgotten character actor, John Barrett, tipsily wound up his watch before going to bed – and why was that so beautiful? But it was. And the get-in of *Collier*, when Peter's assistant, Barry Hanson, and I looked round to see Peter running out of the stalls. We found him in the alleyway, vomiting blood. An ambulance took him to hospital, where he nearly died: his ulcer had burst.

Bill Gaskill took over *Collier* and *Mrs Holroyd* and Jane Howell took over *The Daughter-in-Law*. Both said afterwards that there'd been nothing for them to do bar run the technicals: the work had been done. Gaskill took daily reports to Peter in his hospital bed. Wired up and half-unconscious, he was determined to protect the austere beauty of his shows. There's a scene in *Collier* where the bread burns in the oven. Gaskill suggested mildly that he was thinking of arranging for dry ice to simulate the smoke. Peter was outraged. 'Dry ice?' he croaked through his oxygen mask. 'Who do you think I am? Franco Zeffirelli?'

A year or two later I was in deep trouble, having opened the Theatre Upstairs with three ill-chosen plays, all very badly done. I knew that my next request for a pay packet was likely to be embarrassing, and I had the sense to realise that my only hope was to get in someone cleverer than myself to help me out.

Peter had just finished his third play, *Over Gardens Out*. I remember my intoxication at the grace and simplicity of the dialogue. Quite recently I came across my diary of that time and found that I'd written, on a page of its own, the phrase 'the beating heart'. I meant that the dialogue had a transparency that led me into his characters' inner lives.

I programmed the play as quickly as I could, along with a revival of Peter's earlier play, *The Sleepers' Den*. Everything went right for the shows and, after that, for the Theatre Upstairs as well, though not for Peter. His *Duchess of Malfi* in the main house was eagerly awaited. There was a cast of sixteen, eight playing principals, eight playing everyone else. Bill Dudley designed it, with a line of salvaged doors up each side, and the predominant colour was ochre. In the Lawrences, Peter had played with physical choreography in a realistic context: here there was no realism, instead a formal, almost mannerist, interplay of bodies, faces packed together like a Giotto. The actors were young and unfamiliar with the fruity acting that people expect in Webster. I can't describe how deeply the show was disliked by everyone except for a few fans. The critics hated it, so did the Royal Court grandees and the audience was mostly not present. All I can say is that I'm sure all the criticisms were very justified, but I'd never seen a show like that before and I've spent the last thirty years looking at bits of it repeated all over the place, in theatre, in opera and in dance. Peter had shot something new into the ether, and it landed. What it cost him was enormous. I've often wondered what it's like to give everything you've got – twice – and to receive two such devastating rebuffs, one from your own body, and one from the world.

When talking about Peter, there's a potential cause of confusion, which is whether one's talking about the playwright or the director. It's a confusion that he has done nothing to dispel. All his plays in this collection were first directed by himself, all (except for *The York Realist*) in his distinctively stripped-out, impressionistic style. On an open stage, where even a single chair stands out as a major visual statement, different places coalesce into one, one group of characters counterpoints another, memory nudges its way into actual time, just as in life. A extremely good director, who had just read *Cardiff East* and quite fancied directing it, complained to me that since the action was all over the place, and there weren't any stage directions, nobody but Peter could direct it anyway, and that this was doubtless what he intended.

Many of his plays, and three in this collection, are set in the community he comes from: working-class life in Wales. It is poor, so poor that you have to stay quiet when the rent man knocks on the door. It is Catholic, it is strong, it is dignified, it is riven with neurosis. It is underpinned by a profound sense of melancholy: Peter never depicts the place of his youth without a sense of sadness and loss. These houses will be pulled down, perhaps already have been; the warmest values are most embodied in people who are old and about to die. Family life, neighbourly support, men's friendships are subverted by insecurity, loss and death. Common to everyone is a class-based attitude to a social system that they both detest as an injustice and welcome as a target of their wit. The dialogue is a political statement: working-class conversation, with its trim vocabulary, its hesitations, its habitual use of shared knowledge and local references, is made as musical and precise as great prose of the Enlightenment.

A recurring figure is the young man who escapes his class, as much as anyone does, and is for ever unable to convey to the people he loves the cost and rewards of getting away from them: young Christopher's destiny in *The Look Across the Eyes*.

In the same way, for John in *The York Realist*, a young man whose natural home, whatever it used to be, is now the world of contemporary theatre, middle-class good taste and art movies, the class divide is both an element of love and an impediment to it. One of Peter's first jobs as an aspirant director was being Bill Gaskill's assistant on the York mystery plays, and no doubt the context of the play owes a lot to this. It's unusual in Peter's writing for its traditional qualities: a sturdy two-act structure, discreetly effective exposition and, uniquely among his plays, the need for a realistic set. The original 'York Realist' was one of the authors of the mystery plays, so called for his success at breathing new life into an old form, and, when I first saw the play I wondered whether Peter had changed his style in a conscious reference to him. What I'm sure he hadn't planned was its huge commercial success at the Royal Court, followed by a transfer to the West End.

Certain Young Men – one of the two explicitly gay plays in this collection – suggests, in its teasingly fractured way, that metropolitan life is as rich in melancholy as that of working-class Wales. The other, *Original Sin*, is his reinterpretation of the inexhaustibly enigmatic *Lulu* plays by Frank Wedekind. Peter assisted on the Royal Court production of Wedekind's *Spring Awakening*, and it was he who introduced me to the very notion of Lulu in the days when that siren beauty – or that blank screen onto which a series of men project their fantasies – used to be reincarnated once a year at the Academy Cinema in the shape of Louise Brooks. 'If only Lulu could be a young man,' he'd say. So here you are.

Nicholas Wright
September 2008

Going the Distance

Recollecting the Green Park is the only way in;
Butting through a sequence of film where nothing
Happens, where there is only stasis and finishing;
Sucking the dryness for the blue about you,
The hectic in the smoke, rose over dark.
Until access comes like oil into tightness,
Pouring warmth over my head. Making you,
First a son managing an inland farm with his mother,
After a father gored, and then head boy and girl
love –
Was she for you what you are?
And you into achieving and with no feeling of
hiraeth.
Until a meeting in a coffee bar in Soho, full of chess
players
And open-necked shirts and dedication to lost causes;
Talking to a woman asserting the significance
Of metropolitan statues, with George the Third
In the Haymarket as the most apposite. And seeing
through
This absence of rock and roll, you, luminous and
swart,
Walking with me into north London in the summer
night,
Past the Craven A factory and on, urgent and
committed
And an early hours fuck on Primrose Hill,
Identifying your enthusiasm for sex and for Court
Theatre plays.
And then in your student room in Gordon Square,

Your ruthless, hetero good nature and your chapel
carefulness,
In an insistence on medicated lubricant.
When you qualified refused to go on the wards, the
laboratory
And the bedroom your place of interest, the epitome
Of a young doctor's care and carelessness, a
transferable, indiscriminate impulse
From your maternal concern to easy liaisons as part
of your bargain.
Me, too young and fearful and unemancipated to
give up comparison
In your seeming to find anything young and
effeminate interesting,
And we hurt with too much and too little. A break-
up in the park
In what was two-part imprudence.
For you, the inevitable political conservatism in
success.
The power you gave me over you always remaining
after
Sometimes tens of years, always reasserted on
meeting;
Until your death took away an unconsidered distant
constant.
So that now in new turmoil, turning over this scrap
between us,
This grief must be my thanks. Sugar on a fire that
would not catch.

Peter Gill

CARDIFF EAST

For Mary

Cardiff East was first performed in the Cottesloe auditorium of the National Theatre, London, on 6 February 1997 with the following cast:

Neil Daniel Evans
Stella June Watson
Tommy Matthew Rhys
Annie Gwenllian Davies
Darkie Andrew Howard
Anne-Marie Lowri Palfrey/Stacey Nelson
Ryan Alex Parker/Richard Pudney
Michael Kenneth Cranham
Shirley Melanie Hill
Billy Mark Lewis Jones
Marge Susan Brown
Dolly Elizabeth Estensen
Vera Di Botcher
Carol Lisa Palfrey
Len Karl Johnson
Charlie Windsor Davies
Bingo Caller's Voice Anthony O'Donnell

Directed by Peter Gill
Designed by Alison Chitty
Lighting by Andy Phillips
Music by Terry Davies

Characters

Neil

Stella

Tommy

Annie

Darkie

Anne Marie

Ryan

Michael

Shirley

Billy

Marg

Dolly

Vera

Carol

Len

Charlie

Bingo Caller

The play takes place on the east side of Cardiff

When the play begins:

Darkie, Shirley, Billy, Marge, Dolly, Vera, Carol, Len and Charlie are sitting together at the back.

Not all of them are facing front.

Michael, Stella, Neil, Tommy and Annie are placed as indicated at the beginning of the first section.

Anne Marie and Ryan enter from the sides.

After this, when characters leave the main action, they rarely leave the stage. Possibly the children do.

ONE

Michael, right. Stella, right of centre, waiting. Neil in bed, left of centre, asleep. Annie, left, about to take a pill. Tommy, left, crosses Annie to Neil.

Neil Who's that?

Stella Is that you?

Tommy It's all right, it's me.

Neil What?

Tommy Sssh.

Stella No.

Neil You can't come in here.

Tommy I've got to. Sssh.

Annie Perhaps I won't take one.

Neil Get out, Tommy.

Tommy I can't.

Neil Go on.

Tommy No.

Neil Tommy. Get out.

Tommy Come on, don't be like that.

Neil is sitting up in bed.

Annie If I could sleep without anything, that would be a good thing. It would be.

Neil How did you get in?

Tommy The key was under the mat.

Neil Oh Jesus.

Tommy What?

Neil I should have brought it in with me.

Tommy Well, you didn't.

Neil Oh Christ.

Tommy What?

Neil I said to leave it out for me because I thought I lost mine.

Tommy How did you get in?

Neil I had it with me, I found it in my pocket. Have you brought it in?

Tommy Yeah, yeah, it's on the table. See how good I am? They'll think you brought it in.

Tommy begins to get undressed.

Neil I hope I've still got my key. Don't get undressed.

Tommy Yeah.

Neil Where's my key? Give me my trousers.

Tommy What?

Neil Give me my jeans, go on.

Tommy, trousers round his ankles, hands Neil a pair of jeans from the floor.

Thank fuck, here it is. No it isn't, where is it?

Neil gets out of bed.

Tommy What's the matter with you?

Neil I keep losing things.

Tommy Get back in bed.

Neil No, I got to find my key.

Tommy No you haven't. Get back in bed, go on.

Neil gets back into bed.

Neil You're not stopping here, Tommy, I told you.

Tommy I've got to.

Neil I told you, you can't.

Tommy Yeah.

Neil No.

Tommy I've got to.

Neil You can't. What you undressed for?

Tommy I'm sleeping here.

Neil You're not.

Tommy Yeah, I am.

Neil You can't.

Tommy I've got to. Come on, let me in.

Neil Tommy, no.

Tommy Come on.

Neil What you doing here anyway? Why didn't you go home?

Tommy I owes my mother money. My father put the bolt on the door. Come on, Neil, come on, eh?

Neil lets Tommy into bed.

You're good to me, you are.

Neil Am I?

Tommy Don't be like that. I'm sorry, Neil.

Neil All right then, shift over.

Tommy Don't you want me here?

Neil No.
I wonder where my key is?

Tommy No, don't worry, you'll find it.

Neil I hope I haven't lost it.

Tommy Don't worry, you'll find it in the morning.

Neil Come on then, and keep your hands to yourself.

Tommy I might.

Darkie comes from the back to Stella.

Darkie You still up?
Mam.
You're up late.

Mam.
What's the matter, eh?
Mam?

Annie It would please him if I didn't take one. He's a nice boy. He says I'll feel better if I come off them. I've been taking them twenty, twenty-five years. Oh well, he's a nice boy.

Neil Move over.

Tommy What?

Neil Go on, move over.

Darkie What's the matter?

Stella You know.

Darkie What?

Stella What time is this, then?

Annie I should say my prayers, that's what I should do.

Stella What time is this, then?

Darkie I don't know what time it is.

Stella Oh, that's nice.

Darkie Don't let's have an argument. You weren't waiting up for me. If I was in, you'd be up, don't blame me, all right?

Stella I was waiting up for you.

Darkie What was you waiting up for me for?

Stella I don't know, I'm stupid, that's why. I was afraid you was stopping out and I didn't know.

Darkie Mam, when did I last stop out? What if I was stopping out? If I was stopping out, I would have told you. I'm going to bed out of this.

Stella I can't trust you no more.

Darkie You can.

Stella I can't.

Darkie What?

Stella I can't.

Darkie Why?

Stella And I don't like where you hang about.

Darkie What?

Stella You goes to some places, I know you. You don't have any money. You earns good money, what are you spending it on?

Darkie Did you get your wages? Did I pay the TV?

Stella Yes.

Darkie You can't wait up for me like this, I can't have it.

Stella You don't know what it's like. I can't go to sleep if you're not in. I was expecting you earlier.

Darkie Did I say I'd be in early? Did I say what time I'd be in?

Stella No.

Darkie I can't go on with this, I thought we'd stopped all this. What's started this up again?

Stella I don't know. It's silly.

Darkie If I was in, you'd have gone to bed by now.

Stella I might have, I suppose.

Darkie You would have.

Stella I might have.

Darkie Why don't you go to bed now?

Stella What you shoving me off to bed for? I can't sleep.

Darkie Why don't you take something?

Stella No, I don't take that rubbish, I've had all that before.

Darkie Do you want me to get you something?

Stella No thank you.

Darkie I will.

Stella No, I don't want anything.

Darkie I'll have something.

Tommy What's the matter?

Neil You are. My mother will kill me if she finds you in here.

Tommy No she won't, she likes me, she won't mind.

Neil Won't she?

Tommy I've stayed here enough times. I must have stayed here millions of times, she won't mind.

Neil What about the morning?

Tommy What about the morning? Are you working?

Neil You know I'm not.

Tommy Will she come in here?

Neil No.

Tommy Will your father come in here?

Neil He won't come in here.

Tommy Will Denise?

Neil No.

Tommy Will Tony?

Neil No.

Tommy See.

Neil How can he?

Tommy What?

Neil He's married.

Tommy Well then, there we are.

Neil Oh . . .

Tommy Will Terry?

Neil He's away playing rugby. My mother might come in.

Tommy Will she mind?

Neil No.

Tommy Right then.

He lights two cigarettes.

Do you want a cigarette?

Neil No.

Tommy I'll have one. Do you want one? Do you, Neil? Do you want a cigarette?

Neil I wonder where my key is.

Tommy Don't worry.

Neil Right, I'm going to sleep.

Tommy No, don't go to sleep, I've lit you a fag.

Tommy gives Neil the cigarette.

Neil Where have you been?

Tommy Where do you think?

Neil Why didn't you stay in her house?

Tommy Nah, she does my head in.

Neil I thought you liked her.

Tommy I do. There's too much hassle. I come home.

Neil reaches for an ashtray.

Neil Where'd you go?

Tommy In town.

Neil Did you walk back?

Tommy No, I got a taxi.

Neil You haven't got no money.

Tommy I know. I didn't pay.

Neil Oh no.

Tommy I stopped in the main road.

Neil Yeah –

Tommy By Darkie Jones's house.

Neil And?

Tommy And then I said to the man, like, I had to go in to get the money.

Neil Yeah?

Tommy So I went like down the side and then down the back and over the fence and down the gully and up the side street and up here.

Neil A driver's going to be faster than you one of these days. It's not funny. You're going to get a driver who'll give you a good hiding.

Tommy You've done it.

Neil Only with you I've done it. Why didn't you go home?

Tommy I told you why I didn't go home. I can't go home.

Neil What you going to do?

Tommy I don't know. I don't know what I'm going to do. And I owes Darkie money.

Neil What for?

Tommy He got some stuff down the docks.

Neil What stuff? You're soft, you are. That's a mug's game, that is. You want to quit that, you do. You don't want to do that, do you hear me, Tommy? Do you? You can't stuff your mother's wages up your nose.

Tommy I know. I'm stopping.

Stella I saw Tracy today.

Darkie Oh aye? Where did you see her?

Stella She come over here.

Darkie What's she want round here?

Stella What's the matter with you? I don't think they're very cheerful. Lisa's off work.

Darkie Oh aye.

Stella I don't think they're very happy.

Darkie I don't suppose they are.

Stella No wonder they calls you Darkie.

Darkie What's the matter? They knows what I think. I told them when he picked up with that piece, what'd happen.

Stella I don't like you talking like that; you know I don't.

Darkie Well, what's her name then? You don't even know her name.

Stella I do know her name.

Darkie They don't ever mention her name. It's all a comedy. She's my age. He thinks he's a kid. He's a rhinestone cowboy. He wants more sense, he's bloody stupid.

Stella She seemed fed up.

Darkie With him?

Stella Not with your father. No.

Darkie She'll have 'em out of there. She's not going to put up with them two much longer. She've got a baby now. I suppose they'll want to come home next.

Stella No, they're thinking of taking a flat.

Darkie Oh yeah? Where they going to find a flat? Do you know what the price of flats are?

Stella Well, Lisa earns good money.

Darkie As long as he never comes back here.

Stella I don't think that's likely.

Darkie You never know.

Stella No wonder they calls you Darkie.

Darkie I'll see him. I'll have a pint with him. I saw him last week.

Stella Did you?

Darkie We had a drink. He's a kid. He dresses like a kid.

Stella Would you mind if they came back home?

Darkie As long as they behaves themselves. No, I don't mind, as long as he don't come back. You wouldn't let him back.

Stella I hope I wouldn't.

Darkie See! He's been gone two years. It's better like this, it's better.

Stella You might go.

Darkie I won't go. If he comes back I'll go. If he comes back here ever I'll be off out of it.

Stella Not likely from what I can see. He's got a new baby.

Darkie takes a pill.

What you taking that for? What's that?

Darkie I got a headache. Sure you don't want anything? A cup of anything? Do you want me to get you something?

Stella No. I'm all right.

Neil How are you going to pay your mother?

Tommy My father's going away tomorrow to work. I'll have to talk to her.

Neil What about Darkie? He'll do you.

Tommy He won't. I'll pay him. He's good, Darkie is.

Neil turns to Tommy.

Neil Why does he let you hang round with him?

Tommy And you. You know.

Neil I don't know.

Tommy You do know.

Neil Always Bobby. You're daft, you are. Put this out for me and let's go to sleep.

Tommy Don't go to sleep, talk to me.

Neil What about?

Tommy Did you go over Susan's?

Neil Yeah?

Tommy You come home.

Neil Yeah.

Tommy You stayed in.

Neil Yeah.

Stella Where have you been, anyway?

Darkie You know where I been.

Stella I don't know where you been. Well, who is she?

Darkie She's just a girl.

Stella You went out with her last night.

Darkie I did.

Stella And the other night.

Darkie I did. And tomorrow night I will.

Stella You'll go now.

Darkie Oh Mam, don't. It's only a girl. I've had girlfriends.

Stella Who is she?

Darkie You know who she is.

Stella Is it serious?

Darkie No, it isn't serious. Don't. No . . . Well . . . don't.

Stella They tell me she got a baby.

Darkie I know.

Stella It's not your baby, is it?

Darkie Look. No. Stop it. No it isn't.

Stella Whose is it? I doubt if she knows.

Darkie Right, that's it. I'm off out of this.

Stella You'll go now.

Darkie I won't go.

Stella Picking up crumbs like your father.

Darkie I'm not like my father.

Stella I knew something like this would happen. You should be married by now.

Darkie If I was married I'd be gone.

Stella I know. You shouldn't be home now, you should be settled by now. This is through me. You'll go.

Darkie I won't go, because I don't want to go. You've got to stop. You've got to. Every time I'm out. I'm not Bobby. Do you want me to go? I'm not my father, I'm not Bobby. Nothing's going to happen to me.

Stella You don't understand, when you know what can happen. I tell you, I know things can happen.

Darkie Yes, I know. It was an accident, Mam.

Stella He shouldn't have been over there. You've got to listen to me. Climbing. Oh dear dear dear. This is why your father went.

Darkie Why? He went because of that other piece.

Stella I couldn't cope.

Darkie You mean he couldn't cope.

Stella Well, I couldn't.

Darkie He couldn't cope. You cooked him meals.

Stella I sometimes think I won't get any better, but I was very bitter, you know, upset, upset when he went after. I wouldn't like to go through that again.

Darkie You don't have to go through any of it again.

Stella I'm so silly.

Darkie You are.

Anne Marie and then Ryan enter quickly from the left, crossing Annie, Tommy, Neil, Darkie and Stella to meet Michael. Billy and Shirley come from the back.

Some of the following action includes Darkie and Stella, who are unaware of it.

Anne Marie Michael. Michael. Oh dear, come on, Michael.

Michael What is it, what's the matter?

Ryan Anne Marie!

Anne Marie turns to Ryan.

Anne Marie Sssh! Sssh! What is it?

Shirley I'll kill you.

Ryan Can you go in and tell them to stop?

Michael Come in.

Billy Shut it.

Anne Marie Why didn't you stay upstairs?

Ryan They're fighting, that's why. They kept quiet and then they started again.

Billy Shut it. Shut it.

Shirley Where are you, you pig?

Michael to the children.

Michael Come in. You go upstairs in the front room.

Shirley Get out, get out. Swine that you are, if you're so clever, if you're so clever . . .

Billy Aye, that's enough of that – shouting like that. What's the matter with you?

Shirley You're a pig, you're a real pig, what you said.

Michael It'll be all right.

The children go to the back.

Billy Shouting like that – what's the matter with you? Loud mouth. You're hopeless, you're nothing.

Shirley Shut up, you. You want setting fire to.

Michael goes to Shirley and Billy.

Billy Ay, ay, you. No . . . Michael. Hey. Hey. What's this?

Shirley Get out, you swine.

Michael What's this, then?

Billy See, she's . . .

Shirley You don't know what you said.

Billy Sssh, sssh, no.

Shirley No.

Billy Sssh. Yes. Well. No. All right, Michael?

Michael Yes.

Billy Where's the kids?

Shirley See you – what you . . . They all right, Michael?

Billy They're all right, don't you worry, aren't they, Michael?

Shirley Lot you cares –

Billy All right, Michael?

Michael Aye, fair. You going to be quiet now? Oh you two.

Shirley I'll kill him. I'll kill you, swine that you are.

Billy You haven't got the nerve. You're weak, you are.

Shirley Honestly, Billy, I'll put your face in, I'll go to the police.

Billy Don't be silly.

Shirley I will.

Michael Quieten this down, eh?

Shirley Oh, Michael, please, get rid of this swine for me, will you?

Michael Come on now, Billy, let's quieten down.

Billy You all right, Michael? Yeah I love him, Michael, I do.

Michael You two.

Billy Where are they?

Michael They're all right.

Billy Go and get 'em in, go on.

Shirley Shut up. They're all right.

The baby starts to cry.

Oh, there's the baby. Get out, get out, get out. I'm ashamed.

Michael Why are you ashamed?

Billy All right eh, Michael.

Shirley I'll kill you.

Billy Aye, aye, aye, aye. That'll be the day. You're hopeless. Get 'em in. Get the baby.

Shirley We'll leave them there, we'll leave them. They're all right, Michael?

Michael They're all right.

Billy goes for the baby.

You had a lot to drink?

Shirley I've had a drink. I've got a right to have a drink.

Michael It's firewater with you two. You get silly and then – It's not even Saturday night.

Shirley He tries to make a fool of me.

Billy carries the baby in.

Shirley You makes a fool out of me.

Billy No, don't be silly.

Shirley Don't shut me up. You do, you do. Give me the baby.

Billy Be more of a lady, ladylike.

Shirley See, he's been like this all day. He's got the needle. See, he's needling me. He's gone quiet now, see, now you're here. Now he's made me lose my temper. He's such a sneak. Get a job, get a job, get a job then, you lazy drunk swine you are. He has a dig.

Billy Aye, aye.

Shirley If he's so clever why doesn't he keep his job? He drunk his redundancy money.

Billy I haven't. You're a liar.

Shirley Am I? No job's good enough. I've got to work, why don't he?

Michael I don't know.

Shirley Because I know people he looks down on, where my dadda worked. I go up the Hayes, on the stalls, on Saturdays. He thinks that's funny.

Billy Fifteen p for your satsumas.

Shirley He thinks that's funny. He makes a fool of my friends. How do I get my veg? You're a pig, Billy, you're a real pig, you're a pig what you said.

Billy What I say? What she talking about?

Shirley Waking the baby up.

Billy She's asleep.

Shirley He's a sneak. He's gone quiet now, now you're here. You don't know, see, you bloody – he thinks he's better than me – he's been making fun of me again in front of my kids because I does a Saturday job where I used to work.

Billy I don't.

Shirley You do.

Billy I don't, I don't.

Shirley He just pushes me. He gets me in this state so I will say anything. He starts me. He makes me feel bad. See what you've done? You're happy now. You're a lazy bloody sod. I don't care, he knows I don't mind, I don't, that he can't find a job. It's not his fault. I don't mind doing this and that when he doesn't earn anything. He earned a few bob last week. He knows that, don't you?

Billy Shall I get them in?

Shirley takes the baby.

Shirley No, leave them, there, they're all right, aren't they Michael?

Billy Yes, they'll be all right.

Michael You quiet now?

Shirley Yeah. He'll go to sleep now, see, now he's caused this. He's give up now.

Michael OK?

Billy What you talking about me for?

Annie I should say my prayers. Look at me. And I've got a perfectly good dressing gown. I wonder if I should go up and dressed?

Michael OK? OK?

Annie And now my leg is starting. Dear. Oh dear.

Michael OK?

Shirley I'm tired.

Michael And me.

Annie I couldn't open a bottle of beetroot this morning and then I thought of Harry. Oh dear. I used to bottle my own.

Shirley I won't sleep.

Darkie You comin' up Mam?

Stella Aye, go on. **Anne Marie** Michael.

Michael It's all right, they're quiet now. Time for bed. Goodnight.

Neil What time you going to work in the morning?

Tommy I'm not going. Packed it in.

Neil Why?

Tommy They put a woman in charge.

Neil So?

Tommy So what. Don't shout at me.

Neil Come on let's go to sleep.

Tommy All right.

Tommy puts his cigarette out. Neil turns on his side.

Don't turn your back.

Neil I sleep on my side. You knows I sleep on my side.

Tommy Come on.

Neil No, leave me alone, you queer bent bastard.

Tommy You like it.

Neil I don't.

Tommy Afterwards you don't, in a minute you will. Give me your hand.

He takes Neil's hand and puts it under the bedclothes.

That's better.

Neil Stop it, Tommy.

Tommy Ssh, ssh, turn into me.

Neil Don't, Tommy.

Tommy Come on.

Neil Don't.

Tommy Come on, Neil.

Neil turns to Tommy.

Yeah, that's right.

Neil Do it quiet.

Annie I can't sleep.

TWO

Michael right. Neil in bed asleep. Marge carries washing to Michael.

Marge Do this for me will you, love?

Michael Good morning, brother.

Marge Good morning, love.

Michael You're early.

Marge My machine's broken, Jimmy's away. I told him it was going, he'll do it when he gets back.

Michael I'll have a look at it.

Marge Oh no, you'll do it for good.

Michael Well, you'll have to get someone in then. Give it here then.

Marge Hang on, let me check Tommy's jeans. He left five pounds in them last week. It come out useless. Have you seen him?

Michael No.

Marge Wait till I see him! His father locked the door on him.

Michael Hurry up, I've got toast on.

He goes to get the toast.

Marge Is the kettle on?

Michael What?

Marge Put the kettle on.

Michael Shall I put the kettle on? Do you want a piece of toast?

Marge No, I don't really want a cup of tea. I've had about six cups. I'm all over the place this morning.

Tommy, already dressed, enters with two cups of tea, a brown envelope and five cigarettes.

Tommy Here.

Neil Did you put sugar in it?

Tommy No, I never put sugar in it, you don't like sugar.

Neil takes one of the cups.

Neil What time is it?

Tommy Late. Your mother left you this.

Neil What?

Tommy You've got to cash it for her, she left a note.

Neil Give it here.

Tommy gives him the envelope.

Tommy And she left you five fags.

He gives them to Neil.

Neil Do you want one?

Tommy I'd rather have a smoke. Got anything to smoke?

Neil These.

Tommy Haven't you? You have. Where do you keep it?

Neil I haven't got any.

Tommy Honest?

Neil I got a little bit.

Tommy Where?

Neil There.

Tommy Where?

Neil My shoe.

Tommy goes to Neil's shoe.

Tommy Here's your key.

Neil Is it?

Tommy I told you.

Neil Gis it here!

Tommy hands Neil the key.

I'll put it safe.

Tommy What else you got in here? Ah, ha.

Neil What?

Tommy Durex.

Neil Put it back.

Tommy I can use it on you.

Neil You fucking won't.

Tommy For protection.

Neil Shut up. Roll up.

Tommy Hang on, hang on.

He begins to make a joint.

Why don't you get up?

Neil In a minute.

Tommy I'm hungry. Do you want something to eat?

Neil After. Give us a smoke first.

Tommy Hang on. Why don't you get up, Neil?

Neil I will.

Tommy Here you are.

Tommy having done the honours, they smoke.

Neil What's it like out?

Tommy Great.

Neil (*indicating the joint*) Gis us . . .

Tommy Get up first.

Neil In a minute.

Tommy No, now. Then you can have this.

Neil gets out and sits on the side of the bed. They smoke.

Marge is holding out a shirt. Michael eating toast.

Marge Whose shirt is this then? Jimmy's. He says he won't wear short sleeves. When he put this on? He's got two other shirts like it he won't wear. He won't put them on. Like you, you haven't put that sweater on, you've had since Christmas.

Michael I will.

Marge What would you do without a machine? There's no launderette, where's the nearest launderette?

Michael I don't know.

Marge Up Crwys Road. For students. To think I used to get real pleasure out of washing his shirts. I didn't have a washing machine for . . . OO . . . I used Mam's. No, he's good. They're all good. They'll all put them in the machine. Tommy – all his decent clothes, he won't let me touch them. When I was washing his shirts when we were first married I could feel his mother watching me.

Michael He gone for long, Jimmy?

Marge He might be back tomorrow. Even now I like to look at their shirts, if I like it, if it looks nice and it suits them. This is a nice shirt. Cotton – whose is it? It's those cheap silk ones I don't like.

Michael What's the matter with you? Talking about shirts? Don't take all the washing out. Shirts. Give them to me. What's the matter with you?

Marge Tommy, I'm checking his pockets.

Michael Our mam used to go through all our things to see if there was lipstick on our handkerchiefs or collars.

Marge Oh, I know what I wanted to ask you. How does 'Ave Maria' go?

She sings the Bach/Gounod 'Ave Maria'.

Michael That's right.

Marge But there's another one.

Michael Yes.

Marge How does it go?

Michael I don't know. Why do you want to know?

Marge The old lady next door, over the back, her sister died. You know, she used to have the fish shop. She wants it for the funeral. She wants Mario Lanza but the crematorium don't have it. You'd think they would.

Michael Why should a crematorium have a Mario Lanza tape?

Marge I think they should.

Michael Oh, you!

Marge They don't even have 'Ave Maria'. I said I'd try and get it for her but I don't know which one to get. She wants one she heard on *Songs of Praise.*

Michael Oh, God.

Marge begins to sing.

Marge 'Ave . . .'

Michael Shut up, Marge.

Marge Well, poor woman. *Songs of Praise.* I love *Songs of Praise.* (*Singing.*) 'The rhythm of life is a wonderful thing . . .' You miserable sod. Lovely. (*Singing.*) 'Morning has broken . . . '

Michael No doctrine. No ideas. No morals.

Marge (*singing*) 'How great Thou art, how great Thou art . . .' You'd never think you were in a seminary.

Billy and Shirley come to the left of Michael and Marge.

Shirley Don't say you're sorry, all right?

Billy I'm not going to say I'm sorry. Where you been?

Shirley Where'd you think I been?

Billy I don't know.

Shirley Down the school, down the nursery. What do you think?

Billy You're lucky I'm not violent. I'm not violent, you know.

Shirley Lucky.

Billy You're fortunate. You don't deserve it. You wants a good hiding, I think. Only I wouldn't.

Shirley You wouldn't.

Billy Have I ever hit you, have I? You ask for it all the time you do, you do.

Shirley Shut it, and go back to bed.

Billy You're used to all that, your old man used to hit hell out of your mother. This was always a rough house.

Shirley I'll get the police to you again, I will. I'll get my case taken up like those women.

Billy Don't talk stupid. Stupid. You couldn't if you tried.

Shirley I will.

Billy Shut it. Shut it, you. You don't know what you're talking about. You're stupid, you look stupid. I'm going out.

Annie goes to Marge and Michael.

Michael Hello.

Annie Hello, do you want to put a bet on, Michael? I'm going down the betting shop.

Michael Oh yes, Annie, thanks. Here it is. I want a ten p Yankee. I've written the horses out, one pound twenty including tax, OK?

Annie Yeah. What about him next door?

Michael Oh, he'll have a bet. They were at it again last night.

Annie T . . . t . . . t . . . t . . .

Michael That was a performance.

Marge Well, she's . . .

Annie I'm going round his father's.

Marge Gambling mad, you lot.

Annie I've had a bet every day since I was fourteen.

Marge Do you like washing, Annie?

Annie I don't much. I don't know what we did without a washing machine. I washed and ironed fourteen shirts on Sunday, that's the first time I've ever ironed a shirt on a Sunday.

Marge Why?

Annie Teresa broke her arm and our Paddy, you know him, he likes an evening shirt. She usually does the shirts on a Sunday so I did them for her. Harry always thought I washed his shirts by hand till the day he died because I always put them on a hanger. He never knew. But then he liked corned beef from the shop, he didn't like it from a tin.

Michael From a tin? Where did he think it came from in the shop?

Annie You couldn't persuade him, he said it was different. I used to cut it thin. He never knew the difference. Like his shirts. There used to be a Chinese laundry in Bridge Street, and when I was little I used to take all the shirts there, my father's and my brothers' collars, and my brothers always said the man would kidnap me. I didn't like to go in by myself. Anyway, one day I went and there was no one else in there and the man came through the curtains from the back of the shop with his big cut-throat razor in his hand, and I ran out screaming and my brother came after him. Poor man, he'd only been shaving. I've always been frightened of Chinamen.

Michael You don't see many Chinamen round here.

Marge Annie, how does 'Ave Maria' go?

Tommy Where we going afterwards?

Neil I don't know, I only just got up.

Tommy I'm going to see Darkie in work.

Neil What for? You owes him money.

Tommy I know. I'm telling him I need a job. He knows a bloke, a builder, I'm going to see if there's any work, you want to come?

Neil What doing?

Tommy I don't know, plastering, anything.

Neil Plastering, you can't plaster.

Tommy I can plaster, I've tried plastering.

Neil You're not a plasterer. It'll be labouring. What else we doing?

Tommy Do you want to go swimming?

Neil Aye, all right. I haven't got any money.

Tommy I can get us in. I know a bloke on the entrance.

Neil I want to go swimming in town.

Tommy Well, we'll get in there, then.

Neil How we going to get in?

Tommy We'll have to borrow off your mother, when we've cashed this.

Neil No.

Tommy How much you got? I got one pound five.

Neil I got fifty p and four fags.

Tommy We can get fags.

Neil How can we get fags? I'm not thieving.

Tommy We can get fags. Darkie'll give us fags.

Neil Why is Darkie like that?

Tommy Because he likes us.

Neil I know that. Why?

Tommy You know why.

Neil I don't see it.

Tommy I keep trying to tell you.

Neil I know you keep trying to tell me. What you trying to tell me?

Tommy Why.

Neil I know why but I don't see it.

Tommy Because of Bobby.

Neil I know. I don't get it.

Tommy Because . . .

Neil You're stupid, you are. I'm getting dressed.

Tommy Because . . .

Neil Don't bother.

Vera comes from the back to Michael and Marge and Annie.

Vera Hello, Michael. (*To Marge.*) I've been round your house, I thought you'd be here. I've been to get a sympathy card for Mrs Walsh.

Marge I've got to do that. You can get any kind of card in that shop but a decent Christmas card.

Vera I think they do nice cards. Do you like this?

Annie 'From the two of us to the two of you.'

Vera No – that's for my neighbour's anniversary – this one.

Michael raises his eyebrows.

Annie That's nice, that's nice – very nicely expressed. Very nice.

Vera That was a right performance in there, I heard.

Michael No, they're all right.

Vera That's always been a rough house; her father was a scrumpy drinker. You going to bingo?

Annie No. This afternoon I might. I'm putting a bet on.

Vera I heard you won ten pounds on the lottery.

Annie I did, I won ten pounds.

Marge He's all right, she's the one.

Michael Shirley – she's all right.

Annie His father was a terrible man for betting. He was my husband's best man, Charlie, they were both terrible for betting and Charlie was worse. He was a bookie's runner one time. There were three bookies in this street.

He was a terrible man for betting. He had the first big payout at the Castle Bingo. He won it.

Marge How much?

Annie Oh, thousands and thousands. He gambled it all away. He's quiet now.

Vera Have you ever been over there?

Annie No, I don't like big bingo.

Vera It's like Las Vegas over there. You should see the Ladies – gold taps and soap dishes. They went the first week, the soap dishes.

Marge What's it like over there?

Vera The toilets – the powder room I should say – you should see them. You going to bingo?

Annie This afternoon I might.

Marge She goes to them all.

Annie Do you?

Marge Yeah. The County, the Splott, the Gaiety –

Annie I've never been up there. I haven't been there since I saw – what was it? – the man who'd lost his arms in the war – Frederick March was in it. Dear. Oh well. Never mind. Well, I'm going in next door to see if he wants a bet.

Vera He still going to Gracelands, next door? He tried to sell the house to go to Gracelands.

Marge He never!

Vera He tried to sell the house to go to Gracelands. For the funeral, mind you. He wanted to sell the house. He wanted to sell the house.

Michael It's a council house.

Vera No, their other house. He had to sell it anyway. That was her mother's house. She moved back home. Still, he got a pool table in there. He haven't done so bad.

Michael Yes, he's got the kitchen like a games room. They live in the front room. He knocked it through.

Vera Well, he used to have a good job. He's handy.

Annie He's all right, it's her I don't like. Rough house when her mother and father were there. He's all right though.

Marge How do 'Ave Maria' go? Vera.

Vera sings the Bach/Gounod 'Ave Maria'.

No, the other one.

Vera tries the Schubert but it resolves into the Bach/Gounod.

Vera Why?

Marge She wants it at the funeral. Mrs Walsh.

Vera Haven't the crematorium got it?

Marge No.

Vera My niece has got it. A compilation disc. We had it for a wedding.

Michael Dear. Dear.

Marge Well, at least it's not Tina Turner, they had Tina Turner the last time I went to the crematorium.

Annie I've never been to a crematorium.

Vera Really?

Annie I've never been to a crematorium, I wouldn't go to one.

Marge tries 'Ave Maria'.

Michael It's one of the conundrums of Christianity, that no one can remember 'Ave Maria'.

Neil Right – I'm getting dressed.

Tommy I'm going home first.

Neil What for?

Tommy To get my trunks. And I want to get changed.

Neil What about your mother?

Tommy She'll be over Michael's by now.

Neil Where's my trunks?

Tommy They're on the line. Where you going?

Neil To wash my face and have a piss.

Tommy We can have a shower in the baths.

Annie is talking to Billy.

Annie Do you want me to put a bet on for you?

Billy Yeah.

Annie What do you fancy?

Billy I'm having a two pound double on the favourite in the 2.30 and the 3.30 at Cheltenham.

Annie I fancy one of them. Do you want a double?

Billy Yeah.

Annie I'm going round your father's. He'll have a bet.

Shirley walks past them without speaking.

What's up with her?

Billy I don't know.

Vera I've got that money, Marge. I told you, you've got to make a fuss. My niece made me do it. She wrote the letter.

Michael What's this?

Vera We went on holiday to Tenerife. She booked the holiday, I took my niece, we always go. The apartment, it was . . . well, you should have seen it! I wouldn't have cleaned my floors with the towels in the bathroom. A very nice boy, the tour operator. Lovely. Tim. Well, the other people were as shocked as us, and we got put in the nice hotel. We had a lovely time, it's volcanic, the one beach. Anyway, she wrote a letter of complaint for me and I got a letter back this morning, with a cheque for fifty pounds. Always complain, see. It's right.

Tommy calls off to Neil.

Tommy What you wearing, Neil? Where's your new Reeboks?

Neil Why?

Tommy Wear 'em.

Neil What you wearing?

Tommy I don't know. I might borrow Phil's new shirt. He won't mind.

Neil Won't he?

Tommy We'll have a day out. Bring your gel with you.

Neil comes back in. Tommy is holding up a shirt.

Wear this.

Neil Shall I?

Tommy Yeah.

Neil takes it and puts it on. Tommy finds another shirt.

Can I wear this?

Neil No, you can't.

Tommy puts the shirt down, Neil finishes dressing.

Tommy Ready?

Neil Yeah. Towel?

Tommy We'll get a towel in my house.

He puts on Neil's baseball cap.

Neil Tommy, for fuck's sake don't wear a baseball cap.

Tommy Yeah!

Annie sings Schubert's 'Ave Maria'.

THREE

Shirley and Michael.

Shirley I haven't come for anything.

Michael What?

Shirley I haven't come for a cup of sugar or anything.

Michael laughs.

Michael Oh. Come in, Shirley.

Shirley I'm going down the baby-minder. She had the baby.

Michael Kids in school? What have you come for?

Shirley Nothing.

Michael Well then.

Shirley You're not going to move, are you?

Michael No. What makes you think that?

Shirley I'm in a panic you're going to leave.

Michael No.

Shirley If you're next door, I'm safe. You're not moving?

Michael You know I'm not moving. What do you mean, safe?

Shirley What? No, he don't.

Michael Where am I going to move to?

Shirley Just don't leave. I'm in a panic you're going to leave. I'll dissolve. I will. I'm dissolving, I'll dissolve, dissolve, I'd be gone. Oh, I'd be glad to be gone. Oh, oh. Don't go, I'm asking you.

Michael Shirley, what is it?

Shirley Say it.

Michael I'm not going anywhere. What's this? What's this? What's this?

Shirley It's just come to me this morning, what if you weren't here? You can't be certain of anything.

Michael Don't be stupid.

Shirley I am stupid, I'm dull. Dull as a stone. Dull as. Dull as. I'm stupid. Do you want me? Do you want to sleep with me? Just don't leave. I'll do anything, you know what I mean? I'm in a panic you're going to leave.

I'll dissolve, I will, I'm dissolving, I'll dissolve, I'll dissolve, dissolve, I'd be gone, I'd be glad to be gone. Don't go. Say it. You've got to say it. Am I pretty? I'm plain.

Michael No, I fancy you, I – Come here. No, don't let's do this.

Shirley You see, you're all the same.

Michael No.

Shirley When I'm walking around here, people tell me I'm happy.

Michael Who tells you you're happy?

Shirley Oh, yes. He used to make me feel so useful, so important. As if I was someone. He was good like that; he had eight O-levels. I don't ask you to understand, just pity. I'm so desperate. I don't want to go to bed feeling so bad every night. Is me only a person who isn't anyone, only me? Only doing things. How is that free? Is you, me? Is my love for him only like our mama, our dada? My kids, who are they? I can see, but can they? Are they like me? His kids. As myself. You see. Do you think somewhere – I'm not asking you to understand. You're not going? I thought, my Christ, if Michael wasn't there. He'd say make the best of it, of everything.

Michael Would he?

Shirley Use everything. Find a new use for old things, live as in a siege, teach yourself to be master of a siege situation.

Michael Would he say that?

Shirley I'm so fed up, I'm fed up. You'd think you'd grow up, you'd be your age.

Michael You're no age, you're just a girl, Shirley.

Shirley Why am I a mother, not a woman? Why are men? It makes me feel bad. Why won't someone break through, why won't someone tell me what to do?

Michael He just drinks, it's simple.

Shirley I know it's simple. Stop me. Please. Don't leave us, will you. Ever. Will you?

Marge and Vera and Dolly.

Marge I don't know who comes home to dinner now.

Vera No one I know.

Dolly My mother-in-law still cooks dinner.

Vera Does she?

Marge The kids don't.

Vera Mine never come home.

Dolly No, nor mine. Neil did sometimes.

Marge Was Tommy with Neil last night, Dolly?

Dolly No.

Marge Where was he now?

Carol wheels her baby at the back.

Vera I see that girl Darkie Jones is going out with, with her baby.

Dolly Where? Oh yeah.

Marge My father used to have a bet, have his dinner, wait for the hooter. (*Nodding at Vera.*) Now she has lunch in town every Wednesday with her sister.

Vera I do.

Dolly Jimmy never came home for dinner, did he?

Marge No, he always eats in work.

Vera Do you have dinner in work?

Dolly No, I'll have something later.

Vera She's a pretty girl. I've never noticed her.

Carol picks the baby up.

Dolly I saw his father's car when I got off the bus, Darkie.

Vera Len Jones, over here?

Dolly Yes, he was in the paper shop.

Marge I'd have knifed him for what he did.

Dolly New car.

Vera New car, new house, new baby.

Dolly They always spend more on the second family.

Vera Don't I know.

Marge You're well off without him, Vera.

Dolly Where'd he come from, Marge?

Marge Round the park.

Dolly Did he?

Marge He was in Michael's class.

Dolly I thought he come from town. He's Italian, isn't he?

Marge No, Dolly, his grandfather was a Somali, your grandfather was Italian.

Dolly No, he was Spanish.

Marge No, Dolly, he was Italian.

Dolly How do you know?

Marge Your mother told me.

Dolly She told me he was Spanish.

Marge He wasn't.

Dolly Well, how did she know?

Marge Well, your mother would know about her father-in-law.

Dolly We didn't know him.

Marge Dolly.

Dolly Well, why don't we have an Italian name?

Marge Why don't you have a Spanish name? They must have changed it. Your grandmother used her maiden name. I don't know where you are sometimes, Dolly.

Darkie is with the baby.

Carol OK?

Darkie Yeah, give him here.

He picks the baby up.

Marge I don't know how Stella Jones didn't knife Len Jones after that, I don't.

Vera She's only a young piece he's with, not much older than their kids.

Dolly Oh, she's years older, she's older than his kids.

Vera She's not much older.

Marge I'm glad of that. Dear oh dear, mine did all that when we were younger. All that heartache. I couldn't go through all that again. I wouldn't.

Dolly Wouldn't you?

Marge No, I wouldn't.

Vera I didn't.

Marge No, you didn't. Dear, dear. He's too lazy now, I'd leave him, now, anyway. I had a rough time; he's as good as gold now. He said before he went away, 'I'm not going with any dirty women, don't start.' He never went with any other women. I thought he did. He was just unreliable. He'd stay out and never let me know. You're so frightened when you're young.

Dolly I'm frightened now.

Marge Do you know, it all came back to me the other week when he went to a big funeral down the docks, and you know what they're like. I knew he'd be late, well, he said he would be, but I was still frightened. I'll be glad when we're on our own and they're all of them gone. I'll be glad when he's gone, Tommy and the other one, Philip.

Dolly Marge, how can you say that?

Marge I can. He's too much of it, staying out all hours, he never tells me, he's unreliable, he's the most unreliable, he's the most unreliable bloody kid. If I had hold of the little scarecrow, I'd put a brick through him. He's the worst of them, he is. Then on Mother's Day I get the biggest, silliest card from him of the lot. He can be a nice kid, he can also be a swine. I just can't cope with the worry of him sometimes, I wish he'd – such terrible things – now when I'm not feeling so bad about him. Not to worry again. I wish he'd go away, join the army, go to sea, they won't have him. The parents, I blame the parents. Why don't they say mother and father? What can I do about Tommy? I don't know what to do about him. They're different kids now than the other ones. He's a man now, yes, but he's been in so much trouble, and that business, you know, with Stella Jones's boy –

Vera You take too much notice of it.

Marge I'll cleave him when I get hold of him.

Vera You won't.

Marge I'll give him a good slap, big as he is.

Dolly I don't think you should hit your children.

Marge I don't think you can help yourself sometimes. I don't see how you could keep your hands off Tommy. He's beyond – It never did any good. You could blind him. I'd give him a slap now. But I know, if it doesn't do any good.

Vera I know. It's bad. My mother used to leather me.

Marge Well, there's a difference between a slap and a beating.

Dolly Is there? Is there?

Marge I was never cut out to be a mother. True. I'm better with other people's kids. Give me Neil. He was always like this, long before that business. Five in the morning, when he was six, the bedroom window was wide open and he'd be gone, miles away. I'd just hope he was with the milkman when he come.

Vera Oh, I like Tommy, yes, he's full of life, Tommy, he cheers you up, he's a lovely old kid.

Marge You can have him.

Dolly And that Bobby was older than them, and she gets on my nerves, Stella Jones, she still blames them, she knows it was her kids' fault. He shouldn't have took them over there.

Marge She don't blame them.

Dolly Don't she. I keep away.

Marge Then it all comes back, see. I could hear them crying, right from the back of the church. I couldn't see him, Tommy, they was all down the front, the children, but I could hear him.

Dolly I didn't go.

Marge I did.

Vera Didn't you go?

Dolly She makes too much of it.

Marge Well, you can't expect people to behave better just because they've had a tragedy.

Dolly Well, you'd think –

Marge It seems as if you'd think somehow they'd be elevated and know better.

Dolly Well, we did what we could – we sent them on a holiday.

Marge (*to Vera*) That was you.

Dolly They all went on that holiday. He was a nasty kid, Bobby.

Marge No, he wasn't.

Vera No, he was just adventurous.

Dolly They shouldn't have been over there. The devil has got into her, Stella Jones, and I don't think she'll ever be happy again.

Vera Are we making a collection for Mrs-over-the-back?

Marge Yes, you take it up.

Vera Thank you.

Dolly I don't like too many flowers. There's too many flowers, it's got too much. I don't believe in it.

Vera Well, what shall we do?

Marge She's like one of those people who say they're going to give a donation, no flowers, someone else's funeral. You wouldn't do it on someone's birthday, 'I gave a donation to a good cause on your birthday.'

Dolly But I don't like too many flowers. I just don't see. I don't know why.

Marge It don't say no flowers by request in the paper.

Vera Well, I'll get a collection up then. We'll have to send a wreath, Dolly. Oh aye. Do you know someone stole my camelias and my primula, not vandals, digging them up, not kids.

Dolly Well, plants are so expensive.

Vera Next door, she's got a clever idea, she mixes lovely artificial flowers next door with her other flowers, you wouldn't know. She's a pretty girl Darkie's with – that girl. Whose baby is it – Darkie's?

Dolly It's not his.

Marge I don't think she knows.

Dolly Have she got a flat?

Marge No, she lives with her mother.

Dolly I bet she'll get a flat. They do it to get a flat, half of them.

Marge Well, she didn't. Girls don't get pregnant to get flats, Dolly, they're too stupid.

Dolly They do, you know.

Marge You listen to anyone, you do, Dolly. She hasn't got a flat, she lives with her mother.

Dolly No, I don't think they should get preferential treatment.

Marge They're too soft to get terminations, most of them, they're too silly. If it was that simple, it would be all right. Anyway, her mother's surrounded by SPUC posters.

Dolly Well, I'm not for abortion.

Marge Well, who's for abortion? You're daft you are, Dolly. It's funny though, these pro-life people don't seem to have many kids. Annie's a decent woman. And she won't have anything to do with it. Anything like that.

Dolly I don't think abortion's right.

Marge Dolly.

Dolly I don't.

Marge You'll upset yourself, Dolly, now.

Dolly That time, Marge, was terrible, it was terrible.

Marge Well, you wouldn't want to go back to them days, would you?

Dolly No. I wouldn't.

Marge Well, there we are.

Dolly Marge, you was good to me, that time. All times with Neil. Always. When we went to the woman, when I was pregnant. When I didn't know what to do.

Marge Don't talk like that, Dolly.

Dolly No, it don't upset me now, I'm just saying, I don't know what I'd do without you Marge.

Marge Dolly, don't now, don't. What would I do? What would I do? Who is it I come to when I have a panic, where is it I come to all hours? I come to you. All hours I come to you. Who else would I run to, eh?

Vera Yes, you don't think enough of yourself, Dolly.

Dolly I wonder if she's had it inoculated? There is a scare about.

Marge Oh, a lot of them are silly.

Dolly My daughter didn't have it done. She says, why should I risk my child's life for anyone else?

Marge Honest.

Dolly Well, perhaps she's right.

Marge Dolly, you can't be trusted, you don't know anything.

Dolly What do you mean? What you laughing at? Marge?

Marge Remember when Menachem Begin died? She thought I meant the Paki in the main road.

Dolly Well, it sounded like him.

Marge Remember round the park – whatsisname –

Vera I'm sure I do.

Marge Mrs thing's son-in-law, Tina Bevan's husband – Carlos.

Vera Yes.

Marge He gave a party the night Franco died. She never knew what the party was for.

Dolly It was a good party.

Vera It's nice, that new baby, it's a lovely baby.

Marge Thank God it's not me.

Dolly Marge.

Marge Could you manage a new baby?

Dolly If I had to I would.

Marge That would be New Labour.

Vera That's a lovely shawl. I think it's hand-knitted, that shawl. I used to knit all my baby clothes.

Marge I never did.

Vera Oh, I did.

Dolly My mother-in-law always did mine.

Marge It's a long time since people had to knit anything. Imagine having to knit again.

Vera I don't mind knitting for a baby.

Dolly Do you always think your baby is different from other babies?

Marge You do. All my children were good babies, I was lucky. No. It's a lovely baby, I've seen it. It's beautiful.

Dolly What's she call it?

Marge Some daft name I expect. Amy Pearl, Heidi Louise. Ellie Lou. Safron.

Marge is making Dolly laugh.

Madison. Dakota. Ebbw Vale . . .

Dolly Marge.

Vera I was sitting in the hairdresser's when I saw him across the street wearing his leather coat, flash bastard, holding hands with this Welsh tart. They had 'Raining in my Heart' on, which I love. I ran out and across and punched him. I made myself look common. He thought I didn't know.

Billy and Marge.

Marge What's the matter with you? You don't look too clever, Billy.

Billy I'm all right. I've been round the park. I set out with no other interest in mind than to feel a bit better. It's wonderful how simple life is when you have a hangover. Life is good. Life is good, Marge, suddenly. I can't let this get me down. I haven't had a drink. I haven't had a drink.

Marge What's the matter with you, Billy? What you carry on like that for?

Billy Oh, Marge, don't. I'm gone.

Marge No job?

Billy No, no job.

Marge Wish you were working?

Billy I wish I was. It's not that I haven't looked.

Marge Our Tommy doesn't look: He's playacting half the time.

Billy I thought I was in line for a caretaking job. It would have done me nice. Oh, don't let's go on. It's a lovely day. Sparkling, sparkling day. Funny how it is over here on a bright day, how bright it is. Must be the reflection off the channel. And then it's so grey when it's raining. Well, I'm off.

Marge Don't go for a drink. I suppose you're going for a drink. Come and get something to eat with me. What you having for your dinner?

Billy I can't go home. I can't go home. I slammed out.

Marge Billy!

Billy I'll have to face the music. I went out this morning. Why is there love?

Marge Oh, Billy.

Billy Why do you need it? You can't tell a baby, a little baby, you love it. It wouldn't understand.

Marge You can talk to a baby.

Billy Oh, you can't only talk to a baby, Marge. You can't just say, 'Why are you crying?' You know that. 'What do you want?' We've all tried that. You can't say, 'Tell me what you want, if you'll stop crying I'll get you what you want,' can you? You try getting a baby down with words. Words won't do. Sex don't do it. My feelings, my feelings.

Marge Come on, pull yourself together. You're not drunk. It breaks my heart to see you like you've given up, Billy. What is it?

Billy I don't know, Marge.

Marge You keep yourself clean – Why did you marry the poor girl, the way you treat her?

Billy Why did I marry her? My father says that. He says she come from a rough house, she's a bit rough.

Marge Oh dear.

Billy That's what you think, all of you. That's what it is. That's what I think's the matter. I think you look down on her. You look down on her.

Marge Don't say I look down on her.

Billy I can't live with her, Marge.

Marge Oh aye. Hey, hey, now then.

Billy I'll have to find her. She's not in Shirley. I'd rather stay out. I don't want to go in. I want to stay out. I'd rather stay with you. I've been bad, Marge, I've been bad. You're great, Marge, you are. Not to be. Ha? You're a good person, Marge.

Marge Go on with you.

Billy He's away – I'll be round.

Marge You'll – like hell you will. Go on.

Billy You are.

Marge You're a silly boy. Go on now, go on, get something to eat. Don't go for a drink, don't.

Billy Not unless you lend me the money. See, I need a drink but I don't need one, I need three, see, and that's it. I've had it. You're a good person, Marge.

Marge Go on.

Billy He's away.

Marge Yes.

Billy I'll be round.

Marge You'll – like hell you will. Go on. I'm a married woman.

Billy I don't mind, I'm bad.

Marge You are, aren't you?

Billy I am.

Marge Are you?

Billy Yes.

Marge Are you?

Billy Very.

Marge Go home – take help.

Billy My old man give it up. He had to. He wouldn't give it up for years.

Marge I know, I know.

Billy My mother – I'm going over to see my father now – or later. Marge, you don't know the half of it. Miserable old bugger. He made her life a misery with his gambling. It's an illness and all that, like me and the booze. We should have been comfortably off. He's settled down now she's gone. It took that, and now all the others won't have anything to do with him. I go round most.

Marge Go round now.

Billy I'll go round now, Marge.

Tommy and Neil and Michael.

Michael What you doing here? Hello, Neil. Looking for work?

Neil Oh aye, yes.

Michael What, over here?

Tommy We went into town to see Darkie, we missed him. My mother been here?

Michael Yes, she's looking for you.

Tommy What she say?

Michael You'll have to ask her.

Neil Have you seen my mother?

Michael No. She'll be in work, won't she?

Neil Not now.

Tommy Come on then, Neil.

Michael You only just got in.

Tommy I know.

Michael Cup of tea, Neil?

Tommy Come on, Neil.

Michael You had your dinner?

Neil No.

Michael You hungry?

He goes out.

Tommy Come on, Neil.

Neil No. What's the matter with you?

Michael (*off*) What do you two want for your dinner?

Neil Anything, honest.

Tommy Hey, hold this to your ear.

He proffers Neil a cup.

Neil What? Oh.

Tommy Go on.

Neil holds the cup to his ear.

Neil What?

Tommy Go on. Can you hear the crowd?

Neil What crowd?

Tommy The crowd in the Arms Park. Can't you hear the roaring and cheering.

Neil No.

Tommy It must be half time.

Len and Stella.

Len I've come to ask you something, Stella.

Stella When they coming home?

Len Things are very difficult with Lisa.

Stella Tracy won't stay without Lisa.

Len They both don't have to go. Well, I think it would be better, it'd be better for them, I think.

Stella Oh aye, I never wanted them to go.

Len Well, it seemed better for them then, didn't it? And for you.

Stella Well, they're grown women now, they ought to know what they want.

Len John won't mind?

Stella This is my house.

Len He seems well. I saw him for a drink.

Stella Yes, he said. He's very well.

Len He's got a girlfriend. That's good.

Stella Is it?

Len Well.

Stella How's the baby?

Len She's fine, she's fine, they're fine.

Darkie comes in.

Hello, son.

Darkie What are you doing here?

Len I came to see your mother.

Stella Have you had your dinner?

Darkie Yes.

Stella Why you home so early?

Darkie Job and finish. We nearly finished yesterday.

Len On in the morning?

Darkie Yes, early. We haven't seen you over here for a bit.

Stella I told you what it would mean.

Len Would you mind?

Darkie No, why should I? As long as they behave themselves.

Stella Why would he mind? This is my house.

Darkie Yeah. Well, I'm off.

Len No, I'll go.

Darkie No. I've got to go out.

Len Perhaps I'll see you Thursday.

Stella Where you off to?

Darkie What?

Stella Where you going?

Darkie I'm going out.

Len Perhaps I'll see you Thursday, then?

Darkie Yeah.

He goes.

Len Well, he seems cheerful.

Stella I'm worried about him.

Len You said he was fine.

Stella I know. I'm worried about him. He worries me.

Len Dear, dear. Oh well, I had to come over, Stella.

Stella Yes, you said.

Len I'll go, Stella.

Stella Well, I would have made you a cup of tea. Have you had lunch?

Len Oh no, I'll go home.

Stella Back to work this afternoon?

Len No, contract finished. Not till next Monday now.

Stella Lucky for some.

Len Yeah. I'll give you some money for the girls. They're both working. Perhaps you'll be a bit better off.

Stella Perhaps I will.

Charlie and Annie.

Annie Do you want anything?

Charlie No thanks, Annie.

Annie You all right?

Charlie Aye, aye, I'm all right.

Annie You owe me two pounds. I put a bet on for you. The 2.30 at Chepstow. What did you fancy?

Charlie Nothing much.

Annie See if it comes up.

Charlie The favourite. That's what I fancied. Did you put it on?

Annie Yes. I did. D'you want a cup of tea?

Charlie I owes you two pounds. No, no, I don't want a cup of tea.

Annie You're a miserable sod, Charlie, moaning to yourself and going on about old age.

Charlie Aye, aye.

Annie You want to get some exercise.

Charlie I never been fitter in my life. Anyway, I don't need exercise.

Annie What, a bloody old age pensioner like you? I saw someone helping you across the road when I was going for the bus last night.

Charlie Must have been me helping them, then.

Annie Well, it was the blind leading the blind then. I saw Billy this morning.

Charlie Oh aye? I haven't seen him.

Annie You have. He was here when I was here on Monday.

Charlie Not today. She don't like it.

Annie There's been some disagreement.

Charlie She's the trouble there. How'd he get tied up with that, can you tell me that?

Annie Well, they've got children now.

Charlie No job.

Annie No job, well, you know how it is. Hard times.

Charlie I worked from when I was fourteen – thirteen – fourteen – till they laid me off. I never missed a day's work.

Annie What you taking about? You were in and out of work all your life, I remember. You worked when you had work, true, true. You and Harry.

Charlie D'you want a cup of tea, Annie?

Annie No, I've had too much tea.

Charlie Sit down, sit down.

Annie I've got things to do. Do you want me to get you a sandwich, make you something?

Charlie No, sit down, sit down.

Annie You going over to the club tonight?

Charlie Oh, I don't know. I don't think so.

Annie I'll do a couple of lines of bingo. I'll call for you. Do you want to come?

Charlie Aye, call for me.

Annie You coming on the outing?

Charlie Where?

Annie Symonds Yat.

Charlie I don't think so.

Annie I'll put your name down.

Charlie How much is it? You going?

Annie Yes.

Charlie You sure?

Annie Yes.

Charlie I might come. You going?

Annie Yes. I'd better be off. Here's your shirts.

She gives him his freshly ironed shirts.

Charlie Thanks, Annie. Very kind. It's the ironing.

Annie Now put them away. You got anything for me to take away?

Charlie No.

Annie Charlie, change that shirt. What's the matter with you? Put a clean shirt on if you're coming out with me. You got the paper?

Charlie Yes.

Annie Where's my two pounds?

Charlie I give it to you.

Annie When?

Charlie When you come in.

Annie You didn't, did you? What I do with it?

Charlie Here, I kept this for you. It's the Catholic paper. She keeps it for me next door.

Annie Thanks.

Charlie There's something in the middle interesting.

Annie Thank you.

Charlie Annie, here, here's your two pounds.

Annie You're a bloody crook, Charlie.

Charlie laughs.

Stella and Darkie.

Stella You're very quiet.

Darkie No, no.

Stella What? You are.

Darkie Am I?

Stella He's gone now.

Darkie Yeah, I see.

Stella I wish he'd come back to us.

Darkie No.

Stella I wish he would. I wish he'd get rid of them. I wish he would. It was worse than Bobby, when your father went.

Darkie No.

Stella It was. It was bad. It was worse than Bobby when your father went.

Darkie No.

Stella It was. This loss of mine. For years, you laugh and joke, at least we did, about who'd go first. I suppose you'll marry some tidy little blonde, I'd say. If you do,

I'll come back and haunt you. What would he say? One of those noises he'd make, more of a snort than a reply really. He always kidded me about that, he always did. You're my boy. That's awful when I've got girls. More than Bobby. You were more wilful. That Tommy Driscoll, that Neil. Swine, little swine. I could hit him every time I see him. Useless they are, the pair of them.

Darkie No, Mam.

Stella What use are they? It was worse when your father went. At least I know where Bobby is.

Darkie No, no, no, no, Mam. No. You're mean, you are. That's what I don't like. Why are you so mean? They was terrified, Mam. They was only little kids.

Stella Aye, some kids. I know where Bobby is now.

Darkie That's what Tommy said to me. I know where Bobby is.

Stella He said it was over, your father, before that.

Darkie I don't listen.

Stella Whether or not we would have drifted apart if it hadn't been for Bobby. We might. You don't have to part, drifting apart.

Darkie Well, she'll keep him up to the mark. Look what you're doing, to make me depend on you. I'm not going to get out of this. You ask me for everything, but where are you for me? Where are you when I want you? Not here, not here, you're not here, you're not here, Mam. What did you do this to me for? You made me like this, caring for you, waiting for you.

Stella I am the devil, this is evil. Hell is a place you go to for allowing yourself to suffer. When suffering seems like sin. I try to say my prayers but I can't empty out my mind. It all seems so sinful. One time I stopped and looked what happened. No, it's up to me, I'm to blame.

Darkie You'll have to try, you will, you'll have to.

Stella How am I going to get out of it? It all goes round and round in my head. Suddenly it comes back. If I'm low, if anything happens.

Darkie What happens?

Stella Something happens.

Darkie I know, I know, and it did happen and it's not going to happen again. You should have moved away like him.

Stella Oh no, I couldn't. Bobby. And now it's getting rough over here. Your father had more sense. And look what I've landed you with.

Darkie You haven't landed me with anything.

Stella You'll go.

Darkie I won't go because I don't want to go. But you've got to stop going on and on every time I'm out. I'm not Bobby. Nothing's going to happen to me.

Stella See, that's your father, that's how he carries on talking. It's awful really then, isn't it – it's wrong really, isn't it? I don't think it can have been sent as a trial. If it's a trial I can't overcome it. No. But it's gone. But when something goes wrong, it comes back. I hear people – grief, they say – coping with it, coping with grief. Do you know what, I don't know. You just grit your teeth and hope it won't last too long this time. They thought that holiday would do the trick. Hot, in the winter. They think that makes up for things in the hot weather. It was a kind thought. What is it?

Darkie I'm tired.

Stella Are you?

Darkie I am, I'm tired.

Stella Why are men always tired?

Shirley and Billy.

Shirley I haven't been to town, as it happens. You think you got me taped.

Billy Give me some money, Shirley.

Shirley You drink because without it you can't feel nothing.

Billy I haven't had a drink, Shirley.

Shirley You can't. You know there's more to you and then you go and have to drink to feel it. I'm tired of this, I am.

Billy I'm going.

Shirley Don't go, you haven't got the money. You haven't got no money, have you?

Billy I'm going.

Shirley I'll give you money else you won't say anything. I don't want to have to pull talk out of you like a lump of sash. When you're drunk you're a bad bugger most of the time. When you're not drunk you're still out of it in another way. There's nowhere for me, you only want me when you're out of it, when you're drunk.

Billy I don't, Shirley.

Shirley And then you get nasty. Nothing goes on unless you're drunk. This is my life. You're in and out of it.

Billy Oh, shut it, Shirley. I can't now.

Shirley Don't tell me to shut it.

Billy For Christ's sake shut it.

Shirley Don't you tell me to shut it.

Billy I'm not afraid of you, Shirley. You won't do anything. You're nothing, you're nothing. You wouldn't do anything if you tried. You don't understand, you're stupid, you're stupid, you're stupid.

Shirley Here, here's some. Some money. Take it. Take it and get out.

Anne Marie comes in.

Here, take her, take her and all. Go with him, go on. Go with your father. Here's money. You see, you see your cruelty. How you make me cruel, how you reduce me to the cruelty I'm capable of. Look at her. Don't dare speak, don't dare. Get out. I don't want you to go. How could you. I'm stuck with these kids. Look at her, look what you did and now it's too late to stop it.

FOUR

Marge, Michael and Dolly, right. Charlie, left.

Marge What's ethics, Michael?

Michael Oh, Marge, how do I know? You think because I spent fifteen years in a religious order I know everything.

Marge Well, you usually have an opinion on everything.

Michael Put it like this: ethics aren't for us, we just have morals. We're not material, there is no us any more, we don't exist, we're not material.

Marge Morals.

Michael Right and wrong, sin.

Marge I know what morals are, I don't understand what ethics are.

Dolly Do you believe in sin?

Marge What?

Dolly Oh, aye, I believe in sin. It's sense. What you have to be careful is, well I believe we have a tendency to sin but you have to be careful as to what you mean by sin. I mean, not everything is a sin, not half of what people think is a sin is what I call a sin and you have to be careful that it isn't like making a cup of tea with a sense of sin.

Michael And you a Catholic. You're a moral relativist, Dolly, you want to watch it. That's what we have a church for, that's what we have churches for, to manage things like that, to teach us what is right and wrong. That's what Radio Four is for. They'll be after you. Moral relativism they call it.

Dolly What's that?

Michael It is the essential message of Our Lord, mercy over justice.

Marge Love.

Michael Yes, love next to justice –

Marge – and not pride –

Dolly – and not to judge –

Marge – and love the poor.

Michael And love the poor and love the poor. I think God is everything that is good and it's our task to make God omnipotent. No, he wasn't a relativist, Our Lord.

He told us to follow Him; on that He was absolute. Our Lord was a contradiction – to learn to love yourself and then to love your neighbour in the same way, that's absolute and relative. The simplest things can have the greatest consequences and if the vilest people unite, then the decent people must unite, just that. I used to remind myself that if you did good acts, something good will come of it.

Enter Annie.

Hello Annie, we've been talking about the state of our souls.

Dolly You should hear what he says, Annie.

Annie He says a lot of things. Pity some of them aren't his prayers.

Billy brings Charlie his winnings.

Billy I brought this for you.

Charlie Oh yes.

Billy How are you?

Charlie Not too bright.

Billy No?

Charlie What's this?

Billy Here's your winnings, Annie asked me to give them to you.

Charlie Should have put more on. Give it to us, then.

Billy Hang on, let me sort it out.

He gives him the money.

I fancied that.

Charlie Yeah, I liked the look of it. Did you put a bet on?

Billy Yeah, mine never come up. One horse let me down.

Charlie Sit down, sit down, son.

Billy No. Do you want anything? Do you need anything?

Charlie No.

Billy Shall I put the kettle on?

Charlie No. I thought you'd be round here yesterday.

Billy No, I didn't come.

Charlie What's the matter with you?

Billy Nothing's the matter with me.

Charlie Well, it's your business. Give me a cup of tea.

Annie shows Michael and Marge a newspaper.

Annie Look at this, Charlie kept it for me. A hundred and ten years and the body is still the same as the day she died.

Dolly Who?

Annie Isn't she lovely?

Dolly Who?

Annie Look at her.

Dolly Who is it?

Annie *The Catholic Times*. Saint Bernadette. Look, isn't she lovely?

Dolly looks at the picture in the paper.

Dolly Ooh, yes.

Annie She's my favourite saint. Only thirty-five when she died. I'd love to go to Lourdes, I would, I'd love to go.

Michael I've been to Lourdes. Dear. Dear.

Annie *The Song of Bernadette* was my favourite film. I saw it in the one and nines. You had to wear a hat.

Michael Will you have a whiskey, Annie?

Annie Oh no.

Michael Annie, you'll have a whiskey. Marge, Dolly?

Marge No.

Annie You're not drinking. You don't drink.

Michael No, not for five years now.

Annie Five years.

Michael This is left over from Christmas. I was given a bottle Christmas twelve month. Annie likes a whiskey.

Annie Yes, I'll have a whiskey, no water mind.

Marge What are we celebrating?

Annie Nothing. My winnings – my horse came up and Charlie's.

Michael You, Marge?

Marge No.

Michael goes for the whiskey.

Annie He never drunk much.

Marge Oh, he did. Not like him next door, but he did. At one time he did.

Michael brings in the whiskey.

Michael I saw your two.

Annie Thank you.

Marge Where?

Michael They was here.

Marge You didn't say. Wait till I catch hold of him.

Michael Oh, let the boy alone, leave him alone.

Marge Always in trouble the pair of them. Taking people's cars.

Dolly They don't. Not now, Marge.

Marge No, but he'll be up to something else. No, I'm getting fed up with him.

Michael He's not so bad.

Marge Isn't he?

Michael He may not be as innocent as Kevin Maxwell or as blameless as Azil Nadir, but he is no worse than a lot of them, Marge.

Marge I don't care.

Michael You're quite right, the poor have to show better. If we don't show better, then what's to be done?

Annie You going to the rugby match on Saturday, Michael?

Michael How do you think I'll get a ticket for an international match in Cardiff? It's easier to get into the Royal Enclosure at Ascot.

Annie This stadium will make a difference.

Michael Oh yes.

Dolly Are yours going?

Marge No, Jimmy will go into town with my oldest and they'll watch it in the Albert. Tommy don't show much interest in sport.

Dolly Nor Neil. I wish he did.

Marge (*pointing at Michael*) He was a good rugby player.

Dolly My husband's not much of a sports man.

Marge Mine is, Jimmy.

Michael Wales will never have a good side again, not without grammar schools, and they say it's a classless sport – they say rugby is a classless sport.

Marge You played rugby.

Michael I did. Your boys played soccer. I don't think worrying about the decline in standards of A-levels is going to make any difference to Tommy and Neil.

Dolly None of our kids got A-levels. I passed the eleven plus.

Marge And me.

Dolly Did Vera?

Marge No, I don't think she did. Or if she did, she didn't take her place up. You know when they talk about our children, they don't mean their children.

Billy brings Charlie a cup of tea.

Billy Here you are.

Charlie Do you want a cup of tea?

Billy No.

Charlie You need a drink.

Billy Yeah.

Charlie Get me my tablets, son.

Billy Who's going to win on Saturday. Scotland?

Charlie Nah.

Billy I dunno. I don't know.

Charlie Get away, man, they haven't got a dog's chance. You got the *Echo*?

Billy Aye.

Charlie Thanks.

Enter Tommy and Darkie.

Annie Hello, Tommy.

Marge Hello, John.

Michael Hello, Darkie.

Darkie Hello.

Marge You.

Annie He's a nice boy.

Marge Is he?

Annie Well, I've never known him to be anything but a nice boy to me.

Marge Where have you been?

Tommy What do you care where I've been? You locked the door.

Marge Your father did. He told you he would.

Tommy We've been swimming.

Darkie I haven't. I been in work.

Marge Did you take one of my towels?

Tommy No. It's on the line.

Marge Did you wash it out?

Tommy No, it'll dry.

Marge I bet you took one of my big towels. You owes me four weeks money.

Tommy All right, don't show me up.

Marge I'll show you up.

Tommy I'll get your money, I'll get your money. I'll get it.

Marge Where?

Tommy I'll get it, don't worry. I went looking for work; Darkie wasn't there, was you, Dark?

Darkie No, I finished early.

Michael Sit down, John.

Darkie I come to see you, Michael.

Dolly Where's Neil, Tommy?

Tommy Neil! He's out there.

Darkie I told him to come last week. I told you last week that last week I told you I'd speak to the man. We finished the job yesterday.

Marge See.

Tommy See what?

Darkie I'm going, OK.

Marge OK.

Neil comes in.

Neil Hiya.

Darkie I'll come round to see you. I wanted to see you, Michael, I'll see you, Michael. OK. (*He goes.*)

Tommy Hang on, Darkie. (*He goes.*)

Dolly Neil, did you go down and get my money?

Neil Yes.

Dolly Thank you. Where is it?

Neil I left it at home on the mantelpiece, I didn't want to have it on me.

Tommy and Darkie are outside.

Tommy Have you got anything, Dark?

Darkie What?

Tommy Have you got something?

Darkie Not here.

Tommy Please, Darkie.

Darkie You owes me money, Tommy.

Tommy I'll get it, I'll get it, I'll get it, I'll get it.

Darkie I'll give you a slap if you don't.

Tommy I'll get it, my mother will give it to me.

Darkie You get it. I'll give you a slap, Tommy. I don't like it.

Tommy Come on, Dark. Please.

Darkie gives Tommy some speed.
Carol wheels on the baby in a pram.

Tommy Thanks, mate.

Tommy goes back in to the others.

Carol What were you giving him?

Darkie Nothing.

Carol I was going round your mother's.

Darkie What you going round there for?

Carol To see if you was in.

Darkie Don't go round there.

Carol Why?

Darkie Don't go round there, all right? My mother wouldn't like it.

Carol What do you mean, your mother wouldn't like it?

Darkie That baby's too hot. Don't go round there. No. Don't go round there. No, don't let's talk about it. Don't go round there, all right? All right? Don't go round there.

Carol What's the matter? What's the matter with you?

Tommy has come in to his mother and the others.

Tommy Coming, Neil?

Marge Tommy, will you keep still for a little while, you're giving me a headache. Where's Darkie?

Tommy With his girl.

Marge What's she like?

Tommy She's a foxy lady.

Marge Will you shut up. What's a foxy lady? Don't take pride in ignorance.

Tommy What weighs more, a pound of nails or a pound of feathers?

Marge Shut up.

Neil Come on then.

Tommy If you drop say a car from a high building at the same time as you drop a five pence, say, which would hit the ground first?

Marge Oh, that boy.

Tommy She's great my mother, she's mad. She's a Communist. You're a Communist, Mam.

Marge Which would hit the ground first?

Michael Ow!

Dolly What is it?

Michael My knee. All the things you thought would never happen to you, you thought were the affectation of old age. Life was one long adolescence. Looking for my reading glasses and finding them down the side of my chair or on my head, and now my knee's hurting me.

Neil Are you coming, Tommy?

Dolly Michael. Have you got anything new from the library?

Michael Yes.

Dolly Anything I'd like?

Michael Have a see.

Marge You're a mystery, Dolly, you're a mystery woman.

Dolly You read.

Michael Here.

He hands Dolly a book.

Dolly Thanks. Oh yeah.

Marge Not what you read. And she draws. Have you seen her drawings? But she only draws cats and then colours them in.

Dolly I like cats.

Marge Most of her life, she thinks life is a Tammy Wynette song most of the time. You do, Dolly. She can't see no harm in anyone half the time.

Dolly I can.

Marge Her husband, he can't do nothing wrong. She gets softer as she gets older.

Dolly But he don't.

Marge Well, I know that, he's my friend, I knew him before you. But they're not perfect, Dolly, mine isn't.

Dolly What's wrong with him? He's as good as gold, Marge, you don't know how lucky you are.

Marge I know, I know.

Michael Aren't you a feminist, Dolly?

Dolly Well, yes, yes, I'm a feminist. I don't have to hate my old man.

Annie I hear these women on the telly; they don't want much do they?

Michael What women?

Annie Those women with a lot of mouth chopsing on about getting their jobs, going on about things they don't know. They want everything wrapped up in the one toffee paper. Not that they're better over here. They have everything, these girls over here. Washing machines, tumble dryer, new jeans, if they want food they take it out of the freezer. They don't know what life is. Well, good luck to them. But they lives in their mother's pockets.

Marge One tiff and then back to mama. Telling their mother their married business. When I went home to my mother she said, 'I know what you're like,' and sent me back. Feminism, it's for women with rich husbands or a university degree. It's too good for the working class.

Tommy Up the working class.

Marge You've got to be in work to be in the working class, Tommy. Or available for work.

Dolly They say everyone's working class now.

Marge Yes. Well, if the junior doctors find it so hard why don't they go over Panasonic for £4.80 an hour?

Dolly My niece is getting married over here. She wants to be married in this parish.

Annie That's nice, that's a nice thought. Isn't that a nice idea?

Dolly Yes, she thinks the doors of the church are nice for the photos, with big hinges.

Marge T . . . t . . . t . . .

Dolly Yes, they're going to be all dressed like the American South.

Michael Christ.

Marge Last week, did you see her over the way, her daughter? It was all Spanish. They wants their heads read. Honeymoons in Guyana, Domenica.

Annie They got it easy. My marriage wasn't celebrated.

Dolly What do you mean?

Annie My husband was a Protestant. So we had no music. No flowers.

Michael Mean, mean.

Dolly Did you have a white wedding?

Marge (*pointing at Dolly*) She did.

Annie No, we didn't have white weddings, we couldn't afford it.

Marge What did you wear, Annie?

Annie Blue. A blue dress and a picture hat. Your mother made my breakfast. You had a nice wedding. You did.

Marge I did.

Annie Yes, that's what it was like then, years ago. You know, there never used to be anybody divorced over here. Divorce, it was a rich person's thing. Well, it was more difficult for people to carry on. You knew where they were, they knew where you were.

Marge Did you have a white dress for your first communion, Annie?

Annie Oh, I did, my mother made it and the veil. It was lovely.

Marge I had a dress with puff sleeves.

Dolly Mine was broderie anglaise. What did you wear, Michael?

Michael I had a grey suit and a sash. The Maltese boys all had white suits, all long trousers. What did you two wear, Neil?

Tommy Uniform.

Marge What wedding was it where the bride's mother's dressed the same colour as the bridesmaids and the grooms ties and waistcoats and the flowers? They had a horse and carriage and photos in Roath Park and they were late for the reception. Bad manners.

Tommy Damian Hibbard's wedding.

Annie That's what I mean, there's more money than sense. Half of them get divorced and half of them don't get married.

Dolly Well, I went to my niece's daughter's first communion and, do you know, there was a child and she was looking over her shoulder at her grandmother, and you know, just before the child went up to take her first communion, she pulled a switch and the dress lit up with fairy lights.

Marge Tommy and Neil had Edwardian outfits for a wedding they went to.

Tommy It was wicked, Mam.

Marge Whose wedding?

Tommy Damian Hibbard. I told you. Darkie was there.

Vera goes to Charlie and Billy.

Vera I've come collecting for a wreath.

Charlie For who?

Vera You know.

Charlie I don't know.

Vera He's terrible. You do. She's got a sister.

Charlie Oh blimey, her. She dead?

Vera Her sister's dead.

Charlie Here, blimey. (*Gives her money.*)

Billy I'll have to give you something later, Vera.

Vera Yes, I'm only starting collecting this afternoon.

Charlie Will you have a cup of tea, Vera?

Vera Thank you. I'll tell you what, it's a beautiful day.

Dolly What was all this like, Annie?

Annie What do you mean?

Dolly What was all here before there was houses here?

Annie Oh, I lived in town. This was all the wilds to me. You'd have to ask Charlie. (*To Michael.*) Your father would have known what was here before they built on it. Years ago . . .

Michael This was all moorland here. This was all moorland caught between two rivers, the Taff and the Rummy river. The old sea wall and the gut that run alongside it must have been built to protect animals. It was so flat and wide, all at sea level. There were all farms out here at one time, not all farms because of the tides.

Annie There was a farm here when I first moved over here. I remember running over to your mother to tell her I had a house of my own, right up there by the farm.

Michael Though whether there was much agriculture or not I don't know – any crops here – not many, I should think. Too salty. Cattle and sheep. The country over the other side of the Rummy, the Lambies then right out towards the lighthouse, there was sheep farming and beyond that it was all marshes and flats drained by dykes, reens, and that was all farming. There was a lot of farming there down by the old low road where there had been smuggling there, and flat like that all the way up to Newport. The old London road, the Newport road, and the Great Western railway fencing it all off. Of course, the old low road is still there out to Marshfield but now Rover Way and the other road and the new housing has cut us off from the sea here and squeezed the river, cut off one of its loops. Over our old house you could see straight across the channel to Somerset and watch the shipping. There were a lot of shipping lanes out there to and from Bristol. All the cargo ships and the warships and the slave ships must have gone past our window.

Annie I saw a ship under sail. I saw the last of the big tea clippers. Marvellous, marvellous sight.

Michael I heard some rich black singer, some rich American rock singer on about this being the land of slavery. I doubt if some farm labourer, speaking Welsh, living here on this land, had ever heard of slavery, paying his tithes. Or America. It was grand to have a bit of country. It's much better than a park could be ever. It was a mean piece of country, this piece of country. It wasn't much, it wasn't beautiful compared with the beauty of what must have been up the valleys or the vale. It's sad when you don't see a Red Admiral on a day like this, or the *Gardening Programme* encouraging people to make wild gardens.

Marge Mine's always been a wild garden.

Michael There's something shocking about all this. Should we let it all go? I don't want to live in a theme park, those theme parks up the valleys. I saw a kids' workshop given by a folksinger down Habershohn Street, teaching the kids nursery rhymes. It makes me uneasy, that. I don't like it. I don't like folk masses. I thank God I never had to do Irish dancing or do bloody Morris dancing. I find all that repulsive, I do. It's all a version of the Royal Wedding.

Marge People have to celebrate their lives. You've got no soul.

Dolly Annie got the *Riverdance* video, haven't you, Annie?

Annie I have. It's lovely. I'd love to see it.

Marge (*to Michael*) You shut up now.

Dolly Can I borrow it, Annie?

Marge D'you remember when Tommy used to go over the farm, before we moved here, to help with the milking and feeding? They had a big herd of cattle and I asked him what the names of the cows were. Of course, I thought cows were still called Clover. There was about two hundred cows and it was all done by electrical identification. I was thinking of the cow with the crumpled horn in the colouring book.

Michael What was it like, Tommy?

Tommy The farm I worked on was a dairy farm, sheep and pigs as well, it was the biggest farm in St Brides. It was a lovely farm, quiet, right against the sea wall, called Walnut Tree. I used to milk three times a day, five in the morning, twelve o'clock and nine o'clock. Hard but very enjoyable. It's not there any more, it's gone, there's a golf course there now.

Annie And of course they got rid of the farm to make the old airport, in the war.

Tommy Oh, don't start on about the war.

Tommy sings 'Congratulations'.

Michael Shut up, Tommy.

Tommy Neil can do Sir Cliff. Come on, Neil. Do Sir Cliff.

Neil No. Leave me alone.

Annie You haven't been in a war, nor you, nor you. You don't remember. Do you remember?

Michael I remember things I can't have witnessed. I remember things that can't have happened. The German plane crash.

Annie It wasn't a German plane. It was a –

Michael Yes, in the next street.

Annie It was a Polish airman who took off from the old airport and he crashed, and Charlie pulled him out. He was a hero, Charlie. He saved him.

Marge Did he?

Annie The King gave him a medal. The King gave him a medal.

Michael I remember my mother put the papal flag out on VE Day, which, considering Pius the Twelfth's less than warm support for the Allied cause, was optimistic. But then my mother always could tell the difference between the office and the man. That's why I became a priest. Ow! It's my knee, it's all right, I'm all right, I'm going to live till I'm a hundred and two and then tell lies about everybody over the club. I'm the only one who hasn't had a bypass over there.

Annie Years ago.

Michael Years ago.

Annie A quarter of tea, loose tea, potatoes in the bottom of a bag, lined with newspaper, a separate bag for the veg. Years ago. Door-to-door callers.

Michael I think it was always scrappy over here, Dolly. This isn't much of a city, is it? What's it got?

Marge It's got enough low life. The likes of the Duchess of York are nothing to the low life in town.

Michael It's a bit fond of itself, like Liverpool.

Annie It's like one big London.

Marge Do you feel Welsh?

Michael What?

Marge Do you?

Michael No, I feel like I'm from here.

Tommy I do, I feel Welsh, me.

Neil And me. I do.

Marge I didn't feel Welsh till I went to Yorkshire, and on the way back I heard a Welsh voice in a buffet car and I started to cry. Where do you feel you come from?

Michael Over here.

Marge What about you, Annie?

Annie I'm Irish.

Michael I feel I come from here. Here. This place. This town, and then South Wales.

Annie You Welsh.

Michael I feel I come from this city, I suppose, but I also – I feel I come from just these few streets. I don't feel like a sturdy, enterprising little islander. Perhaps people like us can't feel the conscience of the nation, perhaps that's why they invented the American dream. I feel foolish and proud to be part of the tradition of these parts, of the Labour movement, of the Methodist tradition, the Welsh and the Spanish miners and the Italian cafés and the English and Welsh and the Irish. And all that meant it wasn't provincial. It was an aim to liberate Britain. The Welsh were the original Britons and it had its roots with King Arthur and Owain Glyndwyr and it was more nearly successful than either of them. Nationalism is just a retreat from something that was greater. The poor bloody Welsh, they did it without killing a sodding one. They should have took up arms. No one gives a toss for them, it seems to me.

Dolly Where was you born, Michael?

Michael I was born over here.

Annie I was born in town.

Dolly Over here. Where was Jimmy born? In the Bay?

Marge No, he wasn't born in the Bay, he was born in the docks.

Dolly Vera?

Marge Round St Peter's Street.

Dolly Charlie?

Marge In town.

Dolly Billy?

Marge No he was born over here. She was born down Portmanmoor Road.

Michael Where were you born, Tommy?

Tommy In hospital.

Michael All sorts born in this town. Where did the Jewish people live? Were people anti-Jewish, Annie?

Annie No, no, there wasn't much anti-Jewish feeling in South Wales, there were always too many Irish people. We never thought the Jews were like the Jews with Our Lord, Jews like the Rapports. Monty Horowitz had a stall in Frederick Street. Your mother was very fond of Monty Horowitz and then, of course, when he got rich, she called him all the names going.

Michael Was there a Jewish quarter?

Annie Jewish quarter? There was no Jewish quarter.

Dolly Cathedral Road?

Annie No, that was all later. Round Frederick Street. I lived in Little Frederick Street. All sorts of people lived down the docks. I don't know, Jimmy's mother would know. Louisa Street, George Street was all Spanish. There was only Spanish people in George Street. Crichton Street, Greek. Christina Street. The Maltese and the Chinese in Bute Road. There were Jewish people in Temperance Town, I think.

Michael What did the Jewish people do?

Annie I don't know, pedlars and that. There were big fights with the Irish.

Marge Low life they must have seemed.

Annie No.

Marge Annie, what about Mary Ann Street? In town. It was supposed to be one of the worst streets in Europe. Worse than the docks or the Bay.

Annie Aye, much worse.

Marge What did you do, you lived in Little Frederick Street?

Annie My mother just made us walk past Mary Ann Street. Quick. I worked for a Jewish man in Cathedral Road. Oh, what a nice man he was. If there was a spot of rain, he'd say, Mrs Donoghue, I'm going to drive you home. The Italians, I worked for them. One family, they used to put Benjiamino Gigli up when he came here, but then they interned the father in the war and called his son up and he was killed in the Italian campaign. Dear, dear.

The following overlaps.

Carol Onde fica isso?

Vera Borrita na mu. Pita pu ina aptos o taramos?

Darkie Waxaan doonaya meel aan ku noolaado?

Stella Mae'n ddrwg 'da fi, 'alla'i ddim eich helpu chi.

Billy C'e lavoro qui per me? Per favore?

Annie Taispeáin dom ce'n áit a bhfuil an sráid seo?

Stella Iawn, 'wy'n gwbod ble ma' fe. Fe af â chi yno.

Dolly Me puede decir donde hay una iglesia católica?

Shirley Per arrivare a questa strada cornu faccio?

Len Ma ha y faa shaqo hadda?

Marge Nil aon áit ag mo pháisti chun dual a chodladh.

Dolly Be' sy'n bod, 'y nghariad i?

Tommy Mi puó dire dove si trova la chiesa catolica?

Neil Me puede decir donde esa esta calle?

Vera Ehete kamia thulia?

Dolly 'Ych chi'n siarad Cymrâg?

Darkie Waa xagee meeshani?

Charlie Eu estou a procurar trabalho?

Neil Tien algun trabajo?

Stella Mae'n ddrwg 'da fi, 'alla'i ddim eich helpu chi.

Billy Psahno yia na vro japu na mino.

Carol Eu estou a procurar un lugar para morar.

Tommy Lle ma' fan hyn, 's gwelwch yn dda?

Stella Be' sy'n bod, 'y nghariad i?

Annie Tá mé ag lork áit chun cónadh ann.

Stella Pam nagých chi'n siarad Cymrag? Pam nagých chi'n siarad Cymrâg?

Michael Why don't you speak English?

Dolly Them Somalis have got the only four-bedroom house around here.

Shirley comes in.

Shirley Oh. I'm sorry.

Michael No. No. Come in, Shirley.

Marge Yes. Hello, Shirley. Come in.

Tommy Hello, Shirley.

Annie Well, I can't stop here chatting. I've got things to do. Thank you, Michael. That was a nice drop of whiskey.

Dolly I've got to go too. I've got to put the tea on. They'll be in. Are you coming with me, Marge?

Annie Tara, then.

Marge Hang on, then. Tommy, do you want anything? It's skittles tonight, Dolly. I'll come with you. Do you want anything?

Tommy What you got?

Dolly Tara.

Tommy Come on then. All right, Shirley. Tara, then.

Shirley, Neil and Michael are left.

Michael Well, you got rid of them for me, Shirley. There's only Neil and me left.

Shirley Yes.

Tommy (*off*) Neil.

FIVE

Tommy, Neil and Darkie are playing snooker. Dolly, Marge and Vera are playing skittles. Charlie and Annie are playing bingo. Michael is giving the answers to a quiz and Len is singing karaoke. A Bingo Caller is calling out numbers. What follows will overlap.

Caller Eyes down for the first line –

Michael And the answer to the first question is –

Caller All the threes, thirty-three.

Michael Keir Hardie.

Len Thank you. Thank you.

Caller Seven and four, seventy-four.

Michael The Welsh centre in the nineteen hundred and five match against the All Blacks was Gwyn Nicholls.

Marge You're next Dolly.

Len 'You took a fine time to leave me, Lucille.'

Caller Clickety-click, sixty-six.

Michael Dic Pederyn was hung in Cardiff Gaol.

Dolly Stick them up then, love.

Len Four hungry kids and a crop in the fields.

Caller Seven and six. Was she worth it?

Michael Shakin' Stevens.

Tommy Come on, Darkie, we're on.

Len 'You took a fine time to leave me, Lucille.' (*And he continues this song to its end.*)

Caller Nine-O, as far as we go.

Michael The *Terra Nova* left Cardiff in . . .

Darkie Rack 'em up.

Caller Unlucky for some, thirteen.

Marge These are nice sandwiches.

Michael Alfred Sisley was married in Cardiff.

Caller And those legs –

After this, catcalls and whistles.

Darkie I'll break.

Michael Penrhrys.

Caller Unlucky for some, thirteen.

Michael The answer is Barry Dock.

Vera I felt like saying, get your arse round here. I said, don't you ever talk to me like that, I said, how dare you?

Caller Kelly's Eye, number one.

Michael Lady Charlotte Guest.

Darkie Where's the chalk?

Caller Four and five, forty-five.

Michael Jim Driscoll won the Lonsdale Belt in –

Marge That was a bolter. Come on, pay up. You're the treasurer, Dolly.

Caller Number ten, Major's den.

Single Voice Good old John.

Other Voices Not for long.

Single Voice Tony Blair.

Other Voices Do your hair.

Michael Owain Tydwr was born in Anglesey.

Vera I broke a nail. She said was it false? I said I don't wear false nails.

Caller Doctor's orders, number nine.

Tommy Shot.

Michael Matthew Arnold.

Caller Lucky for some, number seven.

Dolly These are nice sandwiches, tuna and mayonnaise.

Michael Eleven VCs were won by the South Wales Borderers at Rorke's Drift, Natal.

Caller Forty-five, halfway there.

Tommy In off the cushion, in off the cushion.

Michael The answer is Blaenau Gwent, with a majority of thirty thousand and sixty-seven.

Tommy Yeah.

Michael Richard Crawshay.

Darkie Shut up, Tommy.

Caller One and two, one dozen.

Marge That was wide and all.

Vera Sunshine.

Caller Three and four, thirty-four.

Dolly and Marge sing 'Why Was She Born So Beautiful, Why Was She Born at All?' Vera sings 'You Are My Sunshine, My Only Sunshine'.

Caller Two and three, twenty-three.

Michael The signatory to the American Declaration of Independence, born in Llandaff, was Francis Lewis.

Caller Three and four, thirty-four.

Carol enters. Tommy speaks to her.

Tommy Hello, Carol.

Caller Five and six, fifty-six.

Michael The second Marquis of Bute.

Carol Where's Darkie?

Caller Five-O. Blind fifty.

Tommy He's playing. Darkie.

Caller Two and one, twenty-one.

Vera Her eyesight's so bad she runs after the wrong bus, and then curses the bus conductor.

Caller On its own, number nine.

Michael George Borrow.

Darkie What you looking for me for? What d'you want?

Caller Two and eight, twenty-eight.

Darkie I didn't say I'd come over.

Caller Eight and eight, eighty-eight.

Michael The *Mabinogion*.

Neil Come on, Darkie.

Vera You know me, I'm not a moaner.

Michael Lady Eleanor Butler.

Caller Six and five, old-age pension.

Darkie Tommy, take my next shot.

Carol I thought you might come over.

Michael The first race riots.

Caller Six and nine, sixty-nine.

Darkie Why you got the baby, what's the matter with you?

Charlie House.

Annie I was holding three numbers.

Billy to Shirley.

Billy I'm sorry, I'm sorry.

Carol is singing 'Simply the Best'.

Darkie What you singing for?

Michael Tessie O'Shea.

Charlie gives Annie a drink.

Charlie Here you are.

Caller Eyes down for a full house.

Billy I'm sorry.

Caller Four and four, all the fours.

Carol I can sing if I want to.

Caller Seven-O, blind seventy.

Michael Adelina Patti.

Caller One and seven, seventeen.

Darkie staggers.

Darkie Tommy, Tommy.

Tommy What's the matter, Dark?

Caller Two and one, twenty-one.

Tommy Dark!

Darkie Get Michael.

Tommy What is it? Neil.

Michael Pontypridd.

Billy You're nothing, you're nothing.

Caller All the fours, forty-four.

Darkie I can't. Don't. I can't.

Tommy You can.

Darkie I can't.

Tommy You can, come on, you can do anything.

Billy You're rubbish, you're rubbish.

Tommy You can, come on, you can.

Darkie Tommy, Tommy. Oh. Tommy. Where's Carol? I'm all right.

Caller Two and three, twenty-three.

Michael The Welsh Regiment.

Marge Come on, Dolly.

Annie House.

Caller And now who'll give us a song?

As the scene disperses, Len calls out, 'Anyone want a lift?' Carol continues singing. Vera, Dolly and Marge are laughing.

SIX

Stella is sitting centre, Marge sitting to her right, Tommy's bed to her left. Annie standing to the left of the bed. Michael brings folded washing to Marge.

Michael Here we are, they're all folded except the sheets.

Marge My feet. Thank you, love.

Michael You had too much to drink?

Marge No, you know I can hold my drink.

Michael Do you want a cup of something?

Marge No.

Michael Come on.

Marge What?

Michael (*indicating the sheet*) Fold this.

Marge No, give it to me I'll take it home.

Michael Come on, Marge, don't be lazy, come on.

They fold the sheet together.

Marge Isn't it lovely, the smell of washing off the line? Different from the dryer. There we are, let me sit down. Let me see Jimmy's shirt.

She picks up the short-sleeved shirt.

Michael Is it long before he comes back?

Marge He might be back tomorrow.

She puts the shirt down.

Michael Oh.

Marge I'll be glad to see him, I will.

Michael He's only been gone a day.

Marge I know. But when he's away I get so lonely and then I miss our dad.

Michael Marge, don't start.

Marge Yesterday I was thinking, oh I'll tell dad that. I] miss him. D'you know I love Jimmy so much, I don't think anybody could love their husbands so much, but to know you love your husband so much and then to know that the man on the white charger will never come.

Michael Marge.

Marge Scratch my back, love. I hope there's work when he gets back and I hope this job goes on. I hate it when he isn't in work because he hates it so much. He feels so bad.

Michael I suppose I've never done any proper work, I don't feel like that.

Marge Priest's work.

Michael Not that kind of work. I've done that kind of work.

Marge A bit lower down, love.

Tommy and Neil cross Annie to Tommy's bed.

Tommy See, I told you.

Neil They could still hear us.

Tommy They won't if you keep quiet.

Neil What if your mother comes in?

Tommy She's round Michael's. She won't say anything if you're here.

Tommy begins to undress.

Neil Where's Philip?

Tommy He's gone down his girl's.

Neil How do you know?

Tommy Because I know.

Neil He still going out with her?

Tommy Yeah.

Neil They been going out a long time.

Tommy He's getting engaged. Get undressed, then.

Neil I don't know.

Tommy Well, go home.

Neil I lost my key.

Tommy They might have left one out.

Neil They won't have.

Tommy What did you do with it?

Neil I dunno.

Tommy Wake them up.

Neil I can't.

Tommy Why?

Neil Because we spent the money.

Tommy We never spent all of it, we'll pay her back.

Neil starts to undress.

Neil She'll kill me.

Tommy When do you get your Giro?

Neil Wednesday.

Tommy Pay her then.

Neil She needs it today. I won't be able to go home.

Tommy Stay here till Wednesday.

Neil I thought your father had chucked you out?

Tommy I told you, he's away working. It'll be all right if you're here. I can get round her if my father's gone. You getting into bed?

Neil All right.

They get into bed.

Now keep your hands off me.

Tommy I might.

Tommy feels for Neil under the bedclothes.

Neil Tommy, come on, stop it. I'll make a noise.

Tommy Go on then. Let me do it to you, I won't hurt you.

Neil Do it to your girlfriend.

Tommy I would if she was here.

Neil You just got to find somewhere to put it. You've got to stop this.

Tommy I know, there's a lot of things I've got to stop. Come on.

Neil Do you want me to do it to you?

Tommy No.

Neil See.

Tommy Do you want to?

Neil No, I don't want to. Do you want me to?

Tommy Let me do it to you.

Neil Shut up, Tommy, what's the matter with you? You got a girl, or this week you got a girl. You'll have another one next week. What's the matter with you? I was supposed to go round Susan's, I'm always in trouble with you.

Tommy Oh yeah. The first time I ever thieved anything it was you started it. Don't put it all on me. Why didn't you go round there?

Neil Because I was with you.

Darkie and Carol come to the right of Michael and Marge.

Darkie I got to go.

Carol Don't go yet.

Darkie It's late, I'll have to go.

Carol Why can't you stay?

Darkie Your mother, my mother.

Carol I'm leaving my mother. Darkie, what'll I do, what'll I do? Darkie, we'll have to sort this out.

Darkie There's nothing to sort out.

Carol It's because of the baby, you don't like the baby.

Darkie You know I like the baby, he's a lovely baby. What do you mean, I don't like the baby?

Carol Don't go then. Please, Darkie, please, don't.

Darkie Don't, Carole, I'm not going to do it now. What's the matter with you?

Carol Darkie.

She tries to kiss him.

Darkie What do you want? What do you want me to do? Do you want me to fuck you, I'm not going to, your mother's upstairs.

Carol That didn't stop you this afternoon.

Darkie I've had all that. I've had all that.

Carol You pig. You don't care.

Darkie I do.

Carol You pig.

Darkie You don't even know who the baby's father is.

Carol I do.

Darkie Well, why don't you say who it is?

Carol Because he doesn't matter.

Darkie No, he doesn't. I'm going.

Carol Don't go. Your mother, your mother . . .

Darkie Your mother, my mother. I'll see you tomorrow.

Carol You won't see me.

Darkie I will.

Carol You're angry with me. Are you angry with me?

Darkie I'm not angry with you. I'll see you tomorrow. I will. I will. Tara then.

Billy and Shirley come to the left of Marge and Michael.

Billy I'm sorry, I'm sorry.

Shirley Go to bed.

Billy I'm sorry.

Shirley Go to bed, Billy.

Billy I'm sorry.

Shirley Go to bed, Billy, or I'll kill you.

Billy What?

Shirley Go to bed.

Billy I'm sorry.

Shirley Go to bed.

Billy I'll sleep down here.

Shirley Don't sleep down here, don't sleep down here.

Billy I'll sleep down here.

Marge Mam said you were religious when you were a child. You can't blame Mam.

Michael I don't blame her.

Marge She didn't want you to go in the church.

Michael Yes, and then she didn't want me to leave.

Marge You always associate our Mam with pain. I don't. And you were her favourite.

Michael I was religious young, or I thought I was religious. Life is religious, that's what life is. I think all those poor people who take their lives rationally like I once tried to have lost their vocation. It wasn't hard to be religious in our house.

Marge No. Mothers and sons.

Michael You should know, Margaret.

Marge I do know. What am I going to do? I don't know what to do about him.

Michael Just let him get on with it. What can you do?

Marge But he can't tell right from wrong, Tommy. He can't. And he's so stupid about it.

Michael laughs.

Don't.

Michael Because he needs you more than you can bear.

Marge Don't, Michael.

Michael Well.

Marge I always think of her with a fire lit in the mornings and the winter evenings in this house.

Michael I don't see. There was a papal blessing by the front door. The Sacred Heart in the front room. A crucifix in the front room. Our Lady of Fatima in the other room. That big picture of Our Lady over the mantelpiece and upstairs there was Our Lady of Lourdes and the Black Saint, Saint Martin whatever. There were two sick room sets, one of them luminous. Dear, dear. When I was a child, in May I used to make an altar to Our Lady and I could never get the lilac to stand up in the little glass I used as a vase. I won all the holy pictures in school, I was the champion. Penny catechism, five pence. It was my favourite joke. I never liked going to church until I went on the altar. I don't remember my first communion with particular pleasure. I was frightened by my first confession but then when I was an altar boy I had something to do. The amice, the alb, the girdle, the stole, the maniple, the chasuble, *ad deum qui laetificat juventutum meum*. I served Mass every morning at eight o'clock. Boat, acolyte, thurifer, crucifer, MC. I was a daily communicant. Rugby, scouts, sports, school, the youth club. It all became the one thing. Where I could put all my feelings, all my confusions about what was going on, all my contradictions. Then there was a mission when I was about fourteen, a mission in search of vocations, and it was run by a young priest who made me see, feel, there was something bigger than me and I was less frightened. He reminded me of that boy, you know that young Irish boy I told you about, when I worked in that Aids clinic, the one who made the sermon about Our Lord dying of Aids. He had the same kind of warm fervour.

Marge What was he doing here?

Michael He was on leave from his Bishop to sort himself out. He made this modern stuff feel like the early church, he had talent for the priesthood. They won't have him back, they wouldn't know what to do with him. Later on we heard that the young priest at the mission left the church when I did and later he killed himself. Eventually I realised I had no sense of God, that I had never had a sense of God. I lost God eventually because I realised I had never believed in Him. I'd let my life become nothing but moral details. Then I realised I only understood Our Lord as a human being, I couldn't understand anything beyond that and I was angry. I was full of what my superiors called spiritual pride, but I couldn't find my spirit. I was all dogma and then dogma to combat dogma. I knew when I first went into the Seminary that I was going to leave eventually. All we younger men used to break the bottles of the old drunks with a hammer so that the empty bottles would be indistinguishable in the other rubbish. The women who cleaned the house for us were like our mothers. We were embarrassed seeing our mothers cleaning up for us, caring for us, doing our washing, when we'd taken what we thought were vows of poverty. Our vows seemed silly and people thought we were silly, irrelevant, not to the point, to worry about our vows. I had a vocation then, I had a vocation. If you don't have a vocation . . . It's inexplicable – vocation.

Darkie goes to Stella

Darkie I finished with her, is that all right with you? I'm not seeing her again is that OK? Is that OK?

Stella You can't do that, you can't do that now.

Darkie I can. I can do anything, I can do anything me, I can do anything.

Stella What's the matter with you?

Darkie Nothing.

Stella What's the matter with you, John?

Darkie Oh dear, I feel bad. Nothing.

Stella What's the matter with you, son?

Darkie Nothing's the matter with me.

Michael We had two houses in North America, one in Boston and one in New York, in the Bronx. It was such a shock, it's difficult to imagine how exciting America was then, just to see the shops open late. So glamorous and sordid it was. Piles of dirty snow and cracked pavements and beggars and the homeless. Just like it is here now. And the church was a shock. There were two powerful Cardinals, Cushing, who was a friend of the Kennedys in Boston, and Spellman, who was a very powerful man in New York. It was all quite different to here with Heenan. The church had real influence. It seemed optimistic, America then. There had been reform in the church and I was all for it. I didn't miss the Latin Mass, I missed the Tantum Ergo and Benediction and I missed the Douai version, but I was a fervent ecumenist and I believed that was the way forward. And that all the doubts expressed were a digression. A question of style. But of course all the time there were questions that couldn't be answered. The church seemed to have lost its claim to being the only revealed truth. And the fumbling mixed messages that Paul VI sent out to poor women over contraception made the decision for many of us. And though I was excited, I was sickened by America. We used to go to receptions given by sybaritic American Irish businessmen who were bankrolling us and sending money to Noraid and yet these were men who were pro the Vietnam war.

Marge Perhaps they thought they were sending money to freedom fighters.

Michael Oh, Marge. It's not a matter of whether you want to die for it. But then the Buddhist monks in Vietnam had the moral victory there. It's not a matter of whether you want to die for it, it's whether you're prepared to let other people die for it and which of those other people you let die. They were motivated by simple bigotry, anti-Communist and anti-English, without any analysis of the situation. The virtues of the Irish and the vices of the English need no more rehearsing for me. Ireland without England would be like Germany without the Jews. They were sentimental about their own tragedy. They sang songs about it. They never really thought that it could have been averted. They never put to use an analysis of these things that their church was in theory uniquely suited to. Some of them wouldn't believe that some eight million Russians had died fighting for what turns out to have been a thousand-year Reich of American consumerism. Some of the men I am talking about were in Opus Dei, Marge.

Marge What's that?

Michael It's a sort of intellectual anti-Communist freemasonry. They've just canonised the man who founded it. One of the more warming things about him was that he maintained that there weren't six million Jews killed in the Holocaust, only four million.

Marge Still, four million would be quite a lot.

Michael And the racism, Marge, their attitude towards black people. I understood why the American Irish refused to fight for abolition in the American Civil War, that was perfectly understandable to me. Having been considered the blacks of Europe they certainly weren't going to end up at the bottom of the heap in the promised land. But one nun who I heard later became interested in liberation theology once said to me, 'Ah, but you have to remember our blacks are descended from slaves, yours aren't.' I began to be disturbed by the nature of my relationship with my parishioners. I was interfering in individual lives, that wasn't in the interest of the family or truly of the church. Just the state – whatever – the dominant culture. Not truly the church or its people. Marge, tell me how what has been going on in Rwanda or Bosnia or in Palestine or Israel or even in Northern Ireland can be connected with what happened the sixties, or in what way is it related to the decline of family values? Our Order ran the best borstals and the most efficient agencies to enable working-class girls to give up their babies to middle-class families, and my job seemed to be a form of family planning. One of the greatest sins of empire is the inverse imperialism that it produces, and it has become difficult for us who have been colonised in this way to remember the original sin. I began to look back home with an increasing anger. Living there made me realise that I wasn't Irish. I wasn't Irish, but that I had been brought up, made to feel Irish, that I was genuflecting to a notion of someone else's nationalism and that what I thought was a universal church was being practised as a sect. I wasn't in the church, I was in Ireland, the worst of Ireland, cruel, sentimental, stupid. Do you remember on Saint Patrick's Day that woman who used to come over from Ireland to sell shamrock, the one with the leg-iron?

Marge Yes.

Michael And how we used to sing, 'Hail glorious Saint Patrick dear Saint of our Isle, on Erin's green valley bestow a sweet smile and something something in the mansions above. On Erin's green valley look down in thy love.' Erin. Where's Erin? We were in Swinton Street. My mother had never been to Ireland.

Marge Dad did once, to a rugby match.

Michael The nearest our mam came to Ireland was a bottle of Guinness. I began to be filled with a terrible hatred which I've hardly come to terms with. The western world at least, or, as they now say, the Northern Hemisphere, is going to become one big America. Why were they so worried? All these languages and customs will be like flashes of colour in one big America. The shopping malls will soon make it indistinguishable as to whether one is in Bute, Montana or Ebbw Vale or Ashford or Crossmaglen. Except that I expect they will eventually ethnicise them.

Marge Well, at least we have more money than our mothers. Some of us.

Michael Oh, Marge. It's the unbearable smugness that accompanies their final acceptance that the Reformation has occurred. It's on a par with having formally forgiven the Jews. I used to understand all that. As I saw my final vows – I could see my final vows coming from a long way off. So I got ill. For years I defended the idea of the church, the certain practical things it did, the certain good it did. I defended it out of my own self-hatred. I despised my own cowardice but I hated the alternatives to the church, the salt of the earth, tut tut well done, isn't life a wonderful thing, aren't people wonderful, Christianity, but I resented the narrowness I'd experienced, not having been allowed to listen to Palestrina or having been forbidden to sing songs from the Methodist hymnbook. I didn't lose faith, I lost my faith, I couldn't pray, I never learned to pray, only to examine my conscience. To defend myself even after I had left, for years I was a Defender of the Faith, how it worked, its human organisation, its ability to transform itself into the good of a country as well as the bad. Only when I stopped doing that could I even go into a Catholic church. I served Mass down here the other week. He was stuck. But I was angry with my government for paying for allowing my parents to have me educated by foreign bullies. I should have thrown my hand in with counter-culture, I think. When I left I found I couldn't work. When I taught or did social work, or even when I was in South America that time, I felt I was still doing the same thing, and when I tried labouring I found it was too hard, I should have taken sides. There are sides to be taken. Thrown my hand in. Thrown in my hand. Thrown my hand with who now.

Marge We're lucky to have the time to talk about it, Michael.

Tommy and Neil.

Tommy Why can't you sleep?

Neil I don't know. You. Darkie.

Tommy Why Darkie? He's good, Darkie is.

Neil Why is he good? What was the matter with him? Why is he good to us? What good is he?

Tommy I told you because of Bobby.

Neil I don't see how because of Bobby.

Tommy I'll tell you.

Neil No, you goes on about it.

Tommy I don't.

Neil You do. You don't shut up about it. You goes on about it. You makes a big thing about it. That's all you does. You goes on, you goes on.

Tommy I don't.

Neil You do.

Tommy Ssh, what's the matter?

Neil I want to go home.

Tommy Don't go home, Neil. Ssh.

Shirley shakes Billy.

Shirley Come on, Billy. Come on, Billy.

Billy No. I'm all right. I'm all right.

Stella When they say I should like to have children they want one to say I should like to have children. You had children. I should like to have children but it's become something I use when I feel hard done by. I shouldn't have liked to have had children. I shouldn't have had children. Good thing I didn't. Best thing I ever did. What good would I be for them. I should have . . .

Takes her wedding ring off.

My wedding ring's fallen off. My ring's fallen off. Your ring's fallen off. Look, it's come off. Good, I'm losing weight.

Shirley I could kill you, Billy. Come on, Billy. I'll kill you.

Billy What?

Shirley I'll kill you.

Darkie If she dies do I die? If she dies, what then? If she dies where does that leave me? Have I been like one of those babies carried full term in hope? Given all that comfort and then if she dies I, free, find I have been dead born, born dead inside her, inside me.

Neil It wasn't our fault, we never wanted to go over there in the first place.

Tommy All right, all right.

Neil He made us go over there. He was bigger than us.

Tommy Yeah, yeah.

Neil How old was we?

Tommy All right.

Neil How old?

Tommy I was eight.

Neil Then I was eight, wasn't I? My mother knew I was scared but she thought it was because he was lost. But they kept asking us. Everyone did. We was crying.

Tommy All the policemen on the estate, all the estate in a big line walking across the Tidefields and the estate.

Neil Well, we didn't go.

Tommy Kids couldn't go but you could see them from the window.

Neil I was scared all the time.

Tommy And me, I couldn't tell.

Neil Nor me, I couldn't tell, I was scared all the time.

Tommy Well, that's it, it was because Darkie knew and he asked us afterwards after they'd been searching for days.

Neil And we could tell Darkie.

Tommy I know we told Darkie. That's how they found him.

Neil But I don't see what you mean.

Tommy It was because we told Darkie, because we told him. I'm telling you, I know, because we told him where Bobby was.

Neil I don't see it.

Neil turns away and begins to cry.

Tommy Ssh. Don't worry, come on then. Don't turn away, don't turn away.

Tommy turns Neil towards him.

Neil They think we killed him.

Tommy They don't.

Neil We never did nothing. We told him not to go up there.

Tommy What's the matter with you? Don't, Neil.

Neil Tommy.

Tommy Let me, Neil.

Neil Tommy.

Tommy Let me.

Neil Tommy.

They are struggling.

Michael Goodnight, love.

Marge Goodnight, my darling.

Billy has brought in the knife drawer from the kitchen.

Billy Here we are.

Shirley Don't, Billy.

Billy Here we are.

Shirley Don't, Billy.

She knocks it to the floor.

Billy Go on, pick it up, pick it up. Go on. I'll pick it up. Where's the knife?

Shirley Leave it, leave it Billy.

Billy I'll pick it up for you. You haven't got the guts. Here you are.

He offers her the knife.

Shirley Don't.

Billy Here. Here.

Shirley knifes Billy.

Neil Tommy.

Tommy Let me.

Neil Tommy, Tommy.

Neil grabs hold of Tommy's head and kisses him.

Tommy Yeah.

Billy falls to the floor.

Yeah.

Shirley Come on, Billy, don't be stupid.

Tommy Yeah.

Shirley Billy!

CERTAIN YOUNG MEN

In memory of Michael

Certain Young Men was first performed at the Almeida Theatre, London, on 21 January 1999 with the following cast:

Stewart Alec Newman
Michael John Light
David Jeremy Northam
Christopher Andrew Woodall
Andrew Andrew Lancel
Tony Peter Sullivan,
Robert Sean Chapman
Terry Danny Dyer

Direction Peter Gill
Design Nathalie Gibbs
Light Hartley T. A. Kemp
Sound Frank Bradlev
Casting Toby Whale
Costume Supervisor Charlotte Stuart

Characters

Stewart

Michael

David

Christopher

Andrew

Tony

Robert

Terry

Suggestion of a room able to include all the locations indicated.

On the floor: books, records, clothes, magazines, newspapers, video tapes, cups, beer cans, etc.

No furniture except perhaps for chairs when necessary.

After the characters make their first entrance, they remain on stage during the rest of the play.

And there followed him a certain young man,
having a linen cloth cast about his naked body;
and the young men laid hold of him:

And he left the linen cloth and fled from them naked.

St Mark, XIV, 51–52

ONE

Stewart and Michael.

Stewart Right then.

Michael Are you going to ring?

Stewart I said I'd ring.

Michael But are you going to?

Stewart Yeah. Of course I am, what's the matter with you?

Michael I'd better give you the right number then.

Stewart I've got it.

Michael No you haven't. Here.

He takes a piece of paper with the number on it from Stewart.

Stewart Well fuck me.

Michael Yeah.

Stewart What you do that for? What a liberty. What you do that for? Fuck me.

Michael Haven't you ever done that?

Stewart No I haven't got a phone. Anyway I wouldn't. Why did you do that?

Michael I don't know. In case you rang. I don't know.

Stewart But you asked me to ring.

Michael I know. Will you ring?

Stewart I dunno now.

Michael I thought you wouldn't.

Stewart I said I fucking would. Where's the number?

Michael Where's my pen. I can't find my pen. You got a pen?

Stewart gives him a pen.

Thanks.

He writes the number down and gives Stewart back the paper and pen. Stewart takes the paper and pen; the top comes off. Michael is left holding the pen.

Stewart Honest. You. Honest.

He retrieves the pen and puts the top back on.

Michael There we are. Thanks.

Stewart Right then.

Michael You off?

Stewart Yes.

Michael Are you going to ring?

Stewart I said I would.

Michael Or . . .

Stewart Do you want to leave it then?

Michael If you want to.

Stewart Do you want to? Give me your number.

Michael Or perhaps . . .

Stewart Well I'm off . . . I'll phone you . . . Shall I?

Michael Sorry? What? Oh, yes. You've got the number have you?

Stewart Yes. Oh no. Where is it? What did I do with it?

Michael picks up a scrap of paper from the floor and gives it to him.

Oh yeah. Thanks. I'll see you then.

Michael Yes.

Stewart Thank you for the . . .

Michael Oh that's . . . Listen, ring first OK? Don't . . .

Stewart No.

Michael It might be . . .

Stewart Yeah.

Michael You probably won't ring anyway.

Stewart What do you say that for? You never know. Do you? Eh? Anyway thanks. OK?

Michael Yes.

Stewart And I'm sorry about the . . .

Michael Oh that's . . . Listen take care.

Stewart Of what?

Michael I wonder if he'll ring. He might ring. He won't ring. Why should he ring? What if he rings?

Stewart Have you given me the wrong number?

Michael No.

Stewart Only I noticed the number when I came in. You gonna muck me about?

Michael Or . . .
Do you want the number?

Stewart No.

Michael Or . . .
Do you want the number?

Stewart No. Thanks.

Michael Or . . .

Stewart Here we are. OK?

Michael What's your name?

Stewart Stewart.

Michael You don't look like a Stewart.
Do you charge?

Stewart What?

Michael You should charge. You've got the kind of flat and the kind of records. And you live in the kind of street.

Stewart What?

Michael It's so beautiful this street.

Stewart What are you called?

Michael Stewart.

Stewart No. Come on. Come on.

He moves towards Michael.

Michael No.

Michael looks front, as if out of a window.

It's so beautiful this street in this weather.

Stewart Is it? If you think so.

He moves away.

Michael I do. What are they, the trees?

Stewart Trees. Street trees. Are you a student?

Michael I wonder they haven't sold these off. These flats. These cold water flats.

Stewart Why?

Michael They generally do. Sell them.

Stewart Oh yeah.

Michael They do. Do them up. Sell them. They do.

Stewart What do you mean cold water flats? This isn't a cold water flat.

Michael That's what they are.

Stewart You're not in New York you know. What *do* you do then?

Michael I like these flats up all those stone stairs. Do you have neighbours?

Stewart Why won't you tell me?

Michael I like the door knob, the broken glass.

Stewart Eh?

Michael This is just the kind of flat where the guy's on the game.

Stewart Do you want to pay?

Michael Yeah.
Or . . .

Stewart I might see you then.

Michael Or . . .

Stewart Thanks.

Michael Or . . .

Stewart No. I'm not.

Michael Or . . .

Stewart Look at all these books.

Michael Or . . .

Stewart I'm off then.

Michael Or . . .

Stewart Do you want to leave it then?

Michael Or . . .

Stewart D'you wanna leave it then?

Michael Or . . .

Stewart Do you wanna leave it then?

Michael I don't know, do you?

Stewart I don't mind, do you?

Michael I don't know, do you?

Stewart I don't mind, do you?

Michael I don't know.
Or . . .

Stewart Shall I see you then?

Michael Perhaps.

Stewart See you then.

Michael Or . . .

Stewart I can see when you're excited.

Michael Or . . .

Stewart I've got plans for you.

Michael Or . . .

Stewart What are you in to?

Michael I'm in to you at the moment. What are you in to?

Stewart Yeah.

Michael Or . . .

Stewart No I'm not.

Michael Or . . .

Stewart Are you scared? What are you scared of?

Michael Or it could be . . .

Stewart Ssh . . . Ssh.

Stewart leads Michael by the arm.

Michael What?

Stewart You'll wake him up.

Michael Who?

Stewart Lenny.

Michael Christ! Who's he?

Stewart The fella I share with.

Michael What?

Stewart Ssh, come on. He won't wake up. He won't mind if he does. He'll be quite happy.

Michael No.

Stewart Yeah! Come on.

Stewart begins to unbuckle his belt.

Michael Or . . .

Stewart Right then!

Michael Oh yes!

Stewart I'm off then.

He doesn't go.

OK?

No response.

OK?

Michael What? Oh yes. Yes.
Or . . .

Stewart Do you want me to ring?

Michael Or . . .
Why don't you ring?

Stewart No. I won't bother.

Michael Or . . .

Stewart Are we here then?

Michael Or . . .

Stewart This is it, then?

Michael Or . . .

Stewart Do you live by yourself?

Michael Or . . .

Stewart Is this all yours then?

Michael Or . . .

Stewart I don't want to hurt you.

Michael Or . . .

Stewart Are you a student?

TWO

Christopher is sitting, smoking a cigarette and reading. David is standing.

David What is it?
Chris.

Christopher What?

David What's the matter?

Christopher What do you mean what's the matter. I'm reading.

David Oh dear.

Christopher I'm alright, honest. What is it?
David.

David It's alright. It's alright.

Christopher Oh Christ. Come on. What?

David Nothing. Give us.

David takes Christopher's cigarette. Christopher lights another.

Christopher I thought you weren't supposed to smoke. You're always telling me not to smoke.

David Well you shouldn't smoke.
I thought you'd look nice in a punt.

Christopher I come from Oxford. I didn't go to Oxford.

You went to Oxford.
It was a nice afternoon. It was.

David No it wasn't.

Christopher Well it doesn't matter does it?

David Thanks.

Christopher Oh Christ.

David Can I have a drink?

Christopher Yeah.

David What have we got?

Christopher What have we got? You can have lager or extra strong lager.

David Yeah.

Christopher goes out.

You think this is it. You think this is . . . Smudge of oil on his cheek. That's the way his hair falls when parted. This is . . . him.
I see him go from startled laughing unbelieving boy to junker-headed sensualist.

Christopher comes in with two cans of lager.

How's that other car?

Christopher OK. OK.

David Nearly finished?

Christopher Very nearly.

David Alvis. Another Alvis?

Christopher Yes another. Greylady.

David Why do you work in a garage?

Christopher What's this now? Why do you work in a hospital? I like working in a garage. What do you want me to do, take a course as a wheelwright?

David That's not what you said yesterday. Don't you want money?

Christopher No I don't want money. Do you? You don't have any money.

David No. But I'm not short of money. You must have earned money.

Christopher I did alright. It's in the house. She's got the house OK? It's hers. Do you want more money. From me?

David No.

Christopher Well shut up then.

I used to work with people who would have gone to a party on the Marchioness. Girls in advertising who eventually wanted to get into films. One chap – no two of the chaps – said they were really writers but they had to pay the bills. Not the prats who stood in the sandwich queue at lunchtime using mobile phones. Bond salesmen playing Trivial Pursuit. But people who said they wanted to make a killing and then get out. We all had to wear red noses for Comic Relief and sponsor one of the partners for the marathon. One of the girls' boyfriends did sponsored abseiling. It was always someone's birthday or leaving party. There was always cake and champagne and grab bags full of bloody stupid presents and afterwards the trek to Covent Garden to get pissed in a tapas bar. I was glad.

David Of the elbow?

Christopher Yes. I was. It meant I didn't have to make a decision. I like cars.

David What's that?

Christopher It's a picture of a 1958 Buick convertible. Well I put up with your pictures. The statutory Matisse.

David You don't like anything. Except for cars. You don't.

Christopher I liked that play. That play.

David What play?

Christopher I liked it.

David What, that political play?

Christopher No, no. That play.

David I don't remember.

Christopher You do. That play.

I want to set fire to him. I want to crash my bike into a moving lorry. Jump off the bridge. Throw him out of a moving taxi. Saved by the bell. Seconds out.

I'm going up for the weekend.

David Oh, are you?

Christopher Yes. To see Jamie.

David This isn't your weekend.

Christopher I know.

David Oh.

Christopher I want to see if he's alright.

David He's alright.

Christopher She says not.

David I took him in didn't I? There's nothing wrong with him. Why does she think that a gluten free diet is the answer to an unhappy child? What's wrong with the child? He's got his imitation Royal Family coat. There's nothing wrong with him.

Christopher How do you know?

David I know.

Christopher You should know.

David I'm not a paediatrician. I'm an obstetrician. I was a paediatrician, briefly.

Christopher I thought you were a gynaecologist.

David I am.

Christopher Of course you think that no woman can give birth without you.

David I do sometimes. And sometimes I hear fathers at parties arrogate the birth of their children to themselves. We were in labour for 32 hours. We didn't properly dilate. We had a section.

Christopher Oh shouldn't fathers be at the birth of their own child?

David Yes, but it's got bugger all to do with the baby. It's a sort of narcissism. There are still women who don't want, can't have the man with them. They don't have someone holding their hands singing Ten Green Bottles. I want to say yes, you can be part of this if you promise to be with the child and its mother in ten years' time.

Christopher How's that woman?

David What woman?

Christopher What woman? All the other women you call cases or patients. This one has a name.

David Women do have names. They have names even if one doesn't know them. Even if you don't use them they have names.

Christopher Alright. How is she?

David Who? Mrs Murray?

Christopher Yes. She's the only one you ever talk about.

David She's back in.

Christopher Again. Why?

David Oh. To be safe. She brought me in a cake.

Christopher Do women still make cakes?

David Mrs Murray does.

Christopher What is it?

David Chocolate.

Christopher Great. Where is it?

David I had to leave it in the ward. I had to.

Christopher Didn't you bring a piece home?

David Perhaps there'll be some left tomorrow.

Christopher She wants to send him away to school.

David Where?

Christopher That school for very gifted parents. Christ knows who's going to pay. That'll be the next thing.

David Who's going to pay?

Christopher I'm not going to pay. I can't pay. He can go to a school locally like everyone else.

David You mean like you and me. She is his mother.

Christopher I know. I know.

David Well she is.

Christopher I know.

David She just is Christopher. Why don't you go back to her?

Christopher What? Why don't I go back to her? She's hard, she's mad, she's stupid, she's narrow, she's an impossibly selfish, materialistic, unlikeable, unkind, spurious . . . Oh forget it. Why don't I go back to her? She wouldn't have me.

David Do you want to fuck her?

Christopher Yeah I'd fuck her. Well you asked.

David You didn't have to say.

Christopher What does it matter?

David You know it does.

Christopher Oh . . .

David You know it does Christopher.

Christopher What is this, are we supposed to behave like some couple now are we?

David Yes.

Christopher You're giving me power. I don't want power.

David You don't want power? You want the power you want not the power I give you that's what you want.

Christopher I'm serious. Why must I be serious when you want to be serious.

David I think I taught you to be serious.

Christopher You want to dominate me dominating you.

David When?

Christopher When you take it out so you can see me see me come in your mouth.

David I somebody once but this nothing with evidence of his once assertive potential but now nothing as far as I'm concerned. He's as empty as he was but I can't get any pleasure of . . . Light up like a child. Illuminating . . . That I made light up. His light. Now nothing most off anyway. This for that and yes I was . . . if . . . of the . . . Then so intelligent.

Christopher You don't like me. You don't. You only fancy me because you think I'm straight. You were only interested in me because I was married. I think you think – no I think you want me to be shagging half London.

David The thing is when I go for a test each month it's only in case you've been fucking around since last month.

Christopher What?

David I always know or if not know in retrospect I realise I have known. If it was me I'd know how to deceive me without you even knowing. You're so selfish you can't even deceive successfully. You really don't want to deceive – you sort of don't mind if someone finds out. You're just careless.

Christopher Once.

David Once. What about? And.

Christopher Yeah alright.

David Bareback.

Christopher No.

David You can't even call her by her name.

Christopher It's you who won't use her name.

David I can't use her name if you won't. It's you who won't call her by her name.

Sometimes when I'm in the clinic you come into my mind with your not as thick as you think dick and I would really like to put your legs in the stirrup and say there there and fit you up.

For you I am someone to have laughs and be free with.

Christopher Yes.

David And free of.

Christopher You're going to make me want to go you know. I don't want to go but you are on your way you are to making me want to leave. You want me to go.

David Above me with that intent fag in the mouth don't disturb me I've got to get this wheel changed it will take some time man at work look. Your fag in the mouth hang on I've got to get this fixed air.

They talk now a lot about the addictive personality. They sometimes . . . They forget people who are spellbound. Addicts under a spell. You are spellbinding and I am under your spell.

Christopher I feel I am letting you down in some way. I don't mean to let you down.

David When are you going?

Christopher Not now.

David Oh not now. When not now?

Christopher Don't let's – not now.

David Well I'm going to bed. I've got to be on duty for 72 hours.

Christopher Well that's fine and fucking dandy.

You're just trying . . . me . . . You're not even trying to make me. You're so . . . in a state you'll do anything for . . . Get out of my head. Get out of it. I'm . . . in and out of you. You . . . I feel I'm driving up the motorway the wrong way.

David What is it?

Christopher It's you when you're so desperate.

David I'm going to bed.
You did look nice in a punt.

THREE

Michael and Stewart.

Michael I didn't think you'd ring.

Stewart I said I'd ring you.

Michael I know you did. I still didn't think you would. Why should you? I wouldn't have.

Stewart Well there's the difference between us isn't it? I wouldn't have said I would ring if I wasn't going to ring.

Michael You didn't say much on the phone.

Stewart Wasn't much to say.

Michael You came round quick enough.

Stewart I didn't.

Michael Oh.

Stewart I took my time. Anyway what's it matter? I wanted to come round.

Michael Good then, you're here.

Stewart Yeah that's right. Well then.

Michael What.

Stewart Come here.

He makes a move towards Michael.

Michael No.

Michael moves away.

Stewart Suit yourself. I can take my time.

He looks down at a pile of books on the floor

You still got all these books then.

Michael Yeah.

Stewart picks up a copy of 'The Gift Relationship' by R. H. Titmuss.

Stewart 'The Gift Relationship.' 'From human blood to social policy.' When was that written? When the world was young? What have you been doing with yourself?

Michael Do you mean today?

Stewart Today, yesterday. What's the matter with you? Do you want me to go? I'm not going.

Michael Or it could be . . .

Stewart I'm gasping for a fag. D'you smoke?

Michael I don't. I'm sorry. I know, let's go and get some. Why don't you go and get some?

Stewart I'm skint.

Michael I've got money.

Stewart Let's go for a drink then.

Michael Oh.

Stewart Yeah! C'mon.

Michael OK.

Stewart D'you play pool? I'll teach you to play pool.

Michael I can play pool.

Stewart You can't play pool. Can you play pool?

Michael Of course. Can you?

Stewart Of course. I'm brilliant. I've kept myself in fags playing pool.

Michael Or it could be . . .
What is it?

Stewart is rubbing his eye.

Stewart I think I've got something in my eye.

Michael Come here.

Stewart No.

Michael Pull your lid over it.

Stewart No.

Michael Go on.

Stewart does so.

Now how is it?

Stewart I think it's better. Thanks. No it's still here.

Michael Come here. Come here.

Stewart No.

Michael Come on. Hold still.

He removes the grit from Stewart's eye.

There we are, look. There we are. OK?

Stewart Thanks.

Michael Or . . .
Can you whistle?

Stewart Course I can whistle.

Michael You know, like this. Can you whistle like this?

With his fingers in his mouth, Michael makes a loud whistle.

Stewart Of course I can.

Michael Go on then.

Stewart attempts and fails.

Michael I thought you couldn't.

Stewart What does that mean?

Michael Or . . .

Stewart How are you?

Michael Good, very good.

Stewart Good.

Michael I wish you hadn't asked that.

Stewart Why?

Michael Now I don't feel so good. I felt fine, now I feel fairly fucking terrible.
Or . . .
What if he keeps his cigarettes in his teeshirt? Oh my God.
Or . . .

Stewart I came down two years ago.

Michael Or . . .
More brutal exchanges don't you think? Regardless of my views on the matter.
Or . . .

Stewart I'm not living anywhere special.

Michael Or . . .
Sometimes I think I'm as intelligent as I pretend to be.
Or . . .

They sit on the floor to talk.

Stewart I came down with this young lassie. We travelled down together. After I got picked up by the police, she went back. I was bevvying a bit. No money. No kip. I was sent down. You couldn't blame her.

Michael Or . . .

Stewart I was in this doss in London and one morning I went to take a piss, and someone came in and said where's Lenny and tried to kick the cubicle door in. So I went into the next cubicle and I pulled myself up to look about, and there he was, Lenny, sitting with his head rolled back and a needle beside him on the floor. Then the superintendent rang the police and said he's dead as far as I can see. Take your time anyway. He's no use to anyone. An old man died in the same doss, so the authorities came to take the body away. They handed him as far as the landing and one of them says 'hey up' to the men below and tipped him over the banister. They never caught him. They put him in a box and carted him off.

Michael Or . . .

They roll towards each other simultaneously, one tumbling over the other as they meet and end up some distance apart, each lying on his back.

Stewart I like being with you. I do. D'you hear me? You. What about you. Hey.

He hurls a book at Michael.

Michael You're beautiful. I know that.

FOUR

Tony sitting. Andrew comes in.

Andrew I'm sorry.

Tony S'alright. Sit down.

Andrew You fed the dog?

Tony Yes.

Andrew You taken him out?

Calls the dog

Tony I have. Leave him. Sit down.

Andrew I'm sorry. I'm late.

Tony Do you want your tea?

Andrew No. I'm alright. You had your tea?

Tony No. I'm having something later.

Andrew I'll make you something.

Tony No. I'll have a cup of tea.

Andrew Yeah. I'll have a cup of tea.
Why haven't you asked me why I'm late?

Tony You'll tell me. I don't have to ask you.

Andrew Why don't you ask me? Don't you want to know? You angry?

Tony No. Why should I be angry? You're not very late.

Andrew Sure you're not hungry?

Tony No I'm not. I'm not angry either.

Andrew Do you want to go out later?

Tony No. Get in first. What do you want to go out for? You only just come in.

Andrew Alright. Keep your hair on. We'll stay in. I don't want go out. We'll stay in. You'll read the paper. I'll watch the telly. I'll read the paper and you'll watch the telly and then we both might watch the telly.

Tony That's right.

Andrew And you won't say anything.

Tony That's right.

Andrew All night.

Tony That's right. I'll listen you you.
Don't you want stay in?

Andrew Yeah. I'll make us something to eat later on.

Tony No. I'll do that. Sit down love.

Andrew Why don't you want to know why I'm so late? I might have been out for a drink with someone.

Tony You might have. But you haven't.

Andrew I might have had an assignation.

Tony Might you.

Andrew I might have.

Tony Don't.

Andrew With –

Tony Don't.

Andrew See. You don't know. Do you?

Tony Who?

Andrew No one.

Tony Who?

Andrew No one. No one.

Tony That . . . In the showroom.

Andrew Sh. Don't sulk. Give us a kiss then.
Come on. No one.

Kisses him.

Tony Be quiet now, for fuck's sake. And have a cup of tea. What's the matter with you? You never used to be like this.

Andrew Like what?

Tony I don't know. Oh all the time asking questions. Why don't you take the dog out?

Andrew No. I used to be docile. Like your mother. Not any more. Not me.

Tony Leave my mum out of it.

Andrew Yes, sonny. No, sonny. Ooh.

Tony Leave it out.
I spoke to her today. She asked how you were.

Andrew She sympathises with me. You're spoilt. She spoilt you.

Tony She did. I am.

Andrew See. Well, I'm not your mother. Not any more, I'm not.

Tony I think among the most stupid things, one of the most stupid things, no, the most stupid, stupid thing, stupid, is to say I'm not your mother.

Andrew Well, I'm not. So don't blame me, and don't start.

Tony For what?

Andrew For not being your mother. Because, I'm not.

Tony I don't want you to be my mother, what you talking about.

Andrew Good. Because I'm not. Going to sulk now. You can't have a conversation.

Tony I can have a conversation. I don't want a conversation. You pretend you want a conversation. You don't want a conversation. What's the matter with you?

Andrew I don't know. I don't know what's the matter with me.
Do you know what they're talking about?

Tony Who?

Andrew The papers, the radio, the telly.

Points to the newspaper.

Here, this. I really don't know what they're talking about half the time. The chosen. Men. Decisions. I really don't.

Tony Who?

Andrew Men. To be a man, you see, you've got to be a clown. You've got to be able to act the fool. I can't act the fool. I can't clown about.
What are we doing together?

Tony Oh don't. What's the matter with you? Not a man. Where you been then?

Andrew Nowhere. I been round Robert's. Nowhere.

Tony Well then, that's it. He's wound you up.

Andrew He's alright.

Tony You come back like this.

Andrew Like what? I can go round there.

Tony Yeah.

Andrew You jealous?

Tony Of him? Get real.

Andrew Why haven't you come out to your mother?

Tony You see, that's him, that is. It's always the same. He winds you up. Why haven't you come out to your mother? Shut up. Shut up.

Andrew I didn't come out to my mother because I didn't want to give her the pleasure of it. I don't want to give her the opportunity of expressing whatever it is she'd want to express. Either way. Give her the chance. But your mother likes you. She worships you.

Tony Your mother likes you.

Andrew No. She doesn't. It doesn't matter. It's your father you're afraid of.

Tony I don't want to come out to no one.

Andrew But you could come out to your mum.

Tony This is all. Shut up. All this is. What are sexual politics? Talking about it. Analysing it. It was his idea to get a gay plumber. Gay plumber. Who wanted a gay plumber?

Andrew I didn't want a gay plumber.

Tony You did. We did.

Andrew I thought we should show solidarity.

Tony Yes. Well.

Andrew No. I don't want. Don't. Don't come that with me. I don't want all this . . . gay. Gay this, gay that.
I thought it would be a good idea to have a gay plumber.
See. Well people are. Blokes are discriminated against.

Tony You're giving importance to what we can't do fuck all about. Let's just keep calm. What's the matter with you tonight? I get upset about what normal people get upset about. What I know about fox hunting? I don't give a toss about fox hunting. See. You get it all out of kilter.

Andrew I can't have views?

Tony That's not what I mean. Yes. But you said what we doing together. You said that last night. I said, talk like you won't be together with no one. Shut up. Let's get on with it. Don't think. Think. Think. You're no better a thinker than what I am. I want to get on with it. You'd be a bundle of laughs in the back of the pictures, you would. You'd be a bundle of laughs in the back of a parked car.

Andrew You can't say it. You never say it.

Tony I don't want to say it.

Andrew I don't want to say it. I do say it though.
On Valentine's Day, who bought you a praline heart?
I wasn't intending to.

Tony Yes.

Andrew You ate it though, didn't you? You don't believe in it, you say it's silly. It don't mean anything. I would. I would do what you want.

Tony What is it you want? What? You've tied me up in some difficult knots.

Andrew I haven't. It's you. You won't shift.

Tony I don't wanna shift.

Andrew You won't beat me. You won't.

Tony I'm not trying to. What you talking about? Don't laugh.

They laugh.

Andrew This . . . Parallelism. The parallel lines of this. On the parallel. We'll never meet. I don't want any more. Yes. Like it was yesterday.

Tony What?

Andrew And today. This morning. I don't want any more. Just don't make it worse.

Tony Make what worse? I don't get, I don't get, I don't, I don't get it.

Andrew It's me. It's me.

Tony What's you?

Andrew I'm not a man. I'm not a leader. I'm not a man. I'm letting my sister do everything. Sort out whether my mother should go into a home. I'm not serious.

Tony What . . . How . . . you not serious?

Andrew Well, listen. No listen. For a start, to start with, men without children aren't serious.

Tony Don't talk about kids. That's all nothing to do with me alright? That's not my concern. What do you want to concern yourself with that for?

Andrew Why can't you talk about anything?

Tony What's this to talk about?

Andrew I wasn't asking anything. I only perhaps wanted to talk about it. I only wanted to talk about what just crossed my mind. I don't think I could bring up a kid.
I realise I hate my mother entirely. Still see that friend of yours, what's his name? It's the victims, the victims I think about. That's my mother. Yeah. 'You don't want to do that.' But mum, I've lived. I've jumped over the fence. 'That's nice then.' I'm not serious.

Tony Look. I don't want to talk about this. I don't want to be a woman. I don't want to talk about it. Grow up. We're not special. This isn't a marriage.

Andrew I know that doesn't mean you don't have to work at it.

Tony You can't let go – can you? Can you though? You won't let it happen between us. There's all the outside, you've got to bring it home. I'm tired of all the outside. And there's plenty to talk about. You take seriously what's yours to be talked about. There's nothing more important than you and me. There's no more. We're not going through all that. That opinion. How we going through it. That. All that. It's not happening to us. It's not what's happening to us.

Andrew But it is happening to us. I'm trying to make it happen see. I don't want no more silent nights.

Tony I don't know what you're talking about.

Andrew You do.

Tony Nah. Don't know. I'm afraid I don't know. I don't know anything about it. I don't know nothing, I'm ignorant, me. Where's the paper gone?

Andrew You do.

He crumples up the paper.

Tony Don't do that to the paper. Fuck. I'll fist you. Fuck it. I'll do you.

What's the matter? Isn't it alright? Here with me.

Andrew Yes. No. Of course it is.

Tony And it's better out there.

Andrew No. I don't know.

Tony No.

Andrew Not the wine bar stuff. Not stuff your face. Hang out, chill out. Clubbing. Football. Go for a run. Go to the gym. Do weights. Oh, I'm in computers, me. Chemical engineering. Oh me, I work in a sports centre. Rented cars, insurance, rental, the retail business. Booking office, quality control, maintenance office, record shop, men's tailoring, computer graphics. And explaining *this*. I'm living with my mate. In a side street, know it? Yes. Original features. Garden flat. Paved garden, music centre, deep freeze, rag rolled walls, uncover that fireplace. Star Trek books. Star Trek video. I don't want to miss Prisoner of Cell Block H. Flat! Investment. Who's paying the mortgage? Ooh. Nice.

Tony I'm paying the mortgage.

Andrew Yes. It's not even mine. Who am I?

Tony Well, you shouldn't worry. You'll get your mother's place, share it with your sister. Talk to her.

Andrew Let's go to a car boot sale. I like car boot sales.

Tony You do.

Andrew Look at this barbie. I got a soap dish. That's me. Plastic! Cool. Plastic toast rack. Look at this plate, that record. Tape for the car. Tape for the car. Annie Lennox. The Tourists.

Tony What's wrong with it?

Andrew That's not life. That's getting a life, that is. Get a life. Get a life. I don't want a life. Life happens between those things.

Tony That's life.
Sit down. Be quiet.

Andrew If I challenge you, you'll go away you will. If I go away, you'll get over it, you will. That's your mother, it is. If I stay, what'll I do? This for a little love.

Tony Not so bad.

Andrew When through all the thoughts I clear a path I think I'm alive. This is alright. This is OK. The light in the sky reflected as my eyes brim. Then this almost . . . feeling. I think of you. I have to love you. I know I must. It's as though I've been born. Or joy or something.

He makes to go out.

Tony Where you going?

Andrew Take the dog out. Judy, here dog.

FIVE

David and Christopher are drinking tea from mugs.

David Not herbal tea. Not herbal tea.

Christopher Yes herbal tea. It's quite nice.

David What's it made of?

Christopher I dunno.

David You don't know what it's made of.

Christopher Drink it.

David I can't drink this.

Christopher Well make a cup of tea then.

David You make better tea than me.

Christopher Yes.

David You do. You do Christopher.

Christopher Drink it.

David It's awful.

Christopher It's good for you. It won't make you so jumpy.

David What's it called?

Christopher Happy Apple.

David It doesn't taste very happy. Anything to eat?

Christopher Nothing.

David What else? There's bound to be something.

Christopher You want me to get you something?

David No thanks. I don't really want anything. I think I've got a temperature. Why did you buy this?

Christopher Just drink it David.

David You're always in a foul mood when you come back.

Christopher You're always in a foul mood when I come back.

David You're always in a foul mood when you take him back.

Christopher I'm not. I'm always a bit sad. Is that alright?

David Do you think I've got a temperature?

Christopher Nope.

David I think I have.

Christopher Here. Nope.

David Get the thermometer.

Christopher You haven't got a temperature. Shut it.

David Christ you're happy.

Christopher Right. Where's the thermometer?

He goes out.

David I rang you. I exist. When you're there I'm here OK.

Christopher comes back in with a thermometer.

Christopher Here. I'll put it in.

David Oh ay.

Christopher puts the thermometer in David's mouth.

Christopher I don't feel responsible – in any way. I look at him in wonder but I don't feel very proud of myself. Of him of him. Oh, of him.
Here.

He takes out the thermometer.

David It's not cooked.

Christopher Nothing see.

David I rang you.

Christopher Yes.

David I rang you. I exist. When you're there I'm here.

Christopher I know. She makes a thing about it. Silently.

David Oh really. You didn't ask me why I rang.

Christopher I know why you rang.

David To see how he was. What was the matter?

Christopher There was nothing the matter. As usual it was a false alarm. You told me so. That's not why you rang.

David No?

Christopher It's the same when she rings here.

David Where did you sleep?

Christopher Where do you think I slept?

David I don't know.

Christopher Look it's not as if I'm there very often.

David Did you like it?

Christopher It was quite pleasant. No it wasn't.

David What's up?

Christopher Nothing. What's the matter with you?

David Why are you allowing her to still have this effect on you? It makes me feel great.

Christopher I suppose I must feel something. I hate her so much. Say something David.

David She's not my kind of girl. She's too winsome. That hair. That Little Miss Muffet outfit. That juvenile miniskirt. You couldn't kill her with cyanide. Why are you making me say all this? You know I don't like her. Girls like a fairy on a Christmas tree. It's not so much her as you. She must be alright. She's got a very nice child. At least I like him. Except she's got this thing about his skin, his teeth, the usual nonsense. Feeding him carrot – no chocolate. What about school?

Christopher Nothing about school. Digs about money.

David What was that nursery school he went to? The rat hole.

Christopher Squirrel Corner.

David It must be the only Montessori school in Hertfordshire. Is he coming next weekend, Jamie?

Christopher Yes. If that's alright.

David It's fine. He can watch me play cricket. What with you under a car and me at the crease, he's not short of healthy role models.

Christopher I feel bad about him. I don't feel responsible in any way. I look at him in wonder but I don't feel very proud of myself.

David Not of him?

Christopher Of him. Of him. Oh of him. Yes of him. What does he make of things?

David Well he knows.

Christopher How?

David Children know. Look don't worry. You wear pyjamas. He wears pyjamas. I wear pyjamas. He wears a dressing gown. You wear a dressing gown. I wear a dressing gown. All we need is Horlicks and a briar pipe. We could get my mother to embroider a Radio Times cover.

Christopher Your mother.

David What do you mean? You like my mother.

Christopher Your father.

David My father. Your father.

Christopher Oh my father. My mother thinks you're a nice boy. How's that woman?

David She's fine.

Christopher She still in?

David Yes. We're going to keep her in. Not long now.

Christopher She got a husband?

David I don't know. I think so. I suppose so.

Christopher Why do you like her?

David I don't know that I do. I think because she's angry.

Christopher Why does she like you? They all like you.

David But she likes me for my mind.

Christopher What's wrong with her?

David Nothing actually wrong with her – but she's had four children – all difficult pregnancies. She's going to name the baby after me.

Christopher I found a letter.

David Where?

Christopher In her sewing table.

David Does she sew?

Christopher Not much but she sews. It was her grandmother's. That's where she keeps her letters. Ones she wants to keep.

David For others to read. What was in it?

Christopher There were quite a few. I knew she'd been seeing someone.

David How did you know?

Christopher I knew. And from what Jamie said. Ages ago. He stays quite frequently it seems.

David You didn't say.

Christopher I'm saying now.

David Who is it?

Christopher An old boyfriend. A friend of her brother's. They're well suited.

David Christ.

Christopher There was nothing about me in the letters.

David Should there be?

Christopher He's a creep. A real creep. He wears his hair in a ponytail.

David What does he do?

Christopher Nothing. This and that. He's got a bookshop and he's split up from his wife and he's got two children – one of them's called Merlin. And he's part of some New Age community and he's given her these crystals. He's healing Jamie's allergy with them.

David Jamie doesn't have an allergy.

Christopher Jamie told me they'd been to a vigil – a candlelit vigil. What can I do?

David Absolutely nothing. I'll have to have a paracetamol. Have we got any?

Christopher What do you want a paracetamol for? I don't know if we've got any.

David I can't have a temperature.

Christopher You haven't got a temperature. Stay there. I'll get you one.

SIX

Michael and Stewart.
Michael sits by Stewart.

Michael Can't you get a job?

Stewart I don't want a job. I've had a job.

Michael I'm sorry. I'm sorry.

Michael gradually moves towards Stewart on his hands and knees but stops before reaching him.

Stewart That's OK.

Michael I just meant. Well.

Stewart What?

Michael You seem.

Stewart What?

Michael I don't know. You're . . . Oh . . . Money . . . You're so . . . I want. Oh . . . Are you OK?

Stewart I'm OK. The giro'll do for me. I've had jobs.

Michael Or . . .
What is it?

Stewart Nothing.

Michael You can tell me.

Stewart Nothing. I'm alright.

Michael Or . . .

Stands.

You're a lazy fucker.

Stewart Well you'd know.

Stands.

Michael You take the action for the deed, that's your trouble.
Or . . .

Stewart Look, Lenny was already on it. I don't do smack or anything much. I can take it or leave it. I'd rather a drink which is just as well on my income. What business is it of yours anyway?

Michael Or . . .

Stewart Look.

He shows Michael his hand.

Michael What?

Stewart Sweating.

Michael That's alright.

Stewart No it isn't. I don't like it.

Michael Come here.

He takes Stewart's hand and licks it.

Stewart You . . .

Stewart makes a fist at him, joking.

Michael Or it could be . . .
Then it could be . . .
Or it could be . . .

Stewart Do you want me to stay?

Michael Or it could be . . . No.
Or . . . No.

Stewart What's the matter?

Michael Or . . .

Stewart What is it?

Michael Or . . . No.
Or . . .

Stewart It's alright.

He tries to comfort Michael.

Michael No.

Michael pushes him away.

Stewart Come on. Come on. What's the matter?

Stewart persists.

Michael No.

Michael pushes him away.

Stewart Come on.

Michael No.

He pushes Stewart away, violently.

Stewart What is it? What is it?

Michael How am I going to get through? A lot of people spend their lives just in drink . . . When you drop dead. Do you want everlasting life? Just to grow old when you come to think of it. Does that worry you? I think the problems start when you start listening to yourself. I know who I am but I don't know where I am. I'm all over the fucking place. This is awful. I could . . . Go away. I have to be by myself. If I could put myself in touch with my feelings I'd probably kill you. It's when you're not here I want you. I want to reach across and hold on to you. To hold you. Only I seem not to be allowed any feelings. I seem not to have feelings except sentimental ones. Or I seem only to have feelings. I seem to be all feelings.

Michael rejects Stewart again.

Don't please. I'm frightened, I'm OK. I walk around and even now when I'm talking . . . If someone had died I'd have some reason for this. I'd have some right to this feeling. If you died. If someone had just died even. If you were dead. But I haven't first call. You see . . . I think . . . You see to dwell upon the ulterior motive for the sake of truth is . . . To overemphasise that everything is dependant upon motive. To emphasise *that* truth is to deny that ulterior motive does not only produce results for the self. To think altruism is only worth measuring by ulterior motive is wrong. Stupid. Or to deny spontaneity. I'll have to get it together. How am I going to get it together?

Stewart You will.

Michael Do you think so?

Stewart You will.

Michael Never mind. I'm in pieces. Not even pieces, scraps. I'll have to get it together. How am I going to get it together?

Stewart You will.

Stewart embraces him.

Michael Do you think so? I don't think I ever will.

Stewart You will.

Michael moves away.

Michael Yet there's another part of me that doesn't give a fuck.

SEVEN

Andrew and Robert.

Robert Did you walk into a door?

Andrew Yeah. Something like that.

Robert How did you do it?

Andrew I could fucking kill him. I could fucking punch him. I could punch hell out of him. Cheek. I'm really mad.

Robert Sit.

Andrew No, I'm too . . . I am. I'm fucking mad at this. No. I can't. I'm sorry.

Robert What you going to do?

Andrew I'm going to kill him. I'm going to fucking kill him. I'm going to break everything up. Smash all the windows and then when he loses his temper again. Then in that case I'll knife him. Or poison the dog.

Robert Apart from that, what are you going to do? Here.

Gives him a drink.

Andrew Thanks.

Drinks.

Christ. I don't know. He went. He fancies himself. I should have knocked him out. I'm furious.

Robert Why didn't you?

Andrew I could have. I could have, I could. I could have him. He thinks he's mister . . . He's stupid, I wouldn't give him the pleasure. I should have, what's this now? Domestic violence. Abuse. What are two grown men doing living together faking all the stupidities of a fake straight relationship, what's all that about?

Robert Ah well. What's all that about. If we only knew what that's all about. Sex. That's what it's usually about.

Andrew No. No, it's not sex. No. I don't want to talk about that. I don't think you should.
There's something wrong about the whole thing.

Robert What?

Andrew Everything. Everything. I don't want to be an imitation of an imitation.

Robert Of what?

Andrew Of everything. Yeah. Everything. Gay pride. Gay shame, that's what this is. No everything. The thing I'm copying. I don't want it or what it stands for. It's a form of what my mother wants.
Did you go to Diana's funeral?

Robert Yes. I thought I should.

Andrew I didn't. That's what I mean. I don't know what it is. But I don't want it. No. Don't laugh.
What's gay culture?

Robert What's gay culture?

Andrew What underpants you got on?

Robert Yes, well . . .

Andrew Calvins.

Robert Yes.

Andrew That's gay culture. That's about the size of it. Don't laugh. The make of your underpants.

Robert Oh I don't . . .

Andrew Well what else. What else has come out of gay culture? Discos. Body fascism. Is there a gay community?

Robert Well in so far as gay men oppress themselves, there's very like what you call a gay community. I can't imagine there's been much of a call for a homeland though. I don't think we need one. Queers we will always have with us. But you're searching for a solution. What if there is no solution to anything.

Andrew I'll just have to go on looking.

Robert Have you ever been to Pride?

Andrew No. I wanted to go. He wouldn't, see. To see what it's like.

Robert Well you should go the once. I only went the once. But it's not me. But then neither is the Last Night of the Proms. So you can't go by me. I wouldn't like the Highland Games. Or the County Show. Or the Welsh National Eisteddfod. Or St Patrick's Day in New York. Or an Orange March. Or the Notting Hill Carnival. Or Badminton or the Cup Final.

I'm not a great fan of the British Legion.

. . . But being queer can be a project like anything else. It's not your particular project. We all have our axes to grind. Why shouldn't being queer be an axe to grind like other people's? It's not something it's easy to avoid. Some people try.

Andrew Well you don't grind the queer axe.

Robert I hope I do in my own way. It's whether you believe in a continuum or categorical differences. For all the apparent freedom these are prescriptive times. There are choices and they want you to make them. For some you've got to wear a suit or at least a jacket. Have what they call a partner. Now there's a word. There's a word for the market place.

Andrew I don't want to have a partner. It makes you sound like a firm.

Robert I think that's the idea. Makes you into a sound financial proposition.

Andrew I doubt if anyone without an income has a partner.

Robert Settle down. Get a mortgage. Join the Rotary Club. Join the party. Take part. It's the price you have to pay for being comfortable.

Andrew I don't want to take part.

Robert Well join the radical wing of the movement. Where to be really queer you have to have someone nail your foreskin to a piece of wood and generally kick up a fuss. All this sounds much better in the original French. It loses a lot in the translation. Transgressive. Now there's a word too. I have a sneaking sympathy for all this. I think queers are still ultimately transgressive. Jouissance. The unkennelled seeking out of the difference. But in English it all takes on a homely air. The transgressors always turn out to sound like George Formby. The rank smell of poppers and leathers and the seeking for jouissance in the wilds of the heath and I'll thank you to keep a civil tongue up my arse. Hoping to star in a cluster fuck but settling for just being Mrs Norman Maine. I don't think that's for you. Nor the New Labour Old Comptom Street cool Brittania queens. The all inclusive, one price, fun and funky, up for nothing, body conscious, size queens. Disco dollies who think you're old at 27. Cock-led love, cock-led lives. Unaffectionate, meretricious, coarse, conventional. I'd rather the Judy queens. They can at least talk about something. The people I'm talking about haven't got the attention span to take in a drag act. Can't you see the funny side of it?

Andrew Only too fucking well.

Robert That's the mainstream. We're just another niche in the market. And that suits everyone down to the ground. Well able and willing to be neutralised. Sentimental, silly, frivolous, a bit of a laugh, very sympathetic listeners, harmless fodder for gay nights on TV. A convenient addition to popular culture, for the whim of TV executives. Part of the dumbing down. Manipulated by people who having had considerable cultural advantages themselves, want to deny it to others because they're too lazy and too greedy to do otherwise. I don't think there is a gay sensibility. Not a stable one. This all part of the straight man's game.

The success of Judy Garland or Barbra Streisand or Maria Callas can't have been decided on by gay men. Or Stephen Sondheim. Even. Even. There have always been straight queens. We're part of their entertainment. It's to do with a struggle that everyone has with the fact of gender. The anger of all of us at being biologically sorted. Look at straight men. Most straight men are male impersonators. We're making a fuss. Look at the fuss they make in the confusion. But all the while for us and our African brothers and sisters there's something that cracks the whole thing open. The demand for viral rights by that little unsentient claimant to life. That undermines the whole show. You want to know why you're with someone. Don't think there's much more to it than knowing who you're spending the weekend with or Easter or Bank Holidays. It's someone to share the torture with.

What's the alternative? That's what most people have concluded. Gay men aren't different from anyone else in that respect. People aren't in couples for the general good. I don't see pair bonding as some predetermined absolute. We're all much the same. Except that women are seen to be more mysterious than men, more inscrutable. Men are quite straightforward. Their selfishness is so entirely predictable.

Andrew But what about people who haven't got a partner?

Robert Or lost one.

Andrew I'm sorry.

Robert Well what are you going to do?

Andrew I don't know.
No it's not my feeling for him that's fake. I don't think. It's something else. If I don't see him it will be alright but I dread the sense of worthlessness at the prospect. I'm so angry. I'm so frightened. I'll collapse. Where's my inhaler? He's so vain. I like vain men. I like a bit of vanity.

Robert You fool. You don't want to put up with it. He done it before?

Andrew Threatened.

Robert I'm worried now.

Andrew He takes a liberty with a privilege. He wouldn't do it again in a hurry. I don't care if it's my fault. It probably is. He'll have to learn to punch the wall.

Robert When did it happen?

Andrew Last night. I went round my sister's. He's been trying to phone me. He been here? He'd be too scared.

Robert What your sister say?

Andrew She didn't say anything. She says her husband doesn't understand her.

Robert What did you do?

Andrew The dark hours went and I got some sleep.
I haven't been to work.

Tony comes in.

Tony You're here then.

Andrew Yeah I am. That's right.

Tony I didn't know.

Andrew No you didn't.

Robert Do you want anything to drink?

Tony Yeah. No I'm alright. Honest. Thank you. Thank you. You coming home?

Andrew No, I'm not.

Tony The dog misses you.

Andrew Yeah. Look I'm going.

Tony Don't go.

Andrew Yeah. Thanks. I'm off.

Robert You sure?

Andrew Yeah. Tara. Tara.
I'll see you.

Tony Why you going?

Andrew So long.

He goes.

Robert Let him go.

Tony Did he tell what happened?

Robert Not really.

Tony Oh dear. Stupid. I wish it hadn't happened. You know. I don't know what to do now. What do you think?

Robert I don't know.

Tony When I first knew him it was before you knew him.

Robert Yeah.

Tony Yeah.

Robert What does that mean?

Tony Nothing.

He didn't know anything. He just was, I don't know, innocent. That's it. Even naive. He didn't know anything about sex. Nothing. That was so sexy about him. He's a little bit Country, I'm a little bit Rock and Roll.

Please don't.

Robert What?

Tony Please don't take him from me.

Robert No.

Tony You're going to take him from me.

Robert I'm not. I'm not. What makes you think. I'm not interested in him.

Tony Please don't tell him I've spoken to you. Will you?

Robert Of course not. Come on.

Tony I'm horny.

Robert Are you? Come on.

Tony Sorry. Thanks. Thank you.
Last night. I came round here. Was he here?

Robert No. He wasn't here.

Tony Where was he?

Robert I don't know. You'll have to ask him.

Tony I was outside here. It was damp in the street.

Robert Why didn't you ring the bell?

Tony No. No I just pulled my coat collar up and watched till the lights went out. Till there was one on in the bedroom.

EIGHT

Andrew and Terry.

Terry No. I like old men. I wanna be old. I can't wait.
I went into care first when I was three. In and out, you know. Then I got out of control. I never went to school. I never went to school, never. Honest. I didn't. I used to nick my mother's fags for her, mate. They were my family, they was all criminals. Thieves. They weren't honest.
My father's family. My father. We don't know where he came from. Not Roehampton. He lives in America now. They was very unaffectionate. I just used to thieve for my mum. I can't go there now. My uncle died. My grandmother wouldn't have me in the flat. She says I'm the worst. I went to boarding school. I did. The masters was OK. It was the older boys, that's what it was. Eighteen-year-olds and that. Abuse, like. I used to get in bed with my mate. Then, like, you're sixteen. You're not in care, are you? Anyway. Out. Off you go.

I like you. I like your voice. Posh. Like your eyes. Your mouth. Look see. Gold filling. I'd like a gold tooth.

Andrew Where you living?

Terry I'm staying with my mate, the other block from my grandmother. I keep out of her way. It's cool.
I'd like to keep lizards. Cold blooded. No I like the feel of them. Cold blooded. I like really scary books. Stephen King. Have you ever read a book by Edgar Allan Poe?

Andrew Do you like girls?

Terry Girls. Yeah, I like girls. Girls all are OK. Aren't they. No. I'm like, well, you fuck a girl easier, like. Obvious. But blokes suck cock better, don't they? Funny that, innit? They're more, like, industrious. Hungry. Not greedy. They go for it. I like blokes. I know more about geezers. Girls are all over you. I've always been round blokes. Most of the girls I know wear knickers to keep, their ankles warm. No. That's not right. I like some girls. I know a girl I like. But she's chirping all the time. Giving it this. Some lyrics don't half come out of her mouth, honest.
What's this then, where you live?

Andrew My mother's flat.

Terry She in?

Andrew No, no. She's in a home.

Terry Oh yeah.
This yours?

Andrew No. My sister wants to sell. But I don't think we can. I don't think it'd be right. She might come back.

Terry You always lived here?

Andrew No I only been here. I left . . . You know, I told you.

Terry Oh, him. You wanna kick him to the kerb mate. He's a dog. You want me in here. Look after you. Get the shopping and that. What's the matter? OK?

Andrew Yeah.

Terry You alright?
You're trying to make me queer, I think. You trying to make me queer. I think you are.

He pulls up his sleeve.

Andrew What's that?

He takes hold of his arm.

Terry No.

Andrew I'm sorry.

Terry No. It's alright. Look.

Andrew What's that? Needle marks.

Terry What? You seen needle marks in ridges like that?

Andrew I'm sorry.

Terry I used to cut myself. Nah. It's alright. I never do it now. See – these are old. I don't do it now.

Andrew What you do it with?

Terry Anything what cuts. Razor blades. It's. Oh well.

Andrew Why?

Terry Why. Well, like they said it's only to get attention. It's . . . no, I can't. I can't explain it. I don't do it no more. I ain't a kid like that no more. No I got more sense now.

Andrew Why you looking at me like that?

Terry Because that's how you was looking at me son earlier.

Andrew Was I?

Terry Yeah. You was. You're cute, ain't you. Come on.

Andrew I always want it to be over. It's the chase, you know. As much as doing it, isn't it? As much as the act.

Terry What? What you talking about?

Andrew No, it's alright.

Terry Well what we gonna do?

Andrew I don't know.

Terry Well suck my cock then. Do you want to? Suck me off then. OK.

Andrew Blimey.

Terry See. You love it. You been a naughty boy.

Andrew You got anything on you?

Terry I haven't got anything. I haven't brought anything on purpose. Live dangerous.

Andrew No then.

Terry Come, you want it. I want it. You want to feel the tip of my cock nuzzling in your arse, don't you? You do.

Andrew Not safe.

Terry Don't be soft. If it's going to get you, it's going to get you. Next time I'll bring loads of condoms.

Andrew No.

Terry I like meeting people like you. You're interesting. I like talking to you. You're good, you are.

You got something to drink?

Andrew No. Tea.

Terry No. Yeah. No, hurry.
Well, what we gonna do?
No. I come down there with my friends. We saw all these geezers hanging about. What was we on? We was on something.

Andrew Oh yeah.

Terry No. I was just walking through there tonight. No. Leave it out.

Andrew Do you want anything?

Terry What?

Andrew Do you need anything, you know. Do you?

Terry No, I don't want money. I don't want your money. No. I don't do nothing for money. No. You can give us a fag, you got one?

Andrew Yeah. Yeah. Yeah. Of course. Do you want them?

Terry What?

Andrew Do you want a keep them?

Terry Thanks mate. Sweet. I ain't got any indoors. I'll have a couple, OK? No I don't want money though. You know I only ever done one bad thing like that, yeah?

Andrew What's that?

Terry Well like I met this bloke and, like I said, like, I'd see him again, you know. And of course I lose his number, right. Straight up. Of course. And then I then I didn't go round there and that. Well, one day, my mate, I owed this bloke money and he had to have it and I was skint. I said to him 'I can't – I ain't got a lot of money.' I'll see you the weekend. And he had to have it, you know. He really did. I had no money nowhere. So I was near his house. The bloke. I thought, oh well. So I rang on my mobile. You got a mobile?

Andrew Yes.

Terry Excellent. You got a pager?

Andrew No. I thought you lost his number?

Terry No. I had, it was on a bit of paper in this jacket. This jacket I was wearing, straight, and he was in. I said, like, if I come would he pay for the cab. Couldn't think of anything else. And it was OK.

Andrew Why didn't you just ask him for money?

Terry No. I couldn't. I couldn't. Honest, I couldn't. So he give money for the cab at the door and I took it and I never went back. That's bad, that's bad, that is. Like a junkie, like, or something, innit. I don't like that. I should give it back. I'm going go over there one day. I am. I know where he lives.

Andrew What did you used to do

Terry What did I do? Thieving. Houses. You . . . Someone says, you know, know where I can get a radio? I don't do it no more.

Andrew You sign on?

Terry Sign on? No. They can keep it. They don't worry me. Them.

Andrew What would you like to do?

Terry What would I like to do? Nothing. What could I be?

Andrew Lots of things.

Terry I could be a TV chef. I like cooking. Or have a chat show – like Montel. Or I could be in a boy band. Yeah.

Andrew Would you steal round here?

Terry Them flats? I would. They can afford it. I wouldn't do something like here. No they wouldn't miss it. I don't do that now. I don't want to go inside again.

Andrew No you don't.

Terry No. I don't. You're right, I know – I shouldn't. Too fucking true. I'm keeping out of it. Oh yeah. I'm sure. I'm not doing that any more. Ain't worth it. As it is they pick on you for anything once they know you, mate. It's worse in prison.

No you can't cure paedophiles, mate. Not if you castrated them, you wouldn't.

Andrew What can you do then?

Terry You'd have to kill 'em, you wanna cure 'em. They don't worry me. I wasn't bothered much, me. It's funny, paedophiles, like, they're the same. Like, if they like, like you when you're fourteen, that's OK. But they're really on somebody who likes nine-year-olds. They're just like anyone else.

Andrew You have taken some action?

Terry No more than what you'd have to take against, my mother, my fucking father. That's alright though, innit. Keep it in the family.

Andrew What have you taken?

Terry No. I don't do drugs. Now. I never done much. Done bit a gear. But I never got . . . I got more sense. I don't drink. A lot do E. The weekend. You know, that's all.

I'd like to kiss you. I would. Straight. I would. Do you want me to fuck you? Do you want to fuck me? I don't mind. I'm coming down. I'm feeling very, you know, like . . .

I'd like to see you. Can I see you?

Andrew You are seeing me.

Terry Come off it.

Andrew Yeah. You can see me. But you won't come round.

Terry If I don't come round, you'll know you can never trust me again. Come on.

NINE

David.

David I took my mother to the Tate for lunch and because she wanted to see the new hang. Hello Mother. How was your train? Where's Mrs Oakley? She usually has her friend with her. They come up to town together as a team. I don't think she likes what she sees. I can't tell. I think she thinks it's her duty. They usually make straight for the Royal Academy. Do you want to see the Pre-Raphaelites now, Mother? No, dear, not yet. And she stands assessing whatever is the most questionable new acquisition there. Installations are what take her particular attention. She usually sniffs at them and says, interesting. And I know she wants to see Ophelia Drowning – because she's sent me a postcard of it twice. Then we have lunch and then a matinee. I couldn't face it.

She usually has Mrs Oakley with her. They're old campaigners. They been at it for years. Forays every month or so. Matinees now because of the trains. Did you like the play, Mother? Very interesting, dear. Are you sure you don't need a taxi? No, dear, no. No need. How's Christopher, she says at some point. Goodbye dear. She says, even brighter then.

I don't think I'm incompetent enough. She prefers my brother, who's a hopeless drunk or you because you've done something interesting. I think I challenge her competence. It's as though she's jumped a generation. She's quite from another time. See you soon, dear. When will you be down? Daddy would love it. Daddy wouldn't love it. Daddy couldn't care less. I don't know why I'm being so ungenerous. She's a really good woman. It's just seeing her on the train always makes me think of going back to school.

TEN

Tony and Christopher.

Tony Nice motor.

Christopher Would you like to buy it?

Tony I would. But I wouldn't have the price. Do you want anything?

Christopher You've got a dog.

Tony Do you want a drink? A beer?

Christopher I'm driving.

Tony Well, you're not going yet, are you? You can have a beer. Are you?

Christopher I ought to go.

Tony Why did you give me a lift then?

Christopher Because you like the car. You wanted a lift.

Tony I wanted more than a lift, mate.

Christopher You've had more than a lift.

Tony Yeah. I know. But that was a bit, well.

Christopher Public.

Tony Yeah. And I couldn't see.

Christopher It's not that I don't want to, but . . .

Tony Why did you come in?

Christopher I know. I shouldn't have.

Tony What's the matter? You playing away from home? You married? Are you? Is that it?

Christopher Yeah. I am. Just at the moment and I shouldn't. Are you on your own?

Tony Yeah. Yeah. I am just at the moment. I'm just shagging and drinking at the moment. I'm going to get pissed tonight.

Christopher Why?

Tony Something to do.
You been there before?

Christopher No I haven't. It's quaint, isn't it?

Tony Yeah. It's too handy for me. Near the station. Persuade myself I need a sauna after the long slog. You?

Christopher I was showing the car to someone and I couldn't sell it. There's a classic car garage in one of the arches.

Tony What is it?

Christopher A Hispano Suiza.

Tony Cracking motor.

Christopher I don't think I'll be able to get a price for it though.

Tony You want to stay down here?

Christopher No. Don't make me feel . . . I should go.

Tony No. You don't want to go. She won't know.

Christopher I know she won't.

Tony You coming up?

Christopher I'm so weak.

ELEVEN

Terry and Robert.

Terry I come round. I never phoned because I lost your number. I didn't know whether you'd be in. I was lucky. See, I'm always lucky. I'll bring you luck. Aint you pleased to see me?

Robert Should I be?

Terry I couldn't explain. I want to explain.

Robert Explain then.

Terry See I had to have the money for something.

Robert I thought you had to pay the cab.

Terry I had me mate outside. There was rowing.

Robert Why didn't you come back?

Terry I know. I know. Bad, bad man.

Robert So what you round here for now? You haven't come round to pay it back, have you?

Terry Ain't you glad to see me? I bet you are. Ain't you?

Robert No. I'm not. Why should I be glad to see you?

Terry You are. I'll get you the money, somehow. I'll pay you back. No, I will. I just thought I'd ring the bell. I had to be down here. This way. I thought . . . I'll go if you like. Is that it? OK then. Well you could, like, give us a cup of tea. I'm parched.

Robert I could.

Terry Go on then. Come on, don't be like that. I'm really sorry, I am.

Robert Do you want any money? No, no. You need money, don't you?

Terry I don't want money.

Robert You do. That's why you're here. It's alright. Tell me, is that it?

Terry No, that's not why I'm here. No, no. That's not why I'm here. On my life.

Robert Doesn't matter. Here take it, go on.

Gives him money.

Terry I ain't got no money. I'm skint.

Robert I know. Go on, take it. It's alright.

Terry Thanks.

Robert Don't say anything. Now I'm going to throw you out. OK. I got things to do.

Terry No. Let me stay.

Robert No.

Terry Come on.

Robert No, no. I've got to begin work soon.

Terry So I got to go?

Robert Yeah.

Terry Alright then. So long, mate. I'll see you.

Robert I don't know whether you will.

TWELVE

Stewart and Michael.

Stewart I've been for a drink.

Michael Good.

Stewart I've got to have a piss.

Michael Good.

Stewart I feel sick.

Michael Great.

Stewart Michael.

Michael What?

Stewart Michael.

Michael goes to him.

Michael Sit down, come on.

Stewart No it's alright, I'm alright thanks.

Michael You alright?

Stewart Yeah, you're a pal. I'm going for a piss OK. What's the matter?

Michael Now I feel sick.

He bends over, his hands on his knees.

Stewart No, don't feel sick.

Michael I think I'm going to be sick.

Stewart No you're not.

Michael How do you know I'm not going to be sick?

Stewart Are you gonna be sick? Michael.

He goes to comfort Michael and leans over his back, resting.

Don't be sick: I'm not going to be sick. I'm never sick. Are you alright Michael? Oh, Michael, I'm going for a piss. You coming for a piss? I feel rotten. I'm gonna put my fingers down my throat.

Michael Now I feel really sick.
Or . . .
What is it?

Stewart Leave it out will you.

Michael Hang on. Hang on. Hang on!

Stewart Just leave it.

Michael What's the matter?

Stewart You are.

Michael Or . . .

Stewart I'm going for a drink.

Michael Oh yes.

Stewart Yes.

Michael Oh Christ!

Stewart Yes.

Michael Look, why don't you go for a drink?

Stewart I am going for a drink.

Michael Well go for a fucking drink then.
Or . . .
Are we going to the pictures then?

Stewart I don't know.

Michael Well do you want to go to the pictures?

Stewart I don't know, why should I have to make all the fucking decisions?

Michael Well why should I have to?

Stewart Well why should I?

Michael Don't shout.

Stewart I'll shout.

He sits on the floor.

Michael What is it?

Stewart I'm fucking confused, I can tell you. I've never felt like this before, I can tell you. About any fucker.

Stewart is crying.

Michael Why?

He kneels by Stewart and puts his arms round him.

Why?

Stewart Get off.

Stewart pushes him away, Michael follows him. Stewart turns in to Michael briefly then pushes him violently away again.

You're so fucking clever you are, you ought to be done away with, you. You're sick. D'you know that? You're sick. You're sick, d'you know that. You're sick. You are. You're really sick. You're sick. You really are.

Michael Don't.

Stewart Do you love me? You love every fucker you do.

Michael Come on. Come on, let's go to the pictures.

He takes Stewart by the elbow.

Come on.
Or . . .

Stewart I have to thank you. No. I do.

He grabs hold of Michael.

No, don't fuck about. Thanks. Thanks. Hold still. Thanks.

Michael Or . . .
Hello. Nice to see you.

Stewart Don't start anything.
Don't Michael. Alright?

Michael Very nice.

Stewart I've put the kettle on.

Michael I've been everywhere looking for you. I've been to the pub. I've been to the Irish pub. I've been to all the snooker halls round here. I've been to Sid's Snooker Saloon. You looking for Stewart, you've just missed him. I've been down Portobello to see if you were scoring. I've been in the Elgin, I've been down All Saints Road. I went over to Cold Harbour Lane. All up the Railton Road. I came back here again. I nearly rang the law. I've had a really good time. You?

Stewart What you go over there for? I haven't been over there. How long is it since I've been over there?

Michael I don't know. Where have you been?

Stewart Look I was on the piss. I didn't think I'd better come back.

Michael Where'd you end up?

Stewart I don't know.

Michael You know.

Stewart I don't. Look, it's none of your business where I've been, where I ended up.

Michael Just tell me.

Stewart I'm not telling you, Michael. And if you were so concerned you should have shown some concern earlier. I can go out by my own if I want to, OK? Anyway, I asked you to come with me. I wanted you to come. I'm not staying here with you pulling me to pieces one minute and not talking to me the next. You talk about commitment. You haven't spoken to me for three days. What am I to do?

Michael Why didn't you ring up?

Stewart Because I didn't want to.

Michael I'll pull it on, I will, one of these days.

Stewart Well, you wanted me to go out. Didn't you eh? Didn't you?

Michael I didn't.

Stewart Didn't you?

Michael I didn't.

Stewart Oh yeah. Well, why wouldn't you talk to me?

Michael Where were you, tell me. Please.

Stewart And anyway, what about you, eh? What about you?

Michael What?

Stewart You know.

Michael I don't know. What? There was an old man dying. I worked on.

Stewart You didn't tell me.

Michael Did you mind then?

Stewart No, of course I don't mind. But you didn't tell me.

Michael You haven't said anything about it since.

Stewart Well I'm saying it now. I had to ring and find out where you were.

Michael You didn't tell me.

Stewart To find out if you were working on. I had to make a right fool of myself.

Michael How was that making a fool of yourself?

Stewart Well it was.

Michael Well what do you think I was fucking doing last night? And I haven't been to sleep. And I've got to be up all tonight.

Stewart Now you know what it's like.

Michael Stewart, I worked all night because an old man was dying and they were shorthanded and I spent most of the day with him and I worked on.

Stewart You're stupid you are, anyway.

Michael What do you mean?

Stewart You're more qualified than what any of that poxy lot are. What's the matter with you! You've had an education. You give up a top job in the civil service and now you're a hospital fucking orderly.

Michael Auxiliary.

Stewart And how long's it gonna last?

Michael What?

Stewart What are you going to do next?

Michael What are you going on about? What am I going to do next? What about you? What are you doing? What do you do all day? Sleep, boozer, betting shop, smoke dope, sleep.

Stewart But Michael, you haven't got the necessary to be a tosser like me. What are you doing?

Michael Leave me alone.

Stewart But you're making a mess of yourself.

Michael I'm tired.

Stewart Why'd you give your first job up, eh?

Michael I don't know.

Stewart Why? Tell me.

Michael Don't. Please. Really.

Stewart Go on.

Michael I think I thought it was wrong. And you know . . . Growth.

Michael laughs.

I wanted to do something connected with people. Where were you?

Stewart No.

Michael You've got to tell me.

Stewart I haven't.

Michael Tell me.

Stewart No.

Michael Alright. Put the kettle on.

Stewart It's on.

Michael Go on.

Stewart It's on, it's on. Do you want me to sing to you?

Laughter.

Michael Where were you?

Stewart You'll never find out.

Michael I will.

Stewart I doubt it. Got a paper?

Michael There.

He gives Stewart a newspaper.

Stewart Oh Christ, I've got to change. Have you got any clean underpants?

Michael I've stopped wearing them. They're bad for you.

Stewart Oh aye.

Michael Am I making the tea?

Stewart I don't know. Are you?

Michael Are you?

Stewart I will if you like.

He drops the newspaper.

Michael I'll do it.
Where were you? Tell me.

Stewart Michael. No.

THIRTEEN

Terry and Andrew.

Terry Why won't you talk to me?

Andrew I don't know why I let you in.

Terry I know why you let me in.

Andrew No you don't.

Terry Don't I? No. I'll go then. I only thought we could have a drink, like. Have a few beers. You know. How's your mum?

Andrew Don't ask me about my mum.

Terry No, no. I won't. I lost your number. I did. I did.

Andrew I know you did.

Terry I did. Well, what's the matter then?

Andrew It's no good. It's no good.

Terry I don't know what I'm going to do. I been on the rob again. I ain't got no money. I ain't got no one. I ain't got nowhere.

Andrew Where you sleeping?

Terry Here and there.

Andrew This is no good. Honest. I'm sorry.

Terry I ain't got no one. I'd like to have you. I'd like to be with you. Don't get rid of me. You want me to go.

Don't you? Why? Look. I brought something. I'll protect you.

Andrew Don't.

Terry You liked it. You wanted me to fuck you. I liked it. You're exciting. You wouldn't keep still. Your pukka. I'm good at loving, I am.

Andrew No.

Terry I'll shoot off then. Is that it? Is that it, like?

Andrew Yeah.

Terry Well, yeah. I'll fuck off then. Fuck off then you. Alright. Fuck off. You don't know nothing, you don't. I'm fucking off. Fuck you.

Andrew No. Don't.

Terry Fuck off mate.

Andrew Don't.

Terry Am I staying, then?

Andrew No.

Terry Fuck off, then. I'll be alright.

FOURTEEN

David is sitting reading a letter. Christopher is standing.

David Does Jamie have to wear a kilt?

Christopher No. Why should he have to wear a kilt?

David I don't know. Or velvet.

Christopher No. What's the matter with you? It's only some ceremony in the garden. It's not a wedding. Don't you want to go?

David Not much.

Christopher Well you said you did. You said we had to.

David That's because you said you wouldn't go.

Christopher Oh and because I didn't want to go, you thought I should.

David Well you should go. Jamie wants you to go.

Christopher He wants you to go.

David It's a very nice letter.

Christopher Is it?

David It is. It is, Christopher.

Christopher If you say so.

David It just is.

Christopher Have you seen the invitation?

David No, where is it? Where is it?

Christopher Don't bully me.

David I'm not.

Christopher Just don't.

David You've got to stop this.

He finds the invitation.

I'd have thought they'd have used recycled paper. What is it?

Christopher Don't . . .

David Oh come on.

Christopher Don't.

David Right.

Christopher Sorry.

David Do you want a drink?

Christopher Do you want me to get it?

David She's had the baby.

Christopher Who?

David Mrs Murray. Who else do you know who's having a baby?

Christopher When? You didn't say.

David You didn't ask.

Christopher Oh thanks.

David The husband's a nice chap. At the delivery he fainted. We said it might be difficult. The baby was in distress. Thank God the midwife wasn't the senior midwife. She makes me feel hopeless. We couldn't get hold of the boss or the senior registrar. So I had to deal with it. It was a girl. Safe as houses.

Christopher picks up the invitation.

Christopher What about this? What are you wearing to this? What are you going to wear?

David Shorts.

Christopher No, you can't wear shorts.

David I don't know.

Christopher Wear your linen suit.

David What are you wearing?

Christopher Jeans.

David You can't wear jeans.

Christopher I can wear jeans. It's only in the garden.
You're the most exciting person I've ever met. And the most exhausting. When you're interested, you really are interested. You never forget anything I've ever said about myself – you make me feel I belong to you in some way. As though I'm part of you and I don't like it. Because. Well, it's as though I'm some extension of. That I'm some territory you know very well and are angry at losing. Some part of an empire. And your jealousy is frightening because it makes me feel I don't exist and responsible and angry. That it has nothing to do with me. And I could do without it. I really could. I don't want to feel so important. But you make me feel important in a way I've never felt. As though everything I've thought was something I had to be accountable for. But I sense your loyalty. Somehow I feel it's like a creed – political, religious. I can't imagine not knowing you now. You'd always be there fighting.

David We have to answer this.

Christopher Do we really have to go?

David Yes.

Christopher What's her name?

David Who?

Christopher Mrs Murray.

David Mrs Murray.

Christopher No her name.

David Don't know.

Christopher Do you want a drink?

David Yeah.

Christopher What's she going to call the baby?

David Mrs Murray? Well, she isn't going to call her after me.

FIFTEEN

Stewart and Michael.

Stewart I'm going.

Michael Why?

Stewart Ask yourself.

Michael Where will you go?

Stewart Don't worry about me.

Michael Or . . .

Stewart I don't know what I'm doing here.

Michael Don't you?

Stewart Cut it out, Michael, will you?

Michael Well what did you say that for?

Stewart Because I don't.

Michael Why don't you?

Stewart I don't know.

Michael Why?

Stewart Stop it, Michael, will you?

Michael I don't think this is perhaps what we had in mind.

Stewart I didn't have anything in mind. I think it was you who had things in mind.

Michael Or . . .

Stewart I'm going.

Michael Don't do that.

Stewart No I'm going.

Michael Where will you go?

Stewart Don't worry about me.

Michael I won't.
Or . . .

Stewart This is stupid this is.

Michael What is?

Stewart This is.

Michael Not as stupid as you. I can't do this. This is hopeless. You're so stupid.

Stewart Hey you.

Michael What? What? I'm not scared of you.

Stewart Not yet you're not.

Michael What?

Stewart Alright. Alright.

Michael Or . . .
I thought you were going.

Stewart I am going.

Michael I'm glad to hear it.

Stewart I am.

Michael Well go then, fuck off then.

Stewart I will.

Michael Well go on! Go on! Why don't you just go!
Or . . .

Stewart What is it? Oh blimey, Charlie, shall I come over there?

Michael Oh Christ no!

Stewart I want to.

Michael Well I don't. This is like . . . I don't know what this is like. Like . . . this is.

Stewart Don't Michael.

Michael I'm alright. Don't come over.
Or . . .

Stewart I'm moving out.

Michael Don't do that.

Stewart No, I'm going.

Michael Where will you go?

Stewart Don't worry about me.

Michael Why do you want to do that?

Stewart Why do you think?

Michael Or . . .

Stewart See, I can't handle it. I don't know what I'm up to.

Michael I see.

Stewart Can't you see what I mean?

Michael No.

Stewart Well, I'm not up to it. That's for sure.

Michael Or . . .
I suppose one person can't be held responsible for the effect he has on another, wouldn't you say?

Stewart No, I wouldn't say. I bloody wouldn't say.

Michael Or . . .

Stewart I'll be off then. OK. Is it OK?

Michael What are you asking me for?

Stewart Well come with me.

Michael Or . . .

Stewart Be nice Michael. Be nice.

Michael Or . . .

Stewart Why do you want me to go?

Michael I don't.

Stewart But you do, Michael. I'll go if you'll say.

Michael I don't.

Stewart You do.

Michael I don't! I don't! I don't!

Stewart You see.

Michael Or . . .
Please.

Stewart No, for Christ's sake.

Michael I'll try.

Stewart No.

Michael I will.

Stewart You try.

Michael It's worse for me.

Stewart Oh yeah.

Michael I didn't mean it like that.

Stewart Oh.

Michael Don't go.

Stewart I've got to.

Michael It is possible.

Stewart I know.

Michael It basically seems to depend on whether you can do the washing-up. I'll do the washing-up.

Stewart Oh blimey. I haven't got it, Michael.

Michael Or . . .

Stewart Let's sort it out, shall we?

Michael Or . . .
Or . . .

Stewart What do you want to do then?

Michael Or . . .

Stewart Am I staying?

Michael Or . . .

Stewart Come on, let's go.

Michael Or . . .

Stewart We'll be alright.

Michael Or . . .

Stewart What do you want?

Michael Or . . .

Stewart Just tell me!

SIXTEEN

Tony and Andrew.

Andrew How's the dog?

Tony He's alright. He's fine. My mother's looking after him.

Andrew But he's your dog.

Tony I know. She's got him for a few days.

Andrew See. See.

Tony What?

Andrew I knew you wouldn't feed him.

Tony He's been fed. My mother's fed him. You coming back?

Andrew What are you asking me?

Tony Don't. How can you stay here? Look at it.

Andrew Yes.

Tony I'm sorry.

Andrew I know.

Tony But I am. I'm sorry. I shouldn't have done it.

Andrew Don't keep on. I'm not asking you to say you're sorry. I don't want to hear about it again and again.

Tony Well, that's what started all this.

Andrew Is it?

Tony Isn't it?

Andrew I don't honestly know.

Tony Am I to say sorry for the rest of my life?

Andrew Look, no. Leave me alone.

Tony Well, what's going to happen? Is that going to be it? Don't you miss me . . . at all?

Andrew Yes. Don't be stupid.

Tony Come home. Come back with me. Now.

Andrew No.

Tony You can't stay here for good. You don't like it here.

Andrew We're going to have to sell it.

Tony Well, what you going to do?

Andrew I feel it will always get out of hand.

Tony And you don't want to risk anything.

Andrew I'm angry about what I can't change and what it is you still find in me. I can't find anything any more. I haven't the strength to go unprotected any more.

Tony Don't say that. I've thought, get someone else.

Andrew Have you?

Tony But it's not like that, is it? It's not finished between us. I feel this grief. I should let you go. I'm holding you back. Aren't I? Is that what it is?

Andrew Hold me back. What? I'm going nowhere. I'm so tired of making sense of the senseless. I don't know what I'm trying to do. Accept you for what you are. Which means what? I can accept you for what you are. You can't accept me you can't. I can't accept me.

Tony I don't know what I'm ever going to do without you.

Andrew You will.

Tony I won't.

Andrew You don't have to do without me. I'm not going anywhere.

Tony I was in bed last night and I started involuntarily to think about you.

Andrew Oh, just last night.

Tony It's every morning. I wanted to talk to you.

Andrew What about?

Tony I simply had things to say. Now I've fucked everything up.

Andrew What did you have to say?

Tony Don't be like this. It's not like you. You're not like this. Show some feeling. Come on. Let me. Let's find a way. Teach me. Show me. Please, Andrew. I'm lonely. I'm lonely without you.

Andrew Don't.
I'm not coming back.

Tony Don't be like this. What is it?
I can change.

Andrew I don't want you to change.

Tony What do you mean, you don't want me to change, what's all this?

Andrew Not change. You can't ask someone to change. I didn't ask you to change. You're alright.

Tony How can I be alright? Look what's happened.

Andrew Perhaps I could change. But I don't think you can change back. You're alright as you are.

Tony But how can I be alright as I am? Because I want me to change. I want to change because if I don't I won't have you. But what am I to change? But I don't know how to change.

Andrew I never wanted you to change.

Tony You did.

Andrew I never said change. Did I ever say change? Don't change.

Tony Don't cry. Come back with me. It's alright. I know. I know. But can I see you? Is that it?

Andrew Yeah. Yeah.

Tony I want to fuck you.

Andrew Oh yeah?

Tony Don't. I do.

Andrew Yeah.

Tony Don't.

Andrew Yeah.

Tony Can I?

Andrew Yeah.

Tony Now?

Andrew Yeah.

Tony What, here?

Andrew Yeah.
But I'm not going back.

SEVENTEEN

Stewart and Michael.

Stewart Why didn't you ring?

Michael Couldn't.

Stewart Who brought the letter?

Michael Me.

Stewart You.

Michael I didn't think you'd come.

Stewart Why didn't you think I'd come?

Michael You're pretty diffident. Hence the note.

Stewart You should have rung me. Idiot.

He laughs.

Fool.

Michael You don't ring me. But I'm grateful all the same. Thanks. Honest. Thanks for coming, thanks. Thanks.

Stewart How have you been?

Michael Fairly fucking dreadful.

Stewart Not so bad then.

Michael You?

Stewart Oh me. Of course. You know me.

Michael Don't you want to know?

Stewart What?

Michael Why the letter?

Stewart If you like.

Michael Listen, this is important.

Stewart I know, Michael. Honest, why do you think I've come over, eh? Oh Jesus, listen. There's more at stake for me, you know.

Michael Oh aye.

Stewart Because you'll eventually get fed up with all this. Bound to. And where will that leave me, eh? Can you answer me that? You alright?

Michael I'm alright. You alright?

Laughter.

Stewart I brought this back.

He gives Michael a book.

Michael Did you like it?

Stewart Quite.

Michael I can't see why you couldn't have come round. What a bastard thing to do. Why don't you come round? I just can't bear the feeling that you're not coming round. That I'm not going to see you. But what would happen if you did come round? And yet there have been times in the last week when I have so wanted you to be here. Sitting here. When I've thought of things to say to you. Nothing much. Why? Why? But I'm no better than you, that's the truth of it.

You'd better go, hadn't you?

Stewart I suppose.

Michael Hadn't you?

Stewart If you want me to.

Michael Will you be alright?

Stewart I'll be fine. I'll ring you.

Michael Will you?

Stewart I will. Honest.

Michael But will you?

Stewart I said I would.

Michael You got the number. Where's the number? You got the number.

Stewart I've got the number.

Michael Where's the number? Oh Jesus.

Stewart Shall I ring you?

Michael If you want.

Stewart Do you want me to?

Michael If you like.

Stewart You've still got all these books then?

Michael Do you want to come in?

Stewart Shall we go then?

Michael What's your name?

Stewart Do you want a drink?

Michael Not very far.

Stewart By yourself.

Michael Not very often.

Stewart Where do you live?

Michael No. I don't.

Stewart Where's your jacket?

Michael I don't want to hurt you.

Stewart Are you a student?

Michael Or . . .

Stewart Michael.

Stewart doubles up in pain. Michael holds him.

Michael, it's hurting, it's hurting.

Michael It's alright.

Stewart Michael.

Michael It's alright.

Stewart Michael.

Michael It's alright.
Or . . .

Stewart Come on.

Stewart pulls Michael by the arm.

Michael No.

Stewart Yes. Come on. Come on. Come on!

Michael No.

Stewart Come on.

There is a violent struggle between Michael and Stewart, during which Terry stands and calls looking as at a window.

Terry Are you in? Let me in. Let me in. Are you in? Let me in. Let me in. Let me in.

Michael and Stewart have stopped struggling.

Stewart It's alright.
Do you want to leave it then?

THE YORK REALIST

For Bill

The York Realist received its world premiere on 15 November 2001 at The Lowry, Salford Quays, with the following cast:

George Lloyd Owen
John Richard Coyle
George and Barbara's Mother Anne Reid
Barbara Caroline O'Neill
Arthur Ian Mercer
Doreen Wendy Nottingham
Jack Felix Bell

Director Peter Gill
Designer William Dudley
Lighting Designer Hartley T A Kemp
Composer Terry Davies
Assistant Director Josie Rourke
Dialect Coach Jeanette Nelson
Casting Director Toby Whale

Characters

George

John

Mother
to George and Barbara

Barbara

Arthur

Doreen

Jack

The play is set in a farm labourer's cottage outside York in the early 1960s

One

The living room of a farm labourer's cottage. Leading out of this is a small kitchen which was once the scullery. In the living room, stage right, is an outer door and a window. Left, there is a dresser. At the back is a range no longer used for cooking and, next to this on the left, is a door which opens onto a staircase. To the right is a door into the kitchen where there is a sink under the window, and above the sink a gas water-heater. Nearby, a gas stove and an outer door.

Late afternoon.

George and John in the living-room. George having just let John in.

George Well.

John Yes.

George Aye.

John Yeah . . .

George Well then. Mm . . . Yeah . . . Come in.

John I am in.

George No, come in. Sit down.

John I'm all right.

George I must stink. I haven't changed. I only just come in the door.

John I timed it well.

George You did. You timed it well.
I must stink.

John No. What's the matter with you?

George I was just going to have a wash. I'll just put the kettle on and have a wash. OK?
Had your tea?

John I'm all right. You'd better have your tea, though.
Had your tea?

George No. Not yet.
This is a surprise, though. Isn't it, though?

John Perhaps I should have let you know. You still haven't got a phone.

George No.

John I should have . . .

George No. No. No.

John Just as well. I think that might have . . .

George I'm glad you didn't.
What bus did you get?

John I didn't get a bus.

George What?

John I drove.

George You drove?

John Yes. Why shouldn't I drive?

George You didn't like driving a tractor.
You must have set off early, didn't you? That was a bit of a drive.

John What, six miles?

George No, the drive up. You drive up today?

John No. Yesterday.

George You didn't come over yesterday then?

John No. I didn't get here till late.

George You kept your options open.
What you up for then?

John I'm at the Theatre Royal for the week.

George Oh aye. What's that, a play?

John Yes.
I didn't know whether I should come over or not.

George Why not?

John I dunno. Anyway . . .

George It must be a long drive up in a car. It's five hours on the train.

John Yes. Mind you, the motorway makes it easier. Bit . . . bit . . . daunting.

George I should think so. Well, you're not dependent on the bus tonight are you?

John No.

George You couldn't stay here so easy now. Could you?

John No. No. No.

George You wouldn't have the excuse of the bus with the car.

John *We* wouldn't.

George What?

John Have the excuse.

George No.
Aye, if you stayed here now you could have a proper bath.

John Oh.

George Council grant. Put in a bathroom. Cost me nowt.

John Nowt?

George Nowt.

John That'd have pleased you.

George It did.
They want to take that out. (*indicating the fireplace and range*)

John Going to let them?

George No.

John Why?

George I'm not.
Anyway. I won't be a tick. I still have a wash down here. Used to it.
Yes, they offered to take the range out. I wouldn't let them.

John Oh.

George You said you liked it.

John I do.

George Well then. See.
I better get out of these. You all right a minute?

John Yes. Of course I am.

George Then I'll get the tea after.

John Not for me.
Do you make your own tea then?

George Yes, who else?

John I'm sorry about your mother.

George Yes.

John I wrote.

George Yeah.

John You got it?

George Yeah.

John I thought I shouldn't come.

George Why not?

John Oh.
You managing? You all right?

George Aye. Course I am.
Sure you don't want anything?

John No. But you'd better have something.

George Barbara and Doreen. I have to fend them off.

He goes into the kitchen and begins to wash.
John looks at the fireplace.

John I'm glad you didn't let them take this out.
I said . . .
George.

George's Mother comes on through the door, revealing the stairs.

George What say?

John Nothing.

Mother What am I looking for?

John I said I'm glad you haven't taken out the stove.

Mother Oh yes. Clean pinny. I've got it on. Tt. Tt.

John Can I do anything?

George No.

Mother Do you want a clean shirt, George?

John I'm going to the car.

George What?

Mother Do you want a clean shirt?

John I'm going to get something from the car.

Mother George.

John George.

George What?

John I'm going to get something from the car.

George OK.

John exits.

Mother Do you?

George What?

Mother Do you want an evening shirt?
George.

George What?

Mother Do you want a clean shirt?

George Of course I want a clean shirt.

Mother Do you want one of your decent ones?

George You mean am I going out? I might have to go up later to give him a hand. There's a cow about to calve. So I'm not going out. Right?
Where's the towel?

Mother There's a clean one in here.

George comes into the living room wearing different trousers and without a shirt.

George Give us.

Mother Why are you so late? He's got you doing the work of two men.

George There's Charlie. We manage.

Mother He used to have more than you and Charlie. He needs more than two men. He's always been tight. His father was the same.
What shirt do you want?

George It doesn't matter which one I want. I'm not going out.

Mother Aren't you going to your play?
This'll do you, then.

He takes the shirt she offers and puts it on.

Have you shaved?

George Aye. All right? (*Proffers his chin.*)

Mother Yes.

George I need a new packet of blades.

Mother One of them T-shirts do you?

George Nay.

Mother Under your shirt. Arthur wears them.

George Aye, it's a pair of real jeans I'd like. American jeans. Aye, you get them too big, right? You put them on, right? You get in the bath, right? And they shrink to fit you.

Mother See you shrinking jeans in a zinc bath in here. Come on, your dinner's been ready long since.

George My trousers upstairs?

He goes upstairs. She picks up the shirt and towel.

Mother Doreen's supposed to be calling for me later. I don't really want to go.

He comes back down.

George Where's my trousers?

Mother Here's your trousers and your socks.

George What my trousers doing down here?

Mother Come on. Come on.

George Nay, I'm not changing my trousers down here.

Mother I'll save your modesty and get your dinner. I've put it up for you. It's his fault if it's spoiled. I thought you'd be in before this. I swore I heard you whistling.

George You sit down. I'll get it.

Mother No.

George You're supposed to be taking things easy.

Mother I can't be doing nothing all day. I only just made the beds. I had a lie-down.

George Don't give me too much now.

Mother I already put it up. I told you.

Exits to the kitchen. He changes his trousers.

Mother Did you bring me some milk?

George Yes. Yes. Of course I brought you some milk. Do I ever forget?

She enters with his dinner, holding the plate with a tea towel.

Mother That b— door. That oven door out there . . .

George Mother.

Mother Now watch the plate, it's hot.

George Put these on the line, Mother. (*Gives her his trousers and sits down to eat.*)

Mother They need washing.

George No. Just put them on the line.

Mother No. I'll wash them. They're rotten. They wash easy, these.

George You want a washing machine.

Mother What would I do with a washing machine?

George One of them Rolls. I'm getting you one of them.

Mother No.
Mind you, our Barbara, she swears by hers.

George I'm getting you one. They're cracking. They're not a lot. Weekly they're not.

She goes out into the kitchen with the dirty things.

Hey, Mother. They're going on holiday, the gaffer and her.

Mother (*coming back in*) She always goes on holiday.

George Aye. But they're going to Spain, both of them.

Mother What's wrong with Bridlington?
It's nice for some. He won't go. Who's going to manage for him? He's too mean.

George I shan't worry, me.

Mother He won't go. He'd have to get someone in.
What happened to your play? You haven't been going to your play. Isn't it tonight you go?

George No.

Mother You never went last week neither.

George I know. I never went the week before either.

Mother No.

George You were bad.

Mother That was no reason not to go.

George Leave off, Mother.

Mother It's no bother to me. I thought you'd never stick it.

Barbara comes in through the back door and into the living room.

Mother Is that you, Barbara?

Barbara You seen my lad, Mother?

Mother No.

Barbara You had my lad with you, George?

Mother Don't eat so fast, George. Don't be such a guts.
Do you want a cup of tea, Barbara? I'm going to make one now.

Barbara Have you?

George No. He's too old for us now. I haven't seen him for weeks. We could do with him, too.

Barbara He hasn't been to school.

Mother He should go to school.

Barbara Didn't you give him his dinner up here?

Mother No. I haven't seen him.

Barbara He's going wild, he is.

Mother He's not wild. He's not. He's not a bad lad. He's in with some bad uns on that estate. That's what it'll be. I couldn't live down there.

Barbara Well, I wouldn't like to live stuck up here again, I can tell you, Mother, like you, without a bath and a lavatory outside.

Mother Hear that, George?

Barbara I thought he'd had his dinner up here.

Mother He'll not have gone far. You know lads. Anyway, he finishes school soon. He'll soon be working.

Barbara I thought he might start work with you. Arthur don't want it.

Mother It's hard work on a farm.

Barbara Lucky there's plenty of work about.

Mother Put him to a trade. You can't go wrong.
Have you finished?

George Yes. Nothing wrong with that, Mother.

She takes his plate.

Mother Do you want afters?

George Aye. Go on.

Mother Doreen made me a pie.

Barbara Did she? Hear that, George? Doreen's made you a pie.

Mother She's got a touch with pastry.

George And you, Mother. You have.

Mother I had one time. I can't go baking now. (*She goes into the kitchen and brings back a pie. She serves George a slice.*)

Barbara Doreen making you pies now then, George.

George You can shut it an' all.

Mother Here we are.

Barbara You want custard with that.

Mother He won't have custard. He don't like custard.

George What do you mean, I don't like custard?

Mother You don't. Do you want custard?

George No.

Mother Do you want Carnation?

George Aye.

Mother See, he don't like custard.

George That doesn't mean I don't like custard.

Mother Where's the Carnation?

George Telling me what I like.

Mother I'm your mother. I know what you like.

Barbara And don't you see he gets it, Mother.

Mother Now. Now. You. (*She goes out to get the Carnation and then goes back to make the tea.*)

Barbara Our George'll never get married, Mother. You spoil him too much.

Mother Aye.

Barbara Will you, George?

George I got it too good here, Barbara.

Barbara You have.

George And I've seen too much of other people's marriages, Barbara. You and Arthur, for one.

Barbara Oh, you can be nasty.
He can be nasty sometimes, Mother.

Mother gives Barbara and George tea.

Mother What lasses are there round here for him, anyway?

Barbara Doreen.

Mother Do you think?

Barbara She made him a pie. I don't know what he's waiting for.

George I'll not leave you, Mother.

Barbara You know when you're on to a good thing.

George Aye.

Mother You've got more sense.

Barbara You'll be fifty before you know it, wearing glasses and thinking you're eighteen.

George She's a cheeky bitch. Keep this shut a bit, Barbara.

Mother Still, I'd like to see him settled. Someone's missing a good husband.
He doesn't go to his play now, Barbara. That journey's too long for him. I said.

Barbara No, it's not. You catch the right bus.

Mother Right into York.

George Hey. Hey. I'm here, you know.

Mother I knew he'd never stick it.

Barbara Doreen put him in for that an' all.

Mother Well, he was good in that play she put on. Very good.

Barbara He was.

Mother All that way into York with his work, I knew he wouldn't make it.

Barbara No. Well, I'd better go, I suppose.

Mother Finish your tea, love.
Doreen's calling for me later. I promised her I'd go to fellowship with her. I don't feel up to it.

Barbara You'll like it when you get there.

George You didn't used to go to chapel so much, Mother.

Barbara Doreen's very keen on chapel.

Mother I've always gone to chapel.

George On a Sunday, aye.

Mother Here, give me your plate. It wouldn't do you any harm to go to chapel either.

Arthur comes in through the back door and into the living room.

Arthur Don't we get any tea?

Mother Hello, Arthur. (*She goes out.*)

Arthur Stay single, George. You get your tea. No question.

Mother Do you want a cup of tea, Arthur?

Barbara I'll be down. I've been looking for our Jack.

Arthur Well, you just missed him.

Barbara What?

Arthur He's been in and out.
The girls want their tea.

Barbara I'll be down now. Wait till I get hold of him. Where did he go?

Arthur I think he said he was going over, you know . . . What's his name? What's he done anyway? What's up?

Barbara He's not going to school. That's what's up.

Arthur I thought he was a bit quick out.
Nice walk up. Hawthorn's thick. Needs someone down that small field, hedging.

George Oh aye. Let him do that.

Arthur Needs doing. Nice up here, this weather.

Barbara Oh, don't start. You were glad to get out. You don't want to live in that old place up there, do you? You don't want to have to work like our George, do you?

Arthur No. No. Nine-to-five. Nine-to-five. Can't beat it, George.

George You're on shift work.

Arthur Yes. Still.

Barbara Well, what we going to do with that little ferret? It won't be long now before he leaves school. What's he going to do then?

Arthur There's plenty of jobs.

Mother He'll be all right. He can go with George, comes to it.

Arthur He'll not go labouring on a farm, I can help it. He can come to work with me.

Barbara See?

Mother Do you want some pie, Arthur?

Arthur Aye.

Barbara We're going now.
It'll spoil your tea.

Mother gives him some pie.

Arthur You going for a pint later, George?

George I don't know, Arthur. He might want me up there.

Mother You two and your drinking.

Barbara They don't drink much, Mother.

Mother What's too much, some might say.

George Oh, Mother, don't go on. That's chapel talking.

Mother Ay. Ay. Arthur's family was all chapel.

Arthur Aye.

Barbara Father didn't go to chapel much, did he?

Mother What do you know about your father?

George Well, he wasn't much of a chapel man, Mother.

Mother What do you know?

George I know.

Mother No, he didn't, more's the pity.

Arthur Ay. I tell you who was a big chapel man. Skepwith. Remember him? When I worked for him?

George Aye.

Arthur He was a right primitive. Always trying to get the men to sign the pledge. Aye. True.

Doreen knocks and comes in through the front door.

Doreen Oooo.

Barbara Hello, Doreen.

Arthur Hello, Doreen, how are you?

Mother I'm not ready, Doreen. What's the time?

Doreen No, I only popped in to see if you'd remembered.

Arthur It's cracking pie, Doreen.

George It is, Doreen.

Barbara Spoil your tea.

Mother No. I haven't forgotten, Doreen.

Arthur Great.

Mother I don't know whether I'm well enough to go, you know, Doreen.

Doreen Oh, I am sorry.

George Go on, Mother. Don't listen to me.

Barbara Aye, go on, Mother. Do you good to go out.

Mother I don't know.

Doreen You'll come with me. She'll come with me. Won't you? We won't be long.

Barbara Come on then, you. If you see our Jack, Mother, if he comes up here, send him home. And you, George. George.

George Aye.

Barbara Hey, Doreen. He's stopped going to his play, you know.

Doreen I didn't know.

Barbara He doesn't go any more, does he, Mother?

Mother No. He doesn't.

Arthur Well, he was good in that play you did, Doreen. He was. How did you get him to do it?

Barbara He was always good at acting in school.

George Hey. I'm here, you know. Why don't you shut up, Barbara?

Doreen Have you stopped going, George?

George I haven't been for a couple of weeks, no.

Mother Too far for him to go.

George No.

Mother Why don't you go then?

George That's my business.

Mother I knew he'd never stick it, Doreen. I don't know how you persuaded him to go in for it in the first place.

Doreen Well, you'll start up again, perhaps.

Arthur Are you coming, then?

Barbara Aye. Tara, then. Tara, Doreen. You spoil him, making him pies.

Doreen Well, I was baking, you know.

Arthur Tara. You going for a pint then, George?

George I don't know. I'll see how it goes up there.

Arthur I might see you, then. I'll be up the Carpenter's.

They exit.

George Right.

Mother You're not going drinking, are you?

George I don't think so. I might. I don't know.
Our Barbara's too nosy.

Doreen Well, I'll call back for you in a minute, shall I?

Mother Aye, go on.

Doreen Won't be long. (*She goes.*)

Mother She's a good girl. But I don't want to go.

George It'll only be an hour.

Mother I've got the pots to do.

George I'll do them, Mother. You go up and get ready.

Mother There aren't many. I'll do them when I get back.

George I'll do them.

Mother Where's my compact?
You should have put a decent shirt on, you going drinking.

George Mother.

Mother Where is it?

She goes out. George clears pots and goes into the kitchen. John knocks on the front door.

George Is that you, Doreen? She's upstairs.

Another knock.

Come in, Doreen.

He goes to the door to find John, who is dressed differently than before.

Oh.

John I'm sorry. I had no other way of getting in touch with you. We only had an address.

George Come in.

John comes into the room.

John Have I come at a bad time? I'm sorry if I've come at a bad time.

George No. No.

John We wondered where you'd been. So I thought I'd come and see you. I just felt I should come and see you.

George How did you get here?

John Bus.

George Not many buses.

John It's no bother. I've come . . . It's just to say you're so good in the play, you see. And we miss you. It's just . . . It's important for everyone to be at rehearsals, you see.

George I know. I should have rung up. I'm sorry about that. No good on the phone.

John No. I'm sure.

Mother enters.

Mother Have you seen my compact, George?
Oh. I thought it was Doreen.

George This is my mother.

Mother There it is. (*She finds the compact.*)

George He's with the play.

Mother Oh. Are you in it too, then?

George No, he's the assistant director.

John Just came to see where George had been.

Mother See, I told you.

George What?

Mother Well, I'll just powder my nose. Excuse me. (*She goes into the kitchen.*)

Doreen comes in.

Doreen Oo. Oo. You ready? Oh.

Mother I won't be a minute, Doreen. Just tidying myself up.

George He's from the play.
(*to John*) Doreen saw the advert.

John Hello.

George He's the assistant director.

Doreen Oh. That's interesting.

Mother comes in.

Mother He's come to sort out our George.

George Mother.

Mother Well, you ready, Doreen? Where's my coat?

Doreen It's warm, mind. (*She puts her coat on.*)

Mother Right. We won't be long.

Doreen I don't expect you'll be here when we get back.

John No. No. I'll have to be going soon.

Doreen I'm looking forward to the play.

John Good. Good.

Mother Tara then.

John Goodbye.

Mother Don't forget them pots, George.

George Aye.

Mother and Doreen exit.

They've gone to chapel. Doreen, she's very chapel-minded. She told me about the play. Do you want anything? Can I get you anything?

John No.

George No? Sure?

John Yes.

George So.

Look, I can't come. I'm sorry. I shouldn't have taken it on. I'm sorry. Work and that. I have to keep an eye on my mother. She's not been too good. Sorry. I feel bad to leave her, like, if she's poorly.

John I see. No. I understand. I thought it was . . . we made you unwelcome. Or the other people . . .

George No. They were nice. Everyone. Very nice, all of them. I like Peter. Very interesting man. Doesn't put himself out much, does he? But when he stirs himself he can put his finger on it, can't he. Won't take no when he puts his mind to it. Gives you something to think about and I like that, me. Smokes a lot, doesn't he? Funny how he holds his cigarette.

John Yes.

George Like this. (*Demonstrates, holding an imaginary cigarette between his thumb and forefinger.*)

'Is it an action?'

Jesus is a nice fellow. Well, they all are. No, it's not that. They're all very . . . well . . . They would be . . .

Doctors and that. I felt a bit awkward at first, until I got in the swing of it. That's not it. No. I just can't come. Like I said.

John It's . . . There aren't many people like you in it.

George Like me?

John You're so right, you see. You make it sound right.

George Do I? No.

John You do.

George I'm sorry you had to come all this way.

John No. That's all right. I'm glad I did.

George Aye?

John It's lovely here, isn't it? This must be old. How old, do you think?

George Oh, I don't know. Old, I suppose.

John Is it yours? Your mother's?

George No. Blimey, no. No, it's a tied cottage. Belongs to the farm.

John So you rent it?

George Only a few shillings. Part of the wages order.

John What's that?

George Means you get other things with the job. Milk, like. If I had a working dog or owt . . .

John I like that. (*Points to the fireplace.*)

George Want to take it out, that.

John No, don't. I'm sorry. It's . . . I like it.

George Not what my mother says.

John You could still cook on it, look.

George Aye. Used to, my mother says. Good fire. In winter it's cold up here.

John I bet.
Well, I'd better be going then, I suppose.

George No, stay a bit.

John Shall I? I'll have to watch for the bus.

George There's plenty of buses. I'll see you get a bus. You'll get a bus.
You like it up here, then?

John Beautiful.

George I'm used to it, me.
I've got to go up the farm directly. I'll take you, if you like. Show you the other cottage on the farm. Arthur – my sister's husband – they lived there. His family. Till he was moved to a council house. It's empty now.

John What about these? (*indicating the pots*) You said you'd do them.

George Oh, aye. No, leave it. Don't worry about them. Do them when we come back.
I'm glad you came.

John And me. I mean . . .

George Yes. Come on. You fit? Go the back way.

Two

A couple of hours later. The same evening. Jack is in the kitchen.

Mother and Doreen come in through the front door.

Mother Come in, Doreen.

Doreen I'll not stay long. See you in.

Mother I must have a cup of tea.

Doreen I'll get it.

Mother No. I'll get it.
Who's that in the kitchen? George?

Jack No. It's me, Nan.

Mother What are you doing out there?
It's our Jack.

Jack Having a biscuit, if that's OK.

Mother He's eating my biscuits.
Put the kettle on, Jack. (*She takes off her hat and coat.*)

Jack It's on.

Mother Tea, Doreen? Take your coat off.

Jack comes in.

Doreen I'll not be long.

Jack It's boiling, the kettle. Do you want me to make you tea, Nan?

Mother No, you can't make a good cup of tea.

Jack Oh. Thanks, Nan.

Mother Have you been home? Your mother's been worried to death about you. What's up with you?

Jack Aye. Course I've been home.

Mother What you doing up here, then?

Jack I came to see you, Nan.

Mother Oh. He's full of nonsense. You are. Your mother give you a good clip, I hope.

Jack She gave me an earful. I come up here. Can I stay the night?

Mother He hasn't been to school, Doreen.

Doreen Oh. Why's that, Jack?

Jack Dunno.

Mother George must have gone out with your father.

Jack No. My father's in.

Mother He must have gone up to work then. There's a cow sick or something. He does too much for him up there. They could do with you, Jack. You stopped going, George says.

Jack Yeah.
Where you been? To chapel, Nan?

Mother Fellowship with Doreen. Do you good to go to chapel once in a while. What do you say, Doreen?

Doreen Jack was in my Sunday school class. Weren't you, Jack?

Jack Aye.

Doreen Aren't you glad you came now?

Mother I am. He takes a good meeting.

Doreen He does.

Mother I'll make the tea. The kettle'll boil dry.

Doreen Let me.

Mother No. No. Look, he's left these. He said he'd do the pots.

Doreen I'll do them.

Mother No. No. I'm making the tea. I've done most of them already.

Doreen Go on. Let me do them.

Mother No. Will you have a cup, Jack?

Jack Aye.

She goes into the kitchen with the unwashed cups.

Doreen Well, Jack. You'll be finishing school.

Jack Yes.

Doreen What are you going to do, then?

Jack Don't know.

Doreen You'll not go on the farm with George, then?

Jack No. I don't know what to do.

Doreen You'll find something.

Jack Join the army, I might.

Doreen Oh, really, Jack? No. Will you? See the world. Will you?

Jack No. I don't know. I might, though.

Mother enters with the tea.

Mother Here we are. (*Pours the tea.*)

Doreen Jack says he's joining the army.

Mother Never.

Jack I might.

Mother Biscuit, Doreen?

Doreen Thank you.
I mustn't be long.

Mother Join the army? No. He'll get a job. He's not afraid of work, that's one thing.

George whistles before he and John come in through the back door.

George Hello. Hello.

Mother Hello. You still here, then?

Doreen Well, this is a surprise. We thought you'd be gone.

John No.

George We been all over. The cow calved.
Hey, Jack.

Mother Cup of tea?

George Aye.

Jack Thank you.

Mother Jack, get a cup. Two cups.

Jack exits.

I thought you said you'd do the pots?

George Didn't I do them?

Mother No, you didn't.

John I'm sorry. I got in the way. I'm sorry.

Jack comes in with the cups.

Jack George don't do the washing-up, do he?
Do you? Ha.

Mother He can be handy. He can. So you be quiet.

Jack Women's work, that.

Mother Shut it, you.

Doreen Don't you do any washing-up, Jack?

Mother Course he does.

Jack No, the lasses do that.

George Shut it, big man.

Jack D'you have to do much?

George No. I didn't have to do anything. Charlie was back. But he was lucky. I reckon he should've had Humphries out, to have a look at her.

Mother Too mean.

John I've never seen a calf that young.

Doreen Bonny.

John Yes, very.

Mother Here, do you want biscuits?

John Thank you.

George Aye, Mother, we went to have a look at Arthur's old cottage.

Mother Oo. That's falling down.

George He liked it, didn't you?

Mother Did you?

John Yes. I did. I did.

Mother They had a terrible time up there in winter. One thing you can say about this – (*meaning the range*) You can make a good fire if it gets cold.

George How was your meeting, Mother?

Mother Oh, lovely.

George Who took it?

Mother Fred Broadbent.

George Oh, aye.

Mother What was the reading, Doreen?

Doreen looks in the Bible.

Doreen I marked it.
'There is no remembrance of former things. Neither shall there be any remembrance of things that are to come with those who come after.'

George Oh aye.
What do you take that to mean, Mother?

Mother You shut up, you. I think that was very interesting.

George 'Come unto him all ye that labour.' That's what I like to hear.

Mother Makes no difference. You don't go to chapel to hear anything.

Jack What's this play then in York, George? What are they, mystery plays?

George I don't know. Mystery plays. No, don't laugh. Not murder mysteries. What are they, Doreen?

Doreen Don't ask me. John's the one to ask.

George You tell him. You know.

Doreen Well, they're the stories of the Bible and the New Testament. From the Creation to the Last Judgement. Isn't that right?

John That's right.

Jack They old, then?

Doreen Yes. Very old. The time of York Minster.

Jack Who wrote them?

Doreen I don't know.

John No one knows. Some say the monks.

Mother They Roman Catholic plays?

George No. Are they?

John No. Well . . . Um . . .

Jack They're Bible stories, then.

John Yes. Done as plays.

Jack What's the mystery, then?

John Well, each play was done by a guild of tradesmen. Skilled workers. And I suppose they had secrets. Tricks of the trade. I don't really know.

George Like trade unions, Jack.

John That's what they say. I don't know about that.

Jack Was there a farm labourers' play?

John It was all done in the town.

Jack York?

John Yes, and all over. Coventry and Wakefield.

Jack Wakefield?

George Aye, Wakefield.

Jack Blimey, Wakefield.

George Aye. And they did them from dawn till dusk.

Jack No.

George All over York.

Jack No.

George True.

Doreen So you went to see Arthur's old cottage then, John?

George Yes. He liked it. Didn't you?

John I did.

Jack It's falling down.

George No. The roof's still all right.

Mother Did you see a little byre on the side of that cottage, John? Is it there, George?

George Aye, you can see it.

Mother Well, above that byre, that was a place they kept straw and hay. And you could get into that place above the byre from the bedroom of the cottage. Well, years ago, they used to put the kids in there to sleep above the horse, or a cow if they kept one, in the hay. It was warm, you see.

Jack Get out.

Mother They did. That's true. You ask your father.

John I like it. And this too. I like this.

George He says they're going to sell it. Might. Arthur's old place.

Mother Who's going to buy that stuck up there?

John Who owns it, your boss?

George Ha. Ha. No. He's the tenant. The five farms round here are owned by a man from York.

Mother Never see him. You, Doreen?

Doreen No.

Jack I have.

Doreen Fancies himself a bit of a country man. Hunts and that.

Mother Well, he don't live in the big house.

George No. Empty.

Mother Where does he live?

George Old Rectory.

John This is a nice cottage, too. How old is it, do you think?

Mother Must be old.

George He likes the fireplace. Don't you?

Mother Oh, aye. He don't have to clean it. I'd like to take it out. I'd like a grate like Doreen. A nice modern grate. Mind you, it makes a good fire and the boiler works if you needed it.

John I like it.

Mother No. I'd like a modern house. Like Barbara and Arthur got. But I wouldn't want to live down there.

John I like the dresser.

Mother That's years old. I'd like it all modern.

You know Mrs Dorset. Lives by you, Doreen. They had old china. Lustreware. Staffordshire figures. Beautiful old stuff. Do you know, when her mother died she smashed it all with a hammer. Got rid of it all. Everything. Got rid of the old furniture. Got rid of the brass. Chopped up the dresser. Sick of all the years washing and polishing. I don't blame her.

Doreen Well, the man to tell you all about things round here is the man who took the meeting tonight. Mr Broadbent. You know, those old walls where he pens his sheep on the common in bad weather, they were cottages with roofs put up overnight, he says. If you got a roof up overnight you had rights.

Mother They've always been like they are now, as far as I remember.

Doreen And he says they had no stairs. Just a ladder.

Mother That true?

Doreen Yes, apparently.

Mother Well, I can believe it.

Doreen Oh well, I'll have to be off.

Mother All right, dear. Who's going to see Doreen home?

George Jack will.

Mother How you getting home?

John I don't know.

Jack Can I stay here, Nan?

George No.

Mother Can he?

George No. Not tonight. Anyway, who's going to see Doreen home?

Doreen Oh, I'm all right.

Mother No. You see Doreen home, Jack. And mind you go home after. Doreen, see he gets in after, will you?

Doreen Yes. Jack and I will see each other home. Goodnight. It's very kind of Jack. Very nice.

John I hope you'll come and see the play.

Doreen Oh, I'm looking forward to it. Goodnight, then.

Mother Yes. Goodnight.

Jack Tara then.

Doreen Mind you don't miss your bus.

Jack Goodnight, Nan.

Mother Now think on, Jack.

Jack Tara.

Doreen Pleased to meet you.

Jack and Doreen exit.

Mother She's good to me, that girl. Good as gold. She put him in for your play, you know.

John I know.

Mother Well, I'll just wash these and then I'm off to bed.

George We'll do them.

John Yes.

Mother You said you'd do the others and you went walking.

George Don't go on. We'll do them.

Mother I'll just take them out then and get a glass of water. (*She goes into the kitchen with the cups.*) You'll have to watch your bus. You'll miss it. (*She comes back in.*) I said you'll have to be getting your bus.

George He missed the bus half-hour ago.

Mother He never did.

George Yes. Last one's earlier than we thought.

Mother Are you sure?

George He missed it. He'll have to stay here.

Mother Well, you're on the floor unless you want to share.

George Aye. OK with you?

John Yes. Yes.

Mother Are you sure? You'll have to find him a pair of pyjamas. He won't have any pyjamas.

George I'll find him a pair.

Mother I'll get some clean sheets.

George No. Now you go off to bed. Go on.

John I'm so sorry to be a nuisance.

Mother No, love. George should have known about the bus.

George Have you taken your pills?

Mother I'll take them now. Where's the glass for my teeth? Well. Goodnight. You'll be up early, you know. He has to be up. Gets himself up now. Do you want the clock?

George Aye. Better.

Mother It's a bit fast. He's off before I get up now. Doctor's orders. Rest. Rest. Goodnight.

John Goodnight.

George Goodnight, Mother.

She goes upstairs.

John Have I missed the bus?

George I don't know, have you?

John Have I?

George There's one more. She doesn't know.

John Well.

George Yes.
Your eyes are so bright.

John I'm not often in the country.

George Is that what it is, is it, making you look eager, like?

John Yes. Yes, it is. I don't know the country. I find it strange. You wouldn't.

George No. How strange?

John It's as you expect it and at the same time it isn't. The green, for one thing. The hedges and the fields and seagulls so far inland. And the farm. It's all at odds. So old, some of it. I couldn't take it in. It's so old. The stone. The brick. The walls are so old. I couldn't take it in, and then all that pebbledash on the extension. And the cattle shed with the corrugated roof next to the barn with the old stone and the beams and timbers. And the cow smell in the fresh air. And the floors of the cowshed and the smell in the dairy. Such a clinical, cold smell. And the hay in the barn, right up to the roof. Too sweet.

It puzzled me. Just as you thought it would be and yet not. I don't know.

George What about Arthur's cottage?

John I liked it. I did. I did.

George You can see what I can't see. Why did you throw away the flowers you picked?

John Felt silly.

George No.

John Well, then.

George Aye.

John What? Oh.

George Aye. (*Goes towards John.*)

John No.

George Sh.

John I don't know.

George Don't you want to?

John Yes.

George Yes.

John But staying the night.

George It'll be all right.

John Will it?

George Of course it will. Come on. Let's go to bed, shall we?

John Will you come to rehearsals then?

George What, you blackmailing me?

John If you want me to.

George I might. (*Goes towards him.*)

John No.
I'm nervous. It's all . . . Oh . . .

George What, you afraid a copper's going to come up here and arrest us?

John No. Don't be silly.
Yes. No. All right.
Come on, then.

George Hang on.

John What?

George goes into the kitchen. Comes back with a tin of Vaseline.

John What's that for?

George Vaseline. Be prepared.

John No.

George Yeah.

John Will you come to rehearsals?

George That depends on you. Come on.

John What about the noise?

George You noisy, are you?

John Don't be vulgar.

George Don't worry. She sleeps sound.

John Will you come?

George We'll see.
Come on.

They go upstairs.

Three

A month later. Late evening. Mother, Barbara, Doreen, Jack and Arthur come in through the front door.

Arthur Here we are then, Mother. Doreen. Home.

Doreen Thank you.

Arthur Well, we're back. What a night, aye?

Barbara Are you cold, Mother?

Mother Yes, I am.

Barbara I thought it was me.

Doreen I got cold, warm as the evening was.

Barbara I'm chilled to the bone.

Mother You should have worn a vest, Barbara. I warned you.

Barbara Mother.

Mother I put a winter vest on and I'm cold.

Arthur Shall I put a match to the fire?

Mother Aye. Go on.

He does.

Barbara And it was such a glorious day.

Doreen Just get cold sitting, see, summer evenings.

Arthur Still, what a night.

Doreen Wasn't it marvellous? I still can't get over it.

Mother Put the kettle on, Jack.

Jack It's on.

Arthur We should have something stronger. Warm us up. Celebrate.

Mother Drink. That's all you can think of.

Doreen Did you enjoy it, Jack?

Jack Aye, it was cracking.

Arthur We should have taken the girls.

Jack No.

Barbara No. They'd have never sat still. Not all that time. I'm glad we didn't take them, Arthur.

Mother Nay, they'd never have lasted that long.

Arthur I reckon they'd have liked it.

Mother Sit down, Doreen.

Barbara Where you going, Arthur?

Arthur I'm just going out the back. All right? (*Arthur goes out.*)

Mother He arranged very good seats for us though, didn't he?

Doreen He's the assistant director.

Mother He's a good lad. Put our George through his paces. Took our George in hand. Our George did well, and such a cruel part.

Doreen Cruel, the four of them.

Mother Well, I nearly passed out when I saw him. I didn't know where to put myself.

Doreen Well, I thought it was marvellous. Did you enjoy it, Barbara?

Barbara I did. I thought it was great. He started to clap at the end. I didn't know where to put myself. It said not to clap in the programme. Why was that?

Doreen Sacred work, you see. Like *Messiah*, I suppose.

Barbara Oh, aye.

Arthur enters.

Arthur I wish the girls could have seen it.

Mother Nay. They'd not have lasted, Arthur.

Arthur No. I suppose you're right. It would have been too much for them. Pity.

Jack I'm glad, me.

Arthur I'm glad we've got an inside lav.

Barbara Shut up, Arthur.

Arthur It's cold out there. Freezing.

Barbara Have you been to the Abbey ruins before, Mother?

Mother Oh, years ago. I must have.

Barbara I never have. You, Doreen?

Doreen Oh, aye. Always walk from the museum.

Barbara I never have. Jack?

Jack No.

Barbara You ever been there before, Arthur?

Arthur I must have.

Barbara I haven't.

Arthur Go on.
Do you want tea, all of you? (*Goes into the kitchen.*)

Mother They cut quite a lot of the Old Testament out, Doreen.

Doreen Couldn't get it in one evening, you see.

Mother Abraham and Isaac. That's a sad story. Oh, dear. Oh, dear. Breaks your heart.

Barbara I never knew Noah had a wife.

Doreen No. She was funny, wasn't she?

Jack Like our mam when she gets going.

Barbara Cheek.

Jack Aye, Dad?

Arthur What?

Jack Noah's wife, just like our mam.

Arthur Aye.

Jack Or Nan. Bossy.

Mother Cheeky.

Barbara Aye, you.

Mother Nor Pontius Pilate had a wife.

Doreen She was very common, I thought.

Mother What did you like, Jack?

Jack The Devil.

Barbara Yes, you would.

Doreen Jesus was good.

Mother Yes. God had a good voice, didn't he? Very clear. Well, they were all good. There wasn't a weak part.

Doreen It must be a responsibility, playing Jesus.

Barbara Did you recognise that man, Jack?

Jack No.

Barbara Oh, I did. Off the television. I've seen him in something. I know I have.

Arthur enters with the tea.

Did you recognise him, Arthur?

Arthur It was very good. Very good, all of it.
No, I didn't.

Mother You're right, though. A big responsibility.

Doreen For all of them, when you come to think of it.

Barbara Our George was cruel in the crucifixion, though.

Mother Too cruel.

Arthur Very real. Very real.

Mother Too cruel for me. I could have punched our George doing that to him.

Arthur That was clever how they got him down off the cross. One minute he was up there. The next thing he's facing out the Devil. I never saw him get down. Did you?

Barbara No.

Doreen No. I didn't.

Mother No.

Jack Some trick.

Arthur Some magic trick. We'll have to ask George.

Doreen John'll know. He's the assistant director.

Arthur It was very effective, all of it.

Mother It was very Yorkshire, wasn't it? Not that I mind.

Doreen All very Yorkshire.

Jack Jesus Christ wasn't Yorkshire.

Arthur Yes, he was.

Mother No, but you didn't mind.

Jack I didn't mind.

Mother Thank you, Arthur.

Arthur When will they be back?

Barbara Well, he said not long, didn't he?

Mother Our George is tired. Rehearsals and that. Up early and all that. He must be exhausted.

Barbara You look exhausted, Mother. I don't know about George. You must be ready for bed.

Mother Don't shove me off to bed. I haven't finished my tea.

Barbara You must be careful, Mother.

Mother Careful?

George and John come in.

George Aye. Aye.

John Hello.

Doreen Well done.

Barbara Well done.

Arthur Aye.

Jack Aye.

Mother Very good.

Doreen Very good.

Arthur Aye.

Jack Aye.

George What you got the fire lit for?

John You got cold. I was afraid you would.

Doreen Oh, it was worth it.

John Did you like it?

Doreen Aye, I did.

Mother You were a cruel bugger, George.

George Thanks.

Arthur Hey, George. How did he get down off the cross? That's what's puzzling us.

George You'll have to ask John.

Arthur John?

John I can't. Trade secrets.

Jack There's two men.

John No.

Jack There is. There must be.

Barbara Be quiet, Jack, and come on now, we'll have to go.

Jack Well, what's the assistant director do, like?

Doreen He assists the director.

Jack What does the director do, then?

Barbara Shut up, Jack.

George Well, like what Doreen does in chapel shows.

Barbara You know, you were in that play.

Jack No. But what do you do?

John Not a lot.

George He does. He does.

Mother Chase our George up.

George Aye.

Barbara Come on then.

Doreen I'll come with you. Yes. Well done.

Arthur Yes, well done.

Barbara Well done. We were really proud of you, you know.

Arthur Aye, George, when you going on the stage?

Doreen Aye.

Mother He's been a cruel thing tonight. Bad bugger. I didn't know you could be like that.

George Three other actors, Mother.

Mother Yeah, but I could see you enjoying it. Callous. You did.

George That's training, see. Special rehearsals.

Arthur Aye.

John Why didn't you come back at the end?

Arthur You see? I wanted to.

Barbara Mother and Doreen wouldn't, and I wouldn't.

Arthur I wanted to come back. See backstage.

Jack Aye.

John I kept my eye out for you.

Barbara We couldn't do that, could we?

Mother No.

George Yes. Doreen, you'd have liked it.

John Another time. Come again.

Doreen Oh. I don't know.

Barbara Come on then. Goodnight all.
You coming, Doreen?

Doreen Yes.

Arthur Goodnight. Well done.

Barbara Yes.

Doreen Where's my bag?

Barbara Jack?

Jack Aye.

Doreen Goodnight. Thank you.

Barbara Night, Mother.

Mother Night.

Barbara, Doreen, Arthur and Jack go out of the back door.

Mother Oo, I'm tired.

George You looked tired.

Mother Barbara said that, but I wasn't taking any notice of her. She's got too much to say for herself.

George I'll get you a glass of water.

Mother Aye.

George goes into the kitchen.

I did enjoy that, John. Well done.

John Thank you.

Enter George with a glass of water.

Mother Hurry up, love. I feel worn out.

George Here's your glass and your tablets. Do you want a hot-water bottle?

Mother No. Aye.

George Want me to do you one?

Mother Aye.

John I'll do it.

Mother You don't know where it is.

John I do. It's on the hook out there. (*He goes into the kitchen.*)

George You all right?

Mother Aye. Just tired.

George I'll bring it up to you.

Mother Will you? Goodnight, love.

George Goodnight.

Mother Goodnight, John. I'll see you in the morning.

John Yes.

Mother (*to John*) You can have a lie-in. You can.

John comes in.

(*to George*) You'll be tired out, you will.

John Goodnight.

Mother You're not going tomorrow, are you, John?

John No. Wednesday.

George Oh. You're not going Wednesday, are you?

Mother Goodnight. (*She goes upstairs.*)

George Are you, then? Stay, aye? You can stay for a bit, can't you? Holiday. What they say? A break. You've been working hard.

John Not as hard as you.

George Can't you?

John I can't stay, George.
Shall I let the fire go out?

George Aye. Well then.

John What?

George Well, what we going to do?

John About what?

George Oh. Fuck off, John.

John What can we do?

George Stay up here.

John I can't stay up here.

George Don't go. I don't want you to go. You're . . . You . . . Like . . . Mmm . . . Oh, don't.

John Don't. We can't go on now. We're tired. Aren't you tired?

George Good tired, though.
Stay, can't you? You don't have anything to go back for.

John Well, I hope I will have.

George What'll I do? What, aye? Not for ever . . . A bit . . . You see . . . Stay here with me.

John I can't.

George I know. I don't know why I asked.

John Come on. Clear the cups.

John goes into the kitchen. George clears the cups.

George Will you stay till the end, then? Will you?

John Yes. (*He brings in a hot-water bottle.*) Here's the hot-water bottle. Say it's hot.

George takes the hot-water bottle upstairs. John finishes clearing the cups and washes them. George comes down.

I feel as if I live here.
She asleep?

George No. She's worn out, though.

John I wonder, she never says anything. None of them.
It doesn't bother you, does it?

George What? No, it doesn't bother me. You?

John Not with you. But hasn't it ever bothered you? I don't think it has. I don't. Has it?

George No. But I don't look into things like you do.

John Wasn't it hard for you, ever?

George Not really. It wasn't. No. Until I was eighteen I never thought about it. I went out with my mate one night. Next village, after lasses. And we got nowhere and we was full of it. Full of it. It'll have to be you then, I said. And we come home. Home here. Yeah. And it was. And after. It was all right for me. But it wasn't for him. Took it for granted after that.

John Do you see him?

George Aye. And you do.

John Do I what?

George It was Arthur.

John What?

George We were farm boys.
He thinks it never happened. I got on with it.
Is this going to be it when you go?

John Come on, why should it? You can come down to see me. Write to me.

George Aye. I'm a great letter-writer, me.

John Well, George, what can I do?

George Aye.

John You glad you did the play?

George I am. Aye, I am. I am.

John You worked hard. You know how good you are. You know that.

George Get out.

John You are.

George I wish I could do more of it.

John You should try it. I've said.

George Don't be . . . No. Not to . . .

John Pete said.

George He did. He was being kind.

John You could.

George What's the use of talking about it? I couldn't.

John That way . . .

George No.

John We could . . .

George No, John. You've got to be different to me. You've got to be like the little Quaker lass played the Virgin Mary. She's going to acting school in London.

John But you're better than she is. Peter says she's suburban.

George What does that mean? She's got a lovely speaking voice. She's a nice little girl. Very confident. Good luck to her.

John You're more interesting.

George No.
Oh well. Come on. I'm going to bed. Coming?

John Well, we know what it is really, don't we?

George Do we?

John Well, we might as well say it. You can't leave, can you?

George No, I can't.

John I don't think it's because she's ill, see. I think it would be the same if she wasn't ill.

George Oh yeah? How do you make that out?

John I can tell.

George It's you always delving into things. I can't leave her now, can I? Well, can I? Aye? Whatever you say the reason is. Can I?

John No.

George Come on, sweetheart. We'll not solve anything tonight.

They go upstairs.

Four

A *few months later. Morning. George is alone. Arthur comes in.*

Arthur I thought you'd be up here.

George Yes.

Arthur Well, where else would you be?

George Aye.

Arthur I told Barbara you'd gone home. She wanted to be certain. I dunno where she'd think you'd go.

George I couldn't stay any longer, Arthur. I had enough. You know.

Arthur You don't have to tell me. I was glad to get out for a bit. Still, it went off well. Good turnout. Yes. Good crowd. Nice spread. I don't know what they'll do with all that food Barbara and she made. I wanted Barbara to let me get a drink in. But no. You know chapel people. Doreen said it wouldn't do and that. Still, they're not miserable. Said very nice things, you know, very nice.

George Aye.
I could do with a pint. Do you fancy a pint?

Arthur I do. I do. I don't think we'd better, though.

George I don't see why not.

Arthur Oh, you know what they'd say.

George Say what they like. I thought on that too. We could go over to Pickstead.

Arthur They'd still get news of it.

Jack comes in.

George Hello, Jack. You had too much of it, too?

Jack Aye.
(*to his father*) She wants you.
All right, George?

Arthur Are you going back down?

George No, I don't think so. Come for a drink?

Arthur No, I don't think so, George.
(*to Jack*) What does she want me for?

Jack I think they're saying goodbye to all the people.

Arthur Right.

George Aye, Arthur, they've had interest in your old cottage. People from Leeds. He's not selling. He's renting.

Arthur No, he'll not sell. He's not stupid. Selling property on his land.

Jack Leeds. I'd like to go to Leeds.

Arthur What, to work?

Jack Maybe.

George I thought when he helped with the harvest, he'd stay with us.

Arthur Aye. He'll have to find something soon. Won't you?

Jack Aye.

George Gaffer'll take him on.

Arthur Oh well, I'd better see what she wants. I'll miss her not being here. Your mother. I've know her all my life. In and out of here. All my life. Stayed here many a time. Well. (*He goes.*)

George How you managing?

Jack I've never been to a funeral. I was a bit scared. I didn't know what might happen. But it was all right.

George Hey, if you want the job he's willing to take you on, you know. He says he'll take someone on. Up to you, Jack.

Jack Good food.

George You'll be eating that for a week.
I'm going up later. Do you want to come?

Jack I dunno.
Never seen so much tea drunk.

George They like their tea. That's a stimulant.

Jack I didn't know most of the people.

George You know the people from the village.

Jack I know people from the village. All the relatives, I didn't know most of them.

George You know Frank and them.

Jack Oh aye, I know them. Well, I'm off then. All right?

George Where you going?

Jack I'm going into the village. All right?

Doreen comes in the back door.

Doreen It's me.

Jack Tara then.

George Think on, Jack. Jack!

Jack All right. See you later. I'll be up.

George Tara.

Doreen Jack.

Jack goes.

I'll not be long. I missed you leaving, that's all. I must help Barbara clear up. I just popped up. I wanted to see you were all right. For myself.

George I'm all right.

Doreen Anything you want me to do while I'm here.

George No, Doreen.

Doreen I don't mean to intrude, George. Am I intruding?

George No.

Doreen I'll go.

George What's the matter with you?

Doreen You don't want people crowding you. Time like this. I'll go. You want me to go.

George What do you mean, Doreen?

Doreen They all mean well, George.

George Course they all mean well. I know that. But what's that mean to me? Nothing. Nothing. All them flowers. Waste of brass.

Doreen Why are you so hard?

George I'm not.

Doreen Hard on yourself. They have to pay their respects. Barbara found it very comforting, I think.

I shall be lost without your mother. Oh, I'm filling up. Look. Oh dear.

George Nay. Doreen, don't. What is it?

Doreen It's you. You're so sad, I know you are. And I'm sad for you, George. And there's no comforting you. I can't comfort you, can I? I can't. Oh dear. I didn't mean to carry on like this. I just want you to take care of yourself.

George Why wouldn't I take care of myself? I've been looking after things all right these past months, haven't I?

Doreen You have. You have. I'm so sorry.

George I don't want anyone to take care of me, Doreen. Thank you. I don't mean to hurt anyone. I'm just glad it's over. I could only take so much. That's all. I'm all right here.

Barbara enters with a plate of food covered with a cloth.

Doreen Oo, Barbara. I hope you haven't been clearing up by yourself now.

Barbara No. Just brought these up for him.

George No. I don't want anything.

Barbara This'll keep, this. I've put it in here. All right? All right, George?

George Aye.

She comes into the living room.

Doreen They all gone?

Barbara Yes, they've all gone.

Doreen I'm just popping home, Barbara. I'll be back to help. Won't be long. (*Doreen goes.*)

Barbara What's the matter with Doreen?
I'm exhausted. You?

George No. I'm all right. She's just upset, I think

Barbara I haven't taken it all in. Still. I'll go to the cemetery tomorrow.

George What for?

Barbara I'd like to. I didn't take it all in. Look at the flowers again. Didn't you see all the flowers out front?

George No. Not really.

Barbara Anyway, they all asked after you. As they went.

George I was there long enough, wasn't I?

Barbara Perhaps we should have done it up here. Would that have been better?

George No, Barbara.

Barbara She went from home. That's something.

George It's all right.

Barbara We'll have to arrange for the headstone to be done. Under Father's name.

George Oh Barbara, shut up will you?

Barbara Well, we'll have to think of these things.

George Father didn't have a headstone. Did he?

Barbara He did.
We'll have to sort her things.

George She didn't have anything. She didn't leave anything. Just enough to bury her.

Barbara She had you in that club, you know. You'll have to keep up the payments.

George No. You can throw me out with the ashes.

Barbara Don't, George. We'll have to sort her things.

George She didn't have anything.

Barbara No. But some of her clothes, some poor old people could do with them. That coat you bought her last winter. Doreen'll know someone. She never got the wear of it.

George I can't do it. I won't be doing it.
Look at this. (*He takes a box from the dresser.*)

Barbara What?

George Her savings book.

Barbara looks in the book.

Barbara Nothing in it. What did she keep it for?

George I don't know. It was in here with birth certificates and that – her marriage lines.

Barbara Just a penny in it to keep it open.

George There's her wedding ring. You have it now.

Barbara You keep it.

George I don't want anything.

Barbara You know you don't have to stay. You can do what you like now.

George Aye.

Barbara I had a nice card from your friend John. Did I tell you?

George Yes, you did.

Barbara Very nice. Should I send a letter back?

George I don't know.

Barbara Don't you stay in touch?

George Now and then.

Barbara There's nothing to keep you here, you know, George.

George No.

Barbara It's none of my business.

George No.

Barbara I'd like Dad's silver cup.

George OK.

Barbara What about Doreen?

George There's those heavy earrings.

Barbara She don't have pierced ears.

George Well, I don't know. Look, I'm going out, Barbara.

Barbara George, where you going?

George Up to work.

Barbara Today?

George Check a few things. Jack's coming later. I don't know if he'll stick it. We'll see.

George goes out. Doreen comes in.

Doreen All alone?

Barbara He's gone out for a walk. I think he wants to be on his own, Doreen.

Doreen Yes.

Barbara Well, it's hard for him.

Doreen And you, Barbara.

Barbara Oh yes. Oh yes. Well, we'll go. Thanks. Not a lot to do. We needed all those cups. Thank you.

Is there anything you want, Doreen, of Mother's? There isn't much.

Doreen No.

Barbara Well, if there is anything.

Doreen goes to the dresser.

Doreen There's this little thing. We bought it when we went over to Scarborough. Perhaps that.

Barbara Of course. Of course. Anything.

Doreen How will he manage?

Barbara He's quite self-sufficient, Doreen, you know.

Doreen Oh yes. But on his own. Will he manage?

Barbara Well, he will miss her. She was very fond of him, you see. I never minded. I didn't really.

Doreen They got on.

Barbara Yes. He's a solitary one. I think he's not someone for you, Doreen.

Doreen No.

Barbara I don't think he's for marrying, Doreen, you see.

Doreen No. I see that. I'll keep an eye on him, though.

Barbara Come on then. Shall we go?

Doreen Yes.

Mother comes in.

Barbara It's been an awful day for him.

Mother George?

Doreen And you.

Jack comes in.

Jack Nan!

Barbara Right, come on.

Arthur comes in.

Arthur Barbara.

Mother George.

John comes in with a carrier bag, dressed as in the first scene.

John I'm back.

They all go except for John.

George Is there a towel? Is there one there, John?

John Hang on. (*Finds towel.*) Yeah. Yes. Do you want it?

George comes in as he was in the first scene, when he went into the kitchen, but without a shirt.

George Where is it? Oo. Thanks.

John I bought you a shirt in 'Take Six'. Do you want to wear it?

George Oh, thanks. No, it's too good to wear tonight. Thanks. Good, there we are. Where's my clean jeans? Give me my jeans, kid.

He gives him his trousers.

John Thanks. Which shirt?

George Choose one.

John This is good. (*Gives him a shirt.*)

George OK. That's better. Thanks for this. It's great. Where's . . .

John Here we are. (*Hands him shoes.*)

George There we are.

John Yeah.

George Well. (*Looks at the jug of flowers on the table.*)

John These are nice flowers. Did you do these?

George Oh yeah. Doreen. You know Doreen. Very kind. She's been keeping my mother's little garden out there. Barbara ironed these shirts. I can't fend them off.

John You're all right, then?

George Yeah. I am.

John So you're managing, then?

George I'm managing fine. Is that all right?

John I was sorry to hear about your mother.

George You said.

John I didn't feel I should come.

George You could have come. No one would have minded. I'd have liked it.

John I'm sorry.

George No. No. Sorry.

John I thought of not coming tonight. You wouldn't have known. But I couldn't come to York and not see you. You wouldn't have known.

George Why did you come, then?

John You want your pound's worth, don't you?

George What do you mean?

John Don't.

George Well, you said make a break. A clean break.

John You can be hard.

George Aye. I can be hard. What about you? What are you? You're more compassionate, are you?
I think you are.

John Your mother liked me.

George I know. What you say that for?

John I don't know. I don't know.
Look at you. It's just looking at your . . . I can't. When I see your mouth and your hair. Oh please. Come back with me.

George Don't talk soft.

John I know. I know. Stupid.

George If you said jump in the lake, I'd do it. There's not much you couldn't make me do.

John Except what I want you to do.

George I couldn't do what you wanted me to. I had to come back.

John I know. I know. But it's different now. You can do what you like now.

George I couldn't. I couldn't live in London, me.

John You liked it.

George I did.

John There's nothing to keep you here. Is there?

George I live here. I live here. You can't see that, though. You can't see it. This is where I live. Here.

John You liked London.

George I did. I did. It was all right. It was great for a visit. All the visits. But what would I do? Where would I live? In your little room, sleeping in that three-quarter bed? I liked it. You know I did. They were all friendly, your friends. All of them.

And all the things to do. That we did. The picture galleries. That picture house on Oxford Street. The National Film Theatre. All the theatres and the concerts and the chat and everything. The white rooms and brass beds my mother said they had when she was a child. And the white Japanese lampshades and bookcases made out of bricks and planks. And the Whitechapel Gallery and American paintings and the deal tables and the bentwood chairs and the crocheted shawls.

And they were friendly. Very friendly people. Madheads, half of them. And the real coffee. Ugh. And the red wine, worse. And dinner in the night. I liked most of all that play on a Sunday. That was right good. Nearly a fight there was over that. What a lot they were. And the ballet. The ballet. Me. That curtain swinging up. All of it. And they were all nice too. And I enjoyed it all because you did. I'd do owt for you. But what would I do? Where would I work?

John Become an actor. I'd help you.

George I couldn't. It's too late, John.

John No.

George Listen to me speak.

John But that's all changed. I told you. Everything like that's changing. It's different. It's all going to be different. It's going to change. It's changing.

George Is it? I didn't see it. I couldn't learn to speak differently now. I couldn't be in Shakespeare, me. And if I couldn't do that! No. No thanks. Just be some Northerner as a job. Who'd let me do owt else? You know they wouldn't. I wouldn't blame them.

And I'd want to be more, whatever – wide-ranging. It's too late. I've left it too late. You got to be seventeen, eighteen, true. And, you know, I've got no . . . That's it. I'm not ambitious. You've got to be ambitious. I've none. I live here.

John But you're so good.

George That's what you say.

John It's true.

George No.

John It is. It is.

George You come up here. Come up here.

John I can't.

George Why not?

John You know I can't.

George Get a job in York in the theatre. Live here. Drive to York. Or Scarborough. Work from here. Rent Arthur's old cottage. No. No. Stupid. I'm stupid. See you light the kerosene lamp. Cook on a range. Keep a paraffin lamp in the lav. Get your bollocks frozen in winter having a shit outside. Have the pipes froze. Go down that lane in the slush. Cross that field to get to the village. Or move in here with me. Yeah. But how would we explain that? No. We'll have to let it go. See each when we can. As it was.

John Don't be such a bastard.

George Why? How? It was your choice. I was all right. You broke it off. Clean break, you said. All or nothing. Probably right. I thought we could leave it. Let it go as it went.

John We did.

George But it wasn't good enough for you.

John I couldn't just leave it to meet whenever and if.

George But that's what's happened. You came to York. You came over and I'm glad to see you. That's what's happened.

John I can't just let it be, drift apart. I don't feel casual about you. There was nothing casual about it. I haven't come for a fuck. It isn't casual sex. I've had plenty of casual sex.

George Shut up. Talking like that.

John It's all right for you.

George Aye.

John You've got it cosy up here. Tucked up by your sister and Doreen.

George She's all right, Doreen. She is. I like Doreen.

John Why don't you marry her?

George Perhaps I should.

John Better to marry than to burn.

George We're all right as it is.

John As what is?

George Doreen and me. We're sorted.

John Will you marry her then? Will you?

George Well, no. I dunno. I'm all right. Leave it, will you?

John So that's it.

George If you say so.

John I shouldn't have come.

George No.

John You're such a . . .

George What?

John Nothing.

George What? I'm such a what?

John George.

George It's got to be your way.

John No.

George Oh yeah? Why did you come?

John I know. I know. I'm sorry.

George I could fucking kill you.
Don't leave me.

John Come with me.

Doreen comes in.

Doreen Oo. You in?

John Oh Christ. I'm going.

George Fuck it. Don't go. Don't go.

Doreen Here we are.

George Look who's here.

Doreen Well, this is a surprise.

John Hello, Doreen.

Doreen You had your tea, George?

George No, not yet.

Doreen What brings you up here, John?

George He's in York with a play.

John Yes. I have to go. I've got to get back before curtain down.

George No.

Doreen Just for the week?

John Yes.

George Don't go yet.

Doreen We should try and see it, George.

George Aye.

John I must.

Doreen Have you directed it, John?

John Yes.

Doreen That's good. Will you put these in the shed for me, George? They're bulbs. I want to put them out.

George What do you want me to do?

Doreen Put these out there for me, will you?

George Aye, give 'em here. Won't be long. OK? (*George goes out.*)

Doreen So you here for a week? We haven't seen you for a long time. We thought you'd forgotten us. Got your work?

John Yes.

Doreen That's important.

John Yes. That's right. Look, I have to go.

Doreen No, surely you'll have a cup of tea?

John No.

Doreen Are you sure?
George! John's going. George!
He'll be in now. Sit and have tea with us.

John I'm late. I'll have to go. I'm going. OK? Goodbye. (*He goes.*)

Doreen George!

George comes in.

George What? Where's John?

Doreen He had to go.

George What? What do you mean? Why did you let him go?

Doreen You might catch him.

George goes out.

Look at this place. (*Begins to tidy up. Looks at the range.*) We'll have to take that out.

George comes in.

George I missed him.

Doreen You couldn't have. He'll be going for the bus.

George He's got a car.

Doreen Oh. I didn't know. You'll see him during the week.

George Yes.

Doreen I'll make you your tea. I got chops. You like them. (*She goes out.*)

George
Foxes their dens have they
Birds have their nests so gay
But the son of man this day
Has not where his head he may rest.

ORIGINAL SIN

after Frank Wedekind

For John, Deirdre, Bill and Alison

Original Sin received its world premiere in May 2002 at The Crucible, Sheffield. The cast, in order of speaking, was as follows:

Slavin John Normington
Leopold Southerndown Michael Byrne
Eugene Black Adam James
Dr. Edwin Goulderie Paul Imbusch
Angel Andrew Scott
Arthur Southerndown Steve John Shepherd
Hugo Anstruther Andrew Fallaize
Stage Manager Robert Styles
Dresser Barry Howard
Buller David Kennedy
Lord Henry Wantage Richard Cant
Frederick Michael Shaeffer
The Marchese di Casti Piani Clive Arrindell
Weil, Richard Cant
Phillipeau Robert Styles
Baron St Eglise Paul Imbusch
August Andrew Fallaize
Baptiste Michael Shaeffer
Hippolyte David Carr
Bob Paul Child
Mr Tompkins Barry Howard
Euba David Carr
Jack Michael Shaeffer

Director Peter Gill
Designer Alison Chitty
Lighting Designer Hartley T A Kemp
Composer Terry Davies

Characters

Slavin
an itinerant

Leopold Southerndown
a newspaper proprietor

Eugene Black
a painter

Dr Edwin Goulderie
a physician

Angel

Arthur Southerndown
Southerndown's son, a playwright and theatre director

Hugo Anstruther
a schoolboy

Stage Manager *and* **Dresser**
theatre workers

Buller
a strong-man

Lord Henry Wantage
a follower of Angel

Frederick
a footman

The Marchese di Casti Piani
a white slaver

Weil
a banker

Phillipeau
a journalist

Baron St Eglise
one of Angel's guests

August
his protégé

Baptiste, Hippolyte
other guests

Bob
a footman

Policemen

Mr Tomkins, Euba, Jack
Angel's clients

The action of the play takes place in London and Paris in the 1890s

PROLOGUE

Enter Slavin, singing.

Slavin

What's the use of kicking up a row
If there ain't no work about?
If you can't get a job you can rest in bed
Till the schoolkids all come out.
If you can't get work you can't get the sack.
That's an argument that's sensible and sound.
Lay your head back on yer piller
And read yer *Daily Mirrer*
And wait till the work comes round.

(*to the audience*) Anyone who says he can't make a living is a liar. As I am here to show. I've managed. I've managed. It's a matter of priorities and motivation. But that's not to be the thrust of things. No. No. No. Right then. London. 1890. 1890s London. That'll mean something to you. But perhaps I should re-emphasise what you might think is obvious. Fog, for example. Cab horses, for instance. Street lamps lit by gas. London squares and tenement dwellings. East and West. The poor and the destitute, the rich and the powerful. All that. And you'll have thought perhaps of extravagant opulence and gilded youth. The beautiful and the damned. Yes.

Noise of monkeys chattering and screaming. Parakeets. A wolf howling. Big cats snarling.

What's that?

Similar noises.

Oh yes. The street cries of London. Yes. This is to be about the world of men. Of power and cash and the force that seems to drive it all. And if I say, artist and studio and that's where we'll begin, you'll think perhaps of the embankment alongside the river in the mist and the barges and factories and the oily water lapping against the wharves and the bridges dim in the evening light and the little unexploited streets and the north-facing windows and the cold. See where I fit into all this. If I do.

ONE

London. An artist's studio. Prominent, a woman's evening dress on a stand. Unaffected but sumptuous. Near it on an easel, the unfinished portrait of a young man. Leopold Southerndown talking to Eugene Black.

Southerndown (*handing the artist a pair of women's evening gloves*) And these perhaps.

Black Yes.

Southerndown No jewels, I think.

Black No.

Southerndown Flowers? Perhaps not. Here's the photograph I said I would bring you.

Black Perhaps something at the neck.

Southerndown No. My fiancée is essentially unaffected. Simple. No, unspoiled. Her father . . . I don't want too many sittings. That's why you have these to work from. I shall bring her to meet you next week. (*looking at the portrait*) And this?

Black My next sitter. Due now.

Southerndown Adventurous pose.

Black Do you know him?

Southerndown Know him?

Black Dr Goulderie.

Southerndown Dr Goulderie is my physician.

Black This is his . . . protégé . . . Do you know him?

Southerndown No.

Black There he is now.

Southerndown (*giving him the photograph*) Take this.

Enter Dr Goulderie and Angel.

Goulderie Late. Come. Southerndown!

Southerndown Good day.

Angel You're here.

Southerndown I'm arranging for my fiancée's portrait to be painted.

Angel Is she coming to town at last? Is she going to be allowed into society? Shall we meet her? Or are you going to keep her to yourself?

Black Do you know her?

Angel No one's seen her. Her father . . . (*pointing to Southerndown*) She's changed his life.

Black Are you ready?

Goulderie Yes. Come. Let us begin. Is there heat?

Angel Must I change?

Black If you would.

Angel, laughing, goes behind a screen.

Goulderie (*looking at the picture*) You've worked it up since last we were here. What do you think?

Southerndown The flesh. You'll treat the dress like that?

Goulderie Are you using your box tonight at the opera?

Southerndown What are they giving?

Goulderie The new *Tristan.*

Southerndown I don't think.

Goulderie Go. Wagner is better than injections of chloral hydrate. I'll change your prescription. Where's Boy. Boy.

Southerndown Why do you call him Boy? I called him Beauty.

Angel enters, naked except for a long piece of cloth falling over his shoulder like a towel and a chaplet of coloured flowers in his hair.

Southerndown Let me help.

They help to arrange the pose for the painting.

Goulderie (*at the painting, to the artist*) Look at him and then at this. Less refined, more savage. Like some wretched academician with French brush strokes. Less taste. Less delicacy. I'm a physician. I look at what there is. I don't want anything frankly immodest. I want to show it. If I had wanted something piquant I would have arranged it. Paint him as if he was on a plate. Meat or fruit. Paint what is there. Not this. This is coy, this refinement. This is your refinement. Look, do you see refinement? What do you think you see? Turn, Boy. That's it.

Southerndown Let me help.

Goulderie I must go.

Arthur (*offstage*) Papa.

Southerndown Arthur.

Arthur Papa.

Arthur Southerndown enters carrying a sheaf of lilies.

Dr Goulderie.

Goulderie Hello.

Arthur Where shall I put these?

Southerndown Why are you here?

Arthur I want you to come to my rehearsal, Papa. (*to Angel*) Will you come? Dressed like that, you could be in the show. Here, you have these. (*giving Angel the lilies*)

Angel What is it?

Arthur Something entirely new. Something absolutely new. It's an event. Total theatre. Not a word in it. Tumblers, fire-eaters, a great woman with a snake. Music, singing. It's divine. Dancers on tightropes. Tigers and Chinese dragons. It's a show. A show. An opera for all. (*to Angel*) You'd be divine. Dr Goulderie?

Goulderie No.

Arthur Papa?

Southerndown Not this afternoon, Arthur.

Angel Keep us seats for Friday, Arthur.

Arthur Seats. There aren't any seats. You mill about.

Southerndown Come then, Arthur. Doctor?

Goulderie Oh yes. I'll come with you. (*to Angel*) I'll come for you presently.

Angel No, no. I'll send out. Take a hansom.

Goulderie No, I'll send the carriage. No, I'll come myself.

Angel Don't do that.

Goulderie Yes.

Angel No, darling.

Goulderie Yes, my dear.

Angel No. Please.

Goulderie Well. Well. All right. You'll call a cab?

Angel Of course.

Southerndown, Arthur and Goulderie go.

Black These commissions. This painting with another man's hands. These opinions. Put something up and they know what it should be. Prescriptions and judgements and interference. These intolerable opinions. How can you live with him?

Angel Sh. (*Listens.*) No.

Black Would you like to rest?

Angel No. Go on working. He'll be back. I know he will. I don't know why he left me alone with you.

Black No threat. I'm a servant.

Angel What if he comes back? I'm afraid he'll come back.

Black We're doing nothing. Why are you afraid of him?

Angel Sh. There's someone at the door.

Black It's my servant, sweeping the stairs. Be still. I'm painting your hip . . . There . . . Yes . . . Yes . . .

Angel He'll be back, I know. What shall we do?

Black What do you want to do?

Angel I don't know. I don't know what to do. I don't know how to choose. I'm not used to choice.

Black For you and me, the sky is like lead in a coffin. Or else it breaks up into sunlight and lets in the smell of dead orange blossom which no one has worn.

Angel Why has he left me here? He never leaves me alone. He locks me in.

Black Does he?

Angel But without a key.

Black But he must see his patients. He can't be there all the time.

Angel The servants watch me. I can't leave the house.

Black Why do you put up with it?

Angel Because I have to. Paint me in this. (*He puts on the evening dress.*)

Black No, you mustn't.

Angel Why not? Paint me in this. How do I look in her dress? Paint me in her dress. His fiancée's dress. The doctor would like me in this. At home he likes me to dress up.

Black What do you mean?

Angel Paint me.

Black Tell me. What do you mean?

Angel Slave trousers. Hussar's uniform. Midshipman. You know. Pierrot, faun, drummer boy. He sits and watches or plays the piano. After dinner. Sometimes Southerndown is there. Sometimes one of the others.

Black Why don't you leave?

Angel Why don't you give up painting to commission?

Black I'm tired. This light. I can't go on like this. The colours are dancing in my eyes. Please.

Angel We mustn't. He'll ruin you.

Black I don't care.

Angel Don't.

Black Come here.

Angel I mean it. Don't.

Black Yes.

Angel Don't. (*laughing*) Don't. Don't.

Black What do you want? Shall I take my belt to you? Is that what you want?

Angel You'll have to catch me first.

Black Come here then.

Angel You never will.

Black Won't I?

Angel No, you never will. Try it.

Black Come here.

Chase. He doesn't catch him.

Angel I told you. (*as if talking to a cat*) Come on then. Puss. Puss. Come on.

Black catches him. Angel disarms him and he falls on to the floor. Angel climbs a ladder.

I'm climbing into the sun.

Black How did I fall?

Angel I can see all the cities in the world.

Black I'm coming after you.

Angel I can reach the sky.

Black I'm holding up the earth.

Angel Take the stars and put them in my hair.

Black Sheet lightning.

Angel Leave me alone.

Black Come down.

Angel No.

They fall. Angel smashes furniture and china. Mayhem.

I'd like to hunt with a pack of wolves.

Black I've no money to repair all this. You bitch. Look at what you've done. You bitch. I've no one to pour oysters down my throat.

Angel Don't lock the door. He'll be back.

Black I'll belt you.

Angel Will you?

Black I will. He shouldn't have left you.

Angel Will you?

Black No. I love you. Please.

Angel What?

Black Take it off.

Angel It's too cold.

Black Please. Oh please.

Angel You've seen me.

Black That's not seeing you. Please.

Angel Leave me alone.

Black Don't be cruel. Please.

Angel No.

Black Let's go into the other room. Come on. Please.

Angel Why?

Black Because I love you.

Angel What do you want?

Black You know.

Angel In here then.

Black Here!

Angel Don't you want me?

Black You're just being cruel.

Angel You don't want me.

Black I do. I do.

Angel Do you?

Black Yes. Please.

Angel Do you love me, did you say?

Black Take it off, please.

Angel You.

Black What?

Angel Go on.

Black No.

Angel Yes, go on. Go on. Go on.

Black Must I?

Angel Yes, you must.

Black strips to only his shirt.

Unhook me.

In the course of the undressing and kissing Black gets confused.

Black I can't do this . . .

Angel is afraid.

Angel Don't kill me.

Punches Black, who falls.

Black Oh. What is it?

Angel Do you want to kill me?

Black No.

Angel Do you? Do you want to kill me?

Black What?

Angel You've never done this before, have you? Poor boy. How old are you?

Black Twenty-eight. And you?

Angel Eighteen.

Black Love me.

Banging on the door.

Goulderie Let me in.

Angel What shall we do? What shall we do? Look at all this.

Black What are you doing?

Goulderie Open this door.

Angel I'll clear up. He'll kill me.

Goulderie breaks the door open.

Goulderie You dogs. Dogs. Dogs. (*spluttering*) Dogs. (*He collapses.*)

Black Dr Goulderie. (*going to him*) Help me then. Help. Leave all this. Send for a doctor.

Angel I think he's dead.

Black Help me.

Angel His nose is bleeding. He must have hit it. He's too heavy. Leave him. Leave him.

Black I'll go for the doctor.

Angel It's too late.

Black We must do something.

Angel Let him go.

Black No. I'll send for the doctor. (*Exits.*)

Angel He'll get up in a minute. Get up – sweetheart. Come, darling. Get up. Get up. Please, my little one. Get up. He's split his nose. His nose is bleeding. Have you had enough of me? Is that it? What shall I do now? Shall I put something on? What do you want? What shall I do? I don't know what to do. I don't know how to do anything. What will I do? Look at his face. Who'll close his eyes?

Enter Black.

Black The doctor's coming.

Angel Is he? It won't do any good. Close his eyes.

Black What?

Angel We must close his eyes. Will you do it?

Black I can't.

Angel Have you never closed anyone's eyes before this? I'll do it. I'll be dead some day. So will you.

Black Don't say that.

Angel He's staring at me. Look.

Black And at me. I'll do it. (*Closes his eyes.*)

Angel I'm rich now.

Black Tell me something.

Angel Yes.

Black Can you love me? Can you love you? Do you believe in love? Tell me. Can you tell the truth? Can you? Tell me.

Angel I'll get dressed. (*Goes behind the screen.*)

Black (*to Goulderie's body*) If I could change places with you. Will you take him back? Is he mine now? Take my youth. I can't have it. I don't know how to live it. I can't cope with happiness. What if I'm happy? What will I do? I can't. I can't. I love him. I do. You can't hear. Please give me the strength to be happy. Give me the strength.

Enter Angel, fully dressed except for his tie.

Angel Do this for me, will you?

TWO

London. A grand drawing room. The portrait from Scene One finished and hanging on the wall. Angel and Black sitting together in the same chair.

Angel Let me go. Let me go. Stop. (*Gets up.*) You see.

Black follows him.

Don't bite me. We're only just out of bed. (*violent*) Leave me alone. Look, these are yesterday's love bites. Why do you want to mark me?

Black You know I've only to hear you walking and I . . .

Angel I'll go barefoot then.

Black I'll still hear you. What if you die? What if something happens to you? I wake up each morning and I'm frightened that something's going to happen. That a mad dog will bite you. Today I think there's going to be rioting in the streets. And tomorrow will be something else. I'll get an insect bite and that'll be fatal. I know it will. I can't read the papers. I don't like going out.

Angel (*picking up some letters from a pile on a table*) Have you read this?

Black Yes. It's from my dealer in Paris.

Angel And this?

Black From Moscow. An exhibition.

Angel (*reading*) 'The Duke of . . . is pleased to announce the engagement of his daughter, Lady Adelaide, to Mr Leopold Southerndown.' So at last it's official.

Black I can't understand why it's taken him so long to arrange it. A man with his power and position. We must write to him.

Angel Yes, you do it.

Black I owe everything to you. My success. My happiness. My happiness. All my success is due to you. All this great success. I know it. I would be nothing without you. And you belong to me. You belong to me. I've got to work. Are you angry with me?

Angel No, I'm not angry with you.

Black I think I shall go mad.

Angel I'm sure you will.

Black Don't laugh. I feel I'm screaming.

Angel I know, I can hear you. Is it my fault?

Black No. Nor mine.

Angel Whose fault?

Black It is the fault of your beauty.

Angel But I can't help it. I can't help what I am. I wish I was ugly. I wish I was ugly and a child. So that I could grow up again, look forward. How good it would be to know nothing again.

Black It's your fate, your beauty. It's what can make your kisses so mean.

Angel kisses Black.

Where did you learn that?

Angel Before I was born.

Black What is it about you? It's not your beauty. It's something else. Have you got a soul, is that it? Is it that you've got a soul?

Angel I want you now.

Black Do you?

Angel Lock the door.

A bell rings.

Damn it. I've told them to say we're not at home.

Black It might be from my dealer.

Angel It could be from the Queen for all I care.

Black No. I'd better see who it is.

Exit. Angel alone.

Angel Perhaps it's you you you. Perhaps it will be you you you you.

Re-enter Black.

Black It's a beggar. Some old-soldier story. I haven't any change. Will you deal with it? I've got to work.

Goes to his studio. Angel goes to the door and meets Slavin as he enters.

Slavin He's not very impressive, is he? He's not what I anticipated at all. I was expecting something with more dash. He's a bag of nerves for a start. I thought he was going to pass out when he saw me. No stomach, eh?

Angel How could you ask him for money?

Slavin It was very easy, my son. That's why I dragged my poor old bag of bones all this way. I thought you told me he worked in the morning?

Angel He does. How much do you want?

Slavin Fifty if you've got it. A hundred if you're as flush as you seem to be. Two of my clients have absented themselves without prior notice to myself.

Angel I'm so tired.

Slavin That's the two of us. And there's another reason for my call. I wanted to see this place.

Angel And what do you make of it?

Slavin Reminds me of a time fifty years ago when I had a bit of luck. Taste differs, of course. That's all. All Chinese now, I see. I'll be damned if you haven't done well yourself. Look at the carpets.

Angel What do you want to drink? Tokay?

Slavin Hock and seltzer. Does he drink? The artist.

Angel That would be all I need. This stuff affects different people in different ways.

Slavin He a violent chap, then?

Angel If he drinks he's out for the count.

Slavin When he drinks you can get him to spill his guts. Examine his entrails.

Angel No. Thank you. So what have you got to tell me?

Slavin That the streets are getting longer and my legs are getting shorter.

Angel I thought you were dead.

Slavin So did I, my dear. But no. When the sun sets we still have to get up in the morning.

Angel How's the mouth organ?

Slavin I'm a bit short of breath. Wheezy. Wheezy like me and the asthma. I'm looking forward to the winter, I am. My asthma might do me the favour of sending me somewhere where there's no return.

Angel They might have forgotten you where you're going.

Slavin That might be so. They might have thought I was earlier on the bill. But tell me about you. It's been so long. Such a long time since I've seen my little boy. My Angel child.

Angel You called me Angel.

Slavin Well, have you ever heard me call you anything else?

Angel I haven't heard it since time was.

Slavin Is there another way of calling you? What do they call you?

Angel It sounds of a time that is gone.

Slavin Don't dance on the streets now?

Angel No.

Slavin Your old accompanist too old and you too old.

Plays the mouth organ. Angel step-dances. Angel laughs and stops. Puts scent on.

Slavin This is what I hoped for you, all this. What's that?

Angel Scent.

Slavin You smell without it.

Angel Not like you.

Slavin What is it?

Angel Heliotrope.

Slavin Heliotrope. And what do you do with yourself all day?

Angel Laze and sleep. Sleep.

Slavin Is that you? (*pointing to the painting*)

Angel It is.

Slavin And is that good, is it? This is how I wanted it to be. I've always believed in your talent, since you were two big eyes and a wide mouth. I've always wanted this for you. And what do you do with yourself? How's your French?

Angel I sleep most of the time.

Slavin It can be very useful, French.

Angel Yes.

Slavin And you cover yourself in Heliotrope and sleep.

Angel So what do you care?

Slavin Why do I care? What do I care? You say that to me. Who'd rather live till the last day and give up any chance of salvation than leave you down here in a tight corner of any sort. What do I care? Have I no compassion, no human frailty, no empathy or sympathy, no human understanding? What do you feel you are?

Angel An animal.

Slavin An animal.

Angel Expensive, well-trained animal.

Slavin A performing animal.

Angel You trained me.

Slavin I could die happy now. I've made my peace with the Lord. I bear no grudges against anyone. Not even against the old dear who washes me and lays me out.

Angel One thing, they can never wash you again. You'd like that.

Slavin You wash, you get dirty again.

Angel It might bring you back, a good wash.

Slavin We're all rotting. We're all dirty flesh.

Angel Not me. I'm luxurious clean. I'm dipped in scent, and my sheets are made of material that nearly matches my skin. I have flesh like fresh fruit: like a peeled apple.

Slavin Rotting fruit. You're good enough to eat. So am I, a feast, good food, I am.

Angel There's not enough on you for worms.

Slavin Don't give me that talk. Your lovers, they won't put you in a preserving jar. You're all right, you, a young man. A nice bit of flesh, but it's not long before you're an old boot and then, who'll know you then? Even the zoo animals will turn their noses up at you. They're particular about what they eat. Bonemeal you'll be.

Angel Don't.

Slavin Have you forgotten who I am? I dragged you out of a hovel and up west with me. Have you forgotten? You were arse-naked, you were. A little naked boy.

Angel How could I forget? You tied me up by the wrists and belted me. I remember that.

Slavin It was necessary. It was necessary.

Doorbell rings.

Angel Come on, then. (*Gives him money.*) Will that do you?

Slavin That'll be fine. That'll be fine.

Slavin and Angel go out. Angel returns with Southerndown.

Southerndown I don't understand how you can allow that man into your house.

Angel What's the matter with you? What is it?

Southerndown I must speak to you seriously.

Angel What about, I pray? I saw you yesterday. What's so important today that you couldn't have spoken about it to me yesterday?

Southerndown Does he, Black, know that that fellow was here? If I was him I wouldn't let that creature speak to you.

Angel What is it? Tell me. For pity's sake tell me. What is it?

Southerndown I want you to listen to me carefully.

Angel Why are you so formal? He can't hear. He's in the studio.

Southerndown I should have spoken to you yesterday. I was a damn fool.

Angel Will you listen to me? He can't hear. What is it? What do you want to say? Tell me, what is it? What's the matter? What has happened?

Southerndown Be quiet. You're hysterical.

Angel Then tell me what you want to say to me.

Southerndown This is not easy for me. Not at all easy. Your visits . . .

Angel My what?

Southerndown Your visits to me.

Angel My visits to you?

Southerndown Your visits to me. They must stop. Do you understand me?

Angel No, I don't understand you.

Southerndown It's months now since I first realised that it must finally stop. That it would be better for both of us. For me and for you.

Angel Do you want a drink?

Southerndown No, I don't want a drink. Please listen to me. You must give me this undertaking.

Angel What has happened since yesterday?

Southerndown Things have become clear to me.

Angel Have they?

Southerndown I have asked you twice now. Stop coming to see me.

Angel Are you feverish? Are you hot? Let me feel your forehead.

Southerndown No. I'm fine.

Angel And so am I.

Southerndown If you don't want to hear.

Angel I want to hear. Well?

Southerndown If you don't want to hear what I'm saying, I shall simply tell them not to announce you. They won't let you past the front door. I'll treat you as you should have treated that . . .

Angel There is no need. What have I done?

Southerndown You have done nothing.

Angel Don't play games with me. What have I done that is so wrong? Is it because of the announcement of your engagement yesterday? Do you think I will spoil your chances of finally bringing about this marriage? Is it that?

Southerndown It is that in part.

Angel Is she so pure that I can defile her without knowing her?

Southerndown Don't speak of her.

Angel Then I will be silent.

Southerndown I can't any longer live like this. Live with these . . . differences.

Angel That's not it. How did you get her father to agree?

Southerndown He thinks it's right for her. And I was able to help him recently. My newspapers. He was involved in an unfortunate situation. Not entirely of his making. Stupid of him and typical of –

Angel The mother? You could deal with her only too well.

Southerndown You must see that marriage to such a young woman means that I must regulate my life now.

Angel Fine. Fine. Fine. What do I care about visits. We can meet as you arrange it.

Southerndown There is something I can't make you understand. We are not ever going to meet again. Except in the course of things.

Angel Please don't say that.

Southerndown And how anyhow can you go on treating Black like this?

Angel Don't moralise. You hypocrite.

Southerndown He's a decent enough chap. I've grown quite fond of him. I shall miss his company.

Angel Your marriage will provide you with new friends enough.

Southerndown And I want no unpleasantness with Black.

Angel There's no need for what you call unpleasantness.

Southerndown But he's such a child.

Angel Such a fool.

Southerndown If he weren't a fool he would have found out about you a long time ago.

Angel It might be good for him to smell me as I am.

Southerndown Why are you with him?

Angel Because he's so stupid. And because he thinks he's happy with me. And that pleases me.

Southerndown What if he finds out?

Angel He won't. He doesn't want to. His lack of sophistication is too convenient. He has no idea how ridiculous he is. He thinks his outbursts are a sign of temperament. He's the sexual imagination of an eager young clergyman. He doesn't see beyond his paintbrush and his hysteria. He can't see himself and he certainly can't see me. He's blind. He's blind as a new-born kitten.

Southerndown Does he bore you so much?

Angel What do you think? Sometimes I dream of Dr Goulderie.

Southerndown That old lecher. Because he spoiled you.

Angel At least he wasn't unimaginative.

Southerndown Not with his extensive tastes.

Angel Sometimes I still see him above me. I still see his big face.

Southerndown You miss the discipline, don't you?

Angel I dream often that his burial was a mistake and that he wasn't dead. And that he's still with me. That he never went away. Only he walks softly now in his stockinged feet. He isn't angry with me about the painter. Just sad about it. He seems fearful and timid as if he hadn't got permission to be here again. And he seems part of us. Except he doesn't like it that I've thrown so much money away. But he wants to be here. He comes of his own accord.

Southerndown Well, you must educate the painter into the way of things.

Angel He's in love with me. I can't do that.

Southerndown Fatal to be in love with you. But love doesn't quell the animal in us, you must have seen that. Teach him.

Angel He makes me feel so guilty. I can't bear to look at myself. He doesn't know me at all. He calls me all the names that such a lover knows. Such stupid names. Darling, dearest, puss. You know. But he doesn't know me at all. He thinks I am a woman. He knows nothing about women. He knows nothing about men. He wants to be married, I think. He's afraid of life, of what he might really be. I'm a sort of contraceptive. I am. I count for nothing in his neurasthenic picture of things. He either accuses me of coldness and is violent and then weeps with remorse or is frightened by anything frank and withdraws into an attack of sensibility.

Southerndown Some people would be glad of your power.

Angel Let some people have it then. It's so easy. I have only to put on silk pyjamas and cover myself in scent. He's like a dog and then I have to put up with his grunts. He knows no games, no fun. And then he's very much the man and falls asleep. And of course he's an artist, on top of it all, and thinks he's famous.

Southerndown I assisted a little there.

Angel He wouldn't be capable of understanding. He would think me depraved if he knew. He thinks I lived with Dr Goulderie as a sort of innocent. He thinks I'm a child. And yet I'm glad when he's happy. I am.

Southerndown So it is understood. I want my wife to be happy.

Angel What can you see in her?

Southerndown That should be of no concern to you.

Angel She's as young as I am.

Southerndown She's younger.

Angel Oh, I see. There's that, of course. Am I so old, is that it? You'll die of boredom. She'll kill you with her simplicity. I know. She'll be cheerful. That will bore you. or she'll be quiet and that will bore you even more.

Southerndown She's very biddable.

Angel You'll break her open.

Southerndown Don't be vulgar. And don't try to impede any of this. You have set up an establishment with Eugene Black. There can be nothing between us now.

Angel Oh God. Oh my God.

Southerndown I have done all that I could for you. I made his reputation. You have a great deal of cash which results from my setting you up with Dr Goulderie. You move in society. Now let me be free. I want to live the rest of my life in this new way. Don't compromise what is left of your self-respect by begging me for anything.

Angel You don't want me any more. What shall I do? Do you? Do you? You don't. Well, I shall have to try to deal with this. Shan't I? I shall. I shall have to find a way. I shall. Shan't I?

Southerndown Sh. Sh. Beauty. Boy. Angel, child, darling. What is it?

Angel Since yesterday. Overnight. And it's as if you've never known me.

Southerndown It was going to happen one day.

Angel I won't simply be thrown away. I won't be discarded because of your bid for a place in the world. I don't care for how the world treats me. But not you. Not you. It would be wicked of you. You'll kill me. You will.

Southerndown Do you want more money? Will that do it?

Angel No. I don't want more money. If you belong to anyone in the world you belong to me. I belong to you. You have made me what I am. Everything I have you gave me. You made me. Take me back. I'll do anything. I am your slave.

Southerndown I rescued you. I looked after you. I promoted your career. And now you must let me go.

Angel I smell respectability. You want to be respectable. I don't want to be respectable. I am not respectable. I won't be.

Southerndown If you feel anything for me. If you truly feel any of this gratitude. Then I beg you. Beauty.

Angel Do what you want. Marry her. But don't desert me, please. Please. Don't. I beg you.

Eugene Black enters.

Black What's going on?

Angel He's giving me up. When he's told me a thousand times –

Southerndown Be quiet. Be quiet. Be quiet.

Angel A thousand times he's told me. Like a schoolboy. Stammered how there has never been a love like mine.

Black Leave us alone.

Angel Gladly.

Black Leave us alone. Do as I say. Do as I say.

Angel Tell him. Tell. Him. You asked to be told and you tell him.

Black and Angel go out.

Southerndown This will be hard for him to bear.

Re-enter Black.

Black Is this some sort of foolery?

Southerndown No, it is not.

Black What is it then? Tell me.

Southerndown Shall we sit down? I'm fatigued.

Black What has been going on? Tell me. You must tell me.

Southerndown You must have heard.

Black I heard nothing.

Southerndown Or don't you want to hear anything?

Black I don't know what you mean. Have I displeased him?

Southerndown Oh, pull yourself together man. What does that matter? This is not for children.

Black What does he want of me? What did he mean just now? What's going on?

Southerndown You heard him say what is going on. You heard him say it. Can you hear nothing?

Black Does he want to? Behind my back . . . Others.

Southerndown No. No. That's not it. Let it be now. It's in the past now.

Black What is in the past? What is it? That is in the past?

Southerndown Forget it. You have been happy for months. In heaven, it would seem. Grant him that.

Black What has he done?

Southerndown He told you.

Black You. You. How long?

Southerndown I have known him now for fifteen years.

Black You have been deceiving me.

Southerndown Why can't you grow up? This is not the mirror of middle-class domestic life.

Black I don't understand you.

Southerndown Because you won't listen. I came to put an end to it. I came to tell him it was over. It is over. You must help me to make him understand.

Black You have known him for how long?

Southerndown Since he was seven years old. He used to sell my newspapers outside the Alhambra.

Black He told me he was brought up by relatives.

Southerndown I brought him up.

Black A newspaper boy.

Southerndown Yes.

Black Barefoot?

Southerndown Barefoot, a guttersnipe, a street Arab. I am telling you this so that you will try to understand him. So that you won't imagine it to be all his fault. He has done what he can. His standards are not yours.

Black He said I was the only one.

Southerndown He was lying.

Black On his mother's grave.

Southerndown He never knew his mother. Or her grave. She has no grave.

Black You brought him up?

Southerndown I had him brought up and educated by respectable people. Decent people.

Black And what about Goulderie. Where did he get him?

Southerndown From me.

Black But he didn't touch him, did he? Not really. He didn't touch him.

Southerndown Perhaps he told him that I never touched him either.

Black I saw in him my redemption. I thought God had sent him to me. That he was made for me and I for him.

Southerndown The doctor felt much the same thing.

Black Because I was so unhappy.

Southerndown Then accept him for what he is. Or make something of it. Take responsibility for it.

Black Oh God.

Southerndown He has shared all this with you. Grant him that. You have made your life with him. And you have a reputation now. Life is not really over. Don't be such a fool.

Black He told me his life was different. Not that he was . . . That his life wasn't as it was.

Southerndown That's all fooling. Take hold of things. You have money and position. You can't have scruples as well. You love him. Beauty.

Black Who?

Southerndown Him.

Black I call him Darling.

Southerndown The doctor called him Boy. I don't know what his real name is. With such a father. There's little to wonder at.

Black What of his father?

Southerndown He still pursues me.

Black He's still alive?

Southerndown You met him.

Black Where?

Southerndown He was in your house, man.

Black Him? He told me he was lost at sea. That he was lost in a typhoon in the South Seas. Oh God.

Southerndown What is it?

Black Pain.

Southerndown Drink this.

Black My chest. I can't breathe. I can't weep. If I could even cry out.

Southerndown Are you a man? He's worth a million. Who doesn't prostitute himself. You have him. The most beautiful creature in the world.

Black Stop it.

Southerndown This is not a sentimental situation. Take hold of it. Don't lose him. You would be a fool to lose him. Keep hold of him. He is your life.

Black Yes. Yes.

Southerndown He's easy enough to control. You must do it.

Black Yes.

Southerndown Where are you going?

Black To speak to him. To put things right. (*Exits opposite to where Angel has gone out.*)

Southerndown That wasn't easy. He's hard work, that fellow. (*Goes for a drink.*)

Angel enters from the other side.

Where is he? (*Goes to the door which the artist has used to find it locked.*)

Angel What is it? He's with you.

Noise off.

What's that terrible noise? Where is he?

Southerndown Open the door.

Angel Where is he? He's doing this . . .

Southerndown Get me an axe. Open the door. Open the door. Get me something. I mustn't be seen here. Get something. Damn you.

Angel He'll open the door. He is making a scene. He'll come out when the storm has subsided.

Southerndown Damn it, get me an axe. Open the door.

Angel I don't know what to do. Open the door. Perhaps we should send for the doctor.

Southerndown Are you a complete fool?

Doorbell.

What's that?

Angel This is your doing, all this. This is your fault. Eugene.

Doorbell.

Southerndown I mustn't be seen here.

Angel It could be his dealer.

Southerndown Be quiet. If we don't answer they'll think that you are not at home.

Angel What's he doing? The noise. Let us in.

Enter Arthur Southerndown.

Arthur Parliament has been dissolved. There are mounted police in . . . What is it?

Southerndown Be quiet.

Arthur What has happened?

Angel Eugene.

Southerndown Get me an axe.

Arthur You look as white as a sheet.

Noise.

God help us. What's happening?

Southerndown Get me something.

Arthur Let me try. (*Puts his shoulder to the door.*)

Southerndown That is of no use.

Arthur What did he find out, Papa?

Southerndown Damned hysterical fool.

Arthur What did he learn?

Southerndown Shut your mouth. What did you come here for?

Arthur The editors are sending for you. They don't know what to do, they need a leading article.

Southerndown Parliament has been dissolved.

Arthur And rioting.

Southerndown Damn this fellow.

Angel enters with an axe.

Angel Here.

Arthur Give it to me.

They smash the door down, it gives way. They go inside. Noise. They come out.

I must sit down. I'm sick.

Angel Blood.

Southerndown I'm ruined.

Angel All blood.

Arthur What did he do?

Southerndown His razor.

Angel His head. I can't stay here. Come with me. I can't. I must go and change. (*Exits.*)

Arthur I must remember what this was like. (*Makes a note.*)

Southerndown Well, you can send for the doctor now and the police should be sent for. Where is he?

Arthur He's gone to change.

Southerndown He's destroyed all that I had hoped for in this marriage. In there my prospects are covered in blood.

Arthur You'll find some way of handling things, Father. You always do.

Southerndown You'd like that, wouldn't you? To see this marriage come to nothing.

Arthur Certainly I don't look forward to your second family. Certainly I don't. The thought of you with small children isn't attractive.

Southerndown You've spent a fortune, isn't that what worries you? You've squandered all the money I've ever given you.

Arthur When my mother was alive she made it all right for you with him. Didn't she? She somehow understood how to make it seem all right. And when she died you abandoned him to this. Don't you think you should take him in now?

Southerndown If you're so concerned about him, why don't you take him on? Put him in one of your – what are they? Perhaps I'll fund the pair of you. What shall I do about this?

The sound of gunfire.

Arthur The riots.

Southerndown Parliament dissolved, the government falling. That should take the front page.

Arthur Write an obituary. Write an appreciation of him. The artist. That will do the trick.

Southerndown They will have a field day with this.

Arthur They won't – you'll see that they won't.

Enter Angel.

Angel I can't stay here. Come with me, Arthur, will you?

Door knock.

Southerndown What's that?

Angel It will be the doctor or the police. I sent for them. Isn't that what we should do?

Arthur I must look again. (*Goes into the room where Black is.*)

Southerndown We must tell them of his melancholia.

Angel You've a stain here. Let me clean it for you.

Southerndown It's his blood.

Angel I know. He bled easily. I've seen it before.

Southerndown You monster.

Angel Did you think you could escape me?

Re-enter Arthur.

Arthur As if someone had stuck a pig.

THREE

London. Backstage in a London theatre. A scene change in progress: Buller, the strong-man, has finished his act. Slavin and Hugo, a schoolboy in an Eton collar, are threading their way through all this, watched by the Stage Manager.

Slavin We'd better go this way. Careful now. Watch it.

Hugo Do you think he'll see me? Do you think he'll sign my programme?

Slavin Of course he will. Didn't I say he would?

Stage Manager Out of the way. Come on. Come on. (*to Slavin and Hugo*) Who are you, then? What are you doing here?

Slavin Friends of the artist.

Stage Manager Not backstage during a performance.

Slavin My young friend here . . .

Stage Manager Off you go, then. Go on, there's the pass door. Off you go.

In Angel's dressing room we see Angel closely followed by his Dresser and the Stage Manager, and then Arthur. Angel is dressed in imitation of one of the female stars of the music hall.

You've only got five minutes now. Will you be all right?

Angel I think so.

Stage Manager Are you sure now?

Dresser Come on, love.

Angel (*to the Dresser, going behind a screen to change*) Was it all right?

Dresser It was fine. It was fine.

Angel Are you sure?

Arthur I've never seen an audience like it. Never. They're besides themselves, it's a triumph. They love you.

Angel Have you poured me a drink?

Arthur They do. (*Pours champagne and hands it over the screen.*) Here we are.

Dresser Not too much now. We have a performance.

Angel It'll give it fizz. Do you think he's in front? Have you seen him?

Arthur My father?

Angel Yes.

Arthur I don't know. What does it matter?

Angel Are you sure? Do you think he'll come? If he's in, do you think he'll come round?

Arthur If he's in he'll come round. He always has so little time, you know.

Dresser There we are.

Angel She keeping him up to the mark, then? Lady Adelaide, is that it?

Dresser Hold still.

Angel Don't fuss.

Dresser Hold still, then. There we are.

Angel Give me a drink.

The Stage Manager shows Southerndown into the dressing room.

Stage Manager In here. Sir. In here. (*Bars the way to Slavin and Hugo.*) You two. What I say? Off. Shoo.

Slavin The artist is –

Stage Manager Out. (*to Angel*) Five minutes. It's you again next, after the strong-man. How are you doing?

Dresser We're doing fine. Thank you. We know what we're doing.

Angel Who's that? Is it you? It's you. You're in.

Southerndown Quiet. Quiet.

Arthur We were talking about you.

Angel Why have you been so remiss?

Southerndown Remiss? Whose newspapers created all this damned fuss? Eh? They've made this a success, such as it is.

Angel What do you think?

Southerndown There's too much light on the others. Tell them all the light on him. What do you appear as next?

Angel I don't know. Who am I next, Arthur?

Arthur Florrie Forde.

Southerndown Vulgar nonsense.

Angel They seem pleased enough with our efforts. They don't seem to object to what we're doing.

Southerndown Not since my newspapers have been promoting you these past months. (*to Angel*) Have any of your admirers been in to see you? Ha. Ha. I shall go back in front.

Angel Shall we dine afterwards?

Southerndown No.

Southerndown leaves.

Angel I thought he wasn't going to come. He didn't seem to think much of things.

Arthur Take no notice of his endless fault-finding.

Angel comes out from behind the screen, wearing a corset and underpinnings. No wig.

Dresser I'll be outside.

Dresser goes out.

Angel He doesn't know how clever you are. He doesn't understand a talent like yours.

Arthur You were unbelievable, you know.

Angel Do you remember when we first met?

Arthur I was back from school. You were in the drawing room. Dressed in blue velvet. My mother was bedridden then. My father had installed you in the house. I was enthralled by you even then. So was my mother. In awe of you. So young. So important to my father. So pampered by my mother.

Angel They had to hide me.

Arthur Yes.

Angel And I remember how you had a toy theatre and how much it engrossed you. I can see you moving the little figures about so intently.

Arthur I was seventeen when she died. And when he sent you away after I told him I wanted you to stay.

Angel Weren't you jealous?

Arthur No, I wasn't. I challenged him to a duel. I thought it was wrong of him. He thinks I have plans to prevent this marriage now.

Angel He can still see me as an obstacle to that. Is she still so unsophisticated, so quiet, so pure? He wants to get rid of me. That's what all this is about. That's why he's put on this show for you. He's hoping some protector will come along. More champagne.

Arthur Haven't you had enough?

Angel Fill it up.

Arthur I hope you don't leave us. I wouldn't like that.

Angel No.

Arthur You were magnificent, you know. You're in your element here.

Angel It's so exciting. They love it so. What would happen if you put life on the stage? Would that frighten them?

Arthur I think it would.

Angel Well, whatever it is, they like it. Even like this. Even with it dressed up like this. What would happen to them if it wasn't?

Arthur I don't know. I've had enough of the art theatre. I wanted something more popular.

Angel But I mean something else.

Arthur How amazing you are. How original you are.

Stage Manager (*coming through the door with the Dresser*) He's on.

Dresser I know he's on.

Stage Manager Why isn't he ready?

Dresser He'll be ready. Where's your dressing gown?

Stage Manager Quick. He'll be off.

Stage Manager, Dresser and Angel go out, taking Angel's new costume and wig with them, leaving Arthur alone. Arthur drinks champagne and makes a note.

Arthur Act One: Doctor Goulderie. Act Two: Eugene Black. Act Three: who will it be?

Commotion off. Buller carries Angel on, puts him down. The Dresser ministers. Slavin and Hugo in the doorway. The Stage Manager enters.

Stage Manager What should we do?

Arthur What's happened?

Stage Manager He passed out. (*Exits.*) Quick, put on the interlude.

Angel I'm all right, get me a drink.

Dresser Come on, let me undo this.

Angel What happened?

Dresser He fainted. Didn't you, dear? Too hot.

Angel Oh. God. She's out front. She's out front. He's brought her with him. How dare he? Did you know? Let me up. Why didn't you tell me? How dare you?

Dresser Let him lie down. Lie down.

Stage Manager He'll go on, won't he?

Dresser He'll go on.

Angel I won't. Not while she's here. I won't.

Stage Manager What'll we do?

Arthur Change the running order.

Dresser We'll get him on.

Stage Manager I'll come back for you.

Arthur I'm coming.

Angel I saw her.

Enter Southerndown.

Southerndown What is this? What has happened? Out of my way. What is it? What's wrong?

Angel You. How could you do it? Let me up. I'm all right. Let me open and then bring her to see me like this. She's in your box.

Arthur You might have shown some feeling. Isn't this a little brutal?

Southerndown Be quiet. What have you to say that I will listen to? Be quiet. What is this? What is it?

Dresser He passed out. It was them lights, wasn't it, love?

Southerndown Get out.

Dresser What?

Southerndown Get out and you get out. Get out. Get out. Get out.

Stage Manager What shall we do?

Southerndown Get out. Sort it. You sort it. Go.

They all go, leaving Southerndown and Angel.

You've picked up the histrionics easily enough but not the application.

Angel You're making sure, aren't you, that I know my place. Making me appear like this in front of her.

Southerndown You were game enough. And given what you come from, you guttersnipe, you're lucky to be allowed in front of decent people at all.

Angel You can't leave it, can you? It infects everything you feel for me. What I am is where I came from.

Southerndown Nonsense. That's what you trade in. That's what you use. Look at tonight. These gutter hysterics were just an excuse to embarrass a young woman who can hardly keep her seat because of your vulgarity. You're coarse.

Angel I've told you. How often have I told you that I don't care what people think of me. I'm no better than I should be. That's the sum of it. Why should I care about a stupid girl who you bought from a bankrupt aristocrat?

Southerndown You're shoddy stuff, you, aren't you? Eh? This is what you like.

Angel As for coarseness, you'll put her in touch with her coarseness yet. Unlike you, I have never aspired to self-respect.

Southerndown Don't be sentimental. There's gin and a penny gaff about you. Do you think you're any different now from what I found in the streets?

Angel No, thank God. In some ways I'm much the same as I was when I was seven. It's what I've grown into that is so repellent to me.

Southerndown Now. Will you continue with the performance?

Angel Which performance?

Southerndown The one you are paid for.

Angel Which is that? Oh dear. I'm tired.

Southerndown You're not contracted to be tired.

Angel Arthur will understand.

Southerndown Arthur may certainly understand. But I put the money up for this farrago. So this is what you are then, a spoiled performer.

Angel Yes. This is what I've made of all you've given me. No style at all. Have I? Perhaps one of my new-found admirers will take me up. Look. (*Shows him a pack of letters and cards.*)

Southerndown (*picking one up*) Lord Henry Wantage.

Angel Yes. Flowers. Flowers. What he calls his infrequency of flowers.

Southerndown He's not for you.

Angel No. Poor creature. Someone will turn up. One of these. (*dropping the letters*) Perhaps I'll go away. Perhaps I'll go to North Africa with –

Southerndown No. I don't want you to go anywhere.

Angel Why? Why don't you want me to go?

Southerndown Don't look at me. I should go.

Angel Yes. She must be waiting for you. Go then. Go on. I'm not keeping you here.

Southerndown I'll go at the interval. (*He sits.*)

Angel And are you exhausted now? Can't you summon up the energy? With your prodigious energy, can't you find the strength required to marry her? How long an engagement has it been? How many years? You have the energy for everything else. Your schemes. Your newspapers. Your endless capacity for manipulating events. You could give me to Goulderie. You had the energy for that. You could turn the artist into your plaything. You can find the energy to make a duke hand over his daughter against his will. What's stopping you from marrying her, then?

Southerndown Do you flatter yourself that it is you who is stopping me?

Angel Yes. Yes. I do. If you only knew how much pleasure this is giving me. How much I am not regretting this. How I'm enjoying this. You want me to let you go. So that you can put the slum child behind you. But you won't go yourself. You want me to do it. You'll never do it. Try as you will. Get out then. Go then. You see. You won't go. You want me to go. I'm not going. Get out and leave me alone. If you stay you'll make a fool of yourself. You always do.

Southerndown I'm not afraid of you.

Angel I'm not the one you should be afraid of. What do you see in me? You see in me a creature you've imagined, and yet I'm the real thing for you too, aren't I? I'm neither, that's the truth. But you. You swing endlessly between two images of me.

Southerndown Take up with one of these. (*picking up a letter*) I'll be married in a week. And then I'll never have to see you again.

Angel I'll lock all my doors.

Southerndown As there is a God in heaven, I have never hated or regretted anything as I have hated and regretted you.

Angel And all because I was a poor boy.

Southerndown All because you are so wicked.

Angel If you say so. You need to feel that so that you can justify this marriage. Allying that poor creature to someone like you. Oh. Are you going to strike me now? Your wife loved you. But she knew you. This poor girl isn't so wise.

Southerndown Be silent.

Angel Marry her then. Make her perform for you as you have made me perform all this time. Go on. Where's your horsewhip? Do you want me to send for it? Do you?

Southerndown Keep away from me. I must go. I must go home. I can't see her like this. Look at me. Look at me. I can't face them. Any of them. You.

Angel You may be master of all your great enterprises but you'll never be master enough to leave me, will you? You'll never do it.

Southerndown What shall I do? What shall I do?

Angel Here's writing paper. Write this.

Southerndown I can't write.

Angel 'My dear Lady Adelaide.'

Southerndown I call her Adelaide.

Angel 'My dear Lady Adelaide. I write to ask you to release me from our understanding. I cannot in all conscience ask you to link your fate with mine.'

Southerndown Yes. Yes. I can't.

Angel 'I'm unworthy of your love.' Write it. 'The length of our engagement must give some inclination of my ambivalence. I am writing beside the one it is whom I truly love. Forgive me. Leopold Southerndown.'

Southerndown Oh God.

Angel Not oh God. 'My dear.' Post script: 'Do not try to change this.'

FOUR

London. A sumptuous and extravagantly furnished drawing room. Portières, tapestries, several doors, a gallery above. Angel's portrait stands on an easel. Southerndown drinking with Angel and Lord Henry Wantage.

Lord Henry We should be so very honoured if you would come and you might perhaps be amused.

Southerndown What's this?

Lord Henry We intend to re-create for one evening a salon in the French style. In Lord Orchard's rooms in Half Moon Street. He's undertaking the decoration. We are undertaking to dress accordingly.

Southerndown Can anyone come?

Angel No, not anyone. Not you.

Southerndown I didn't think I would be welcome.

Lord Henry I don't think it would interest you.

Southerndown And why not, pray? No. I don't see myself as Madame du Deffand. (*to Angel*) And you, do you see yourself as a bluestocking, then? I think not. Magnificent flowers. Tuberoses. Tubs of tuberoses at Versailles. Hundreds of them every day.

Lord Henry I think you would make a very convincing bluestocking.

Southerndown Ah. Well.

Lord Henry You'll come?

Angel Perhaps. If you promise to stop sending me so many flowers.

Lord Henry Please. I beg you, don't scold me for sending things that are so humble but more expressive than I.

Angel Twelve chrysanthemums yesterday.

Southerndown Chrysanthemums cost the devil to import. Twelve.

Angel That was yesterday.

Southerndown Worth more than these cigars.

Lord Henry You will come.

Angel What shall I wear?

Lord Henry Perhaps more than you are wearing here. More's the pity.

Angel He doesn't like it.

Lord Henry And the artist, do I know him?

Angel I don't think you would have met him.

Southerndown He cut his throat.

Angel Please.

Southerndown Well he did, didn't he? Dammit.

Angel What's the matter?

Lord Henry I must take my leave. Thank you for receiving me. Your servant.

Southerndown Certainly. *À tout à l'heure.*

Angel and Lord Henry go out.

(*alone*) This place is unclean. I thought to spend my last days here. And he defiles every corner of it. Arthur too. I know. I know. He too. (*Takes out a pistol and looks behind curtain.*) Where are you? No one here. That doesn't mean that they haven't been there or that they won't be there. Perhaps I should put a bullet through my brain. Family life. Filth and scum. It's all filth.

Re-enter Angel.

Angel Do you have to go out?

Southerndown What did that fool really want?

Angel You heard what he wanted. Let's take the carriage and drive through the park. (*arms round his neck*)

Southerndown Today I'm going to the Stock Exchange, as I usually do, as you know I do. Today I have to watch everything. Do you want me to lose what little I have in the markets? (*Southerndown injects himself with morphine.*)

Angel You said you would stop that.

Southerndown Did I? I suppose I did. Well, you don't normally see this, do you?

Angel Why are you so sad?

Southerndown I wish I could laugh.

Angel Laugh, try it.

Southerndown I love your profile more than Lord Sheffield does his string of racehorses.

Angel It would be better to die, I think, than to be merely miserable.

Southerndown That sounds fine enough.

Angel I think it would be easy to die.

Southerndown Here we are then. You and I.

Angel Yes, me and you, as I chose it.

Southerndown It was a daring choice. I should laugh.

Angel Try it.

Southerndown I shall.

They go off. Lord Henry enters from another door. Comes in hesitantly. On hearing voices, hides.

Lord Henry I thought he might be alone. Someone's coming. I'll hide.

Enter Buller, Slavin and Hugo. Buller carrying Hugo.

Slavin Come on, boys. There we are. It's good to be home. Who polished those stairs, eh? You could break your neck easy. This place is a death trap. Come on then, don't worry, we'll be all right. Now. What'll it be? Here we are. (*Pours drinks.*) What do you want? It's all here. Will he have one? He'll have one.

Buller He's not big enough, are you? He's not big enough to walk yet, let alone drink.

Hugo You put me down. I'll show who's big enough when the time comes.

Buller He's no more than eight stone.

Hugo Put me down. I shall be expelled from school for this.

Buller We'll give you schooling all right. You'll get your schooling all right from me and this gentleman. Eh?

Slavin Yes, many's the man's won his medals with the person you're going to meet here.

Hugo What shall I say to him?

Slavin Don't you worry. You won't have to say anything. He'll see to that.

Hugo I wrote a poem yesterday.

Buller A poem. What you write a poem for?

Slavin What he write?

Buller A poem.

Slavin Oh, a poem. Very good. (*to Buller*) He promised to see me all right if I arranged a meeting and then left them alone.

Buller He got the cash then?

Slavin His father does. He's an appeal court judge. A cigar? No. Yes. I thought you would.

Hugo Who lives here anyway?

Slavin We do.

Buller Every week we come here when the master's at the Stock Exchange.

Hugo What shall I do with it? Shall I read it?

Buller What's he on about now?

Slavin His poem. Poets are like that. He's going in for elaborate foreplay. Look at his eyes. Look at his eyes.

Buller With eyes like that there's no chance for us. Look at them.

Slavin No chance at all. Have we? We haven't. You're drunk.

Buller Am I?

Slavin You're pickled.

Enter Angel.

Angel What are you up to, eh? What you doing here? Eh?

Buller (*to Slavin*) Your health, you old thief.

Slavin (*to Buller*) Your health, you great ponce.

Angel I'm expecting someone. (*to Hugo*) What are you doing with these two, eh? Don't be shy, eh? Those are not fit companions for you. What are you doing now? With this boy?

Slavin He's not a boy. He's a poet.

Angel Enough. You.

Buller (*to Angel*) Here. Can you lend me fifty pounds? My old woman. My wife, see.

Angel Are you married?

Buller 'Course I'm married. Only she's poorly, see. Bad health. Consumption. I need the cash for her. Ten quid then. Come on, eh? Come. (*Puts his arms round Angel.*) Let's get drunk, eh? Let's get out of here. Let's leave them two. Come on, you want to. You know you do.

Angel Do I?

Buller No. All right. Well then, let's meet then. Out of here. One night. No good here. What do you say?

Angel I don't know.

Buller Don't you? I need the money. Honest I do. Try these. (*Takes his shirt off. Shows his muscles.*)

Angel We all know how big you are.

Buller Try 'em.

Angel Yes.

Buller Come on then. Come on. I don't understand you. I don't. I don't know what you want.

Angel If only your ears were different.

Slavin Who you expecting then? You expecting Lord Henry?

Angel Good Lord, no. God forbid.

Lord Henry hears this.

Buller Who's he then?

Slavin He's going to carry him off.

Angel Indeed he isn't.

Slavin We all want to do that.

Buller Do you want to do that? Take him away from all this?

Slavin We all do.

Buller You don't. I thought he was your boy.

Slavin No.

Buller So who's his father then? I thought you were.

Slavin No. He ain't never had a father. Have you?

Angel What have I never had?

Slavin A father.

Angel No. I'm a physical impossibility. Come on, out you go, he'll be back.

Buller Where we going?

Angel Off you go.

Slavin He's at the 'change.

Angel You never know.

Slavin Gor blimey. In my own home.

Buller I'll sort him out.

Angel Will you? We'll see how big you are if he comes in here. If only your ears were different.

Enter Frederick, a footman.

Frederick Mr Southerndown.

Slavin It's him. Blimey, the bastard's back. That's not part of my plan, not at all. That's not the arrangement by any means. He's become very unreliable. Come on. Give me the key.

Angel What for?

Slavin To lock myself in upstairs.

Angel Shall I see you later?

Hugo goes under the table. Buller hides at the opposite side to Lord Henry. Slavin goes upstairs.

Slavin Give us the bottle.

Enter Arthur Southerndown.

Arthur I've come from the theatre. We're experimenting with electric light. Who in heaven's name is that?

Slavin hasn't yet quite got off.

Angel A friend of your father's.

Arthur I haven't seen him before in my life.

Angel They were in the army together. He's fallen on hard times.

Arthur He's not here is he, my father?

Angel They had a drink and then your father went into the city. I've ordered luncheon.

Arthur No lunch for me.

Angel I've ordered. It's nothing much.

Arthur I can't eat.

Angel You try something. What is it?

Frederick enters with a tray, a bottle of champagne and oysters. Lays the table.

Arthur What's the matter with him? Are you all right?

Angel Let him be, Arthur.

Arthur You seem out of sorts.

Frederick Yes, sir.

He goes. Arthur goes to Angel.

Angel What's this, Arthur?

Arthur You promised.

Angel What did I promise?

Arthur You as good as promised.

Southerndown enters in the gallery.

Southerndown I knew it. My own son.

Angel What have I promised?

Arthur You look flushed.

Angel Do I? When I looked in the mirror a little while ago I wished I was a man.

Arthur Indeed.

Angel And then I wished I was a woman. Then I could marry myself. Be inside myself.

Arthur You envy the pleasure others have in you perhaps, is that it?

Angel Is it? Why are you like this?

Arthur You proposed this assignation as something special. Or you hinted at something special.

Angel Did I? Why are you so, well, overheated?

Arthur You know why. When I'm out riding in the park. When I'm lying in my room. When I'm working. You are in my head. Not in my head, I can feel you. I can smell you. Coming here, rattling in the cab. Everywhere. The thought of you always. The sense of you on my hands, in my nostrils. I smell you. I shall spill over. I can see how a man could be a sex murderer.

Angel I should like to be murdered in that way. Perhaps I would be inside myself then.

Arthur I can sense you all the time.

Frederick re-enters. Clears. Serves another course.

What is the matter with you?

Angel Leave him alone, Arthur.

Arthur Have you got a fever, old man?

Frederick I'm not used to working in the house, that's all. I'm one of the grooms, only in here today.

Southerndown Is he another of them, the groom? Is that it?

Angel Come along, eat something.

Arthur What's this? (*indicating the table*)

Angel Nothing, it's me. My foot.

Arthur Why have you asked me here? Why? You must know how I feel. Why here?

Angel Because I admire you. I respect you. Because I wanted to see you. Is that wrong of me? You have always respected me. You've always stood up for me, Arthur. Always. Even against your father.

Arthur Don't let's talk about all that. That's my unfortunate character.

Angel Don't, you are good, Arthur.

Arthur And I don't want to be good. I'm not good. I'm not just his son. I'm not your brother.

Angel Aren't you? I always think you are my brother. Aren't I allowed that? That's why I've been able to talk to you. Who else can I talk to?

Arthur I'm one of those wicked people who are cursed with an impulse for good.

Angel Arthur.

Arthur Yes. Do you know what it is to be like that and to experience the disintegration of oneself? I'm disintegrating. Sometimes I feel I am. (*He looks under the table.*)

Angel What is it?

Arthur I don't know. I know that the more I try to control myself the more I'm going to pieces. You've always been something to be in awe of. A kind of saint, in spite of your talent for seeming the contrary.

Angel What is it like, this feeling of not being there, then?

Arthur Please don't make me speak of it. Please. I don't want to be the subject of interest over a glass of champagne. The experience to which I allude has been one of the joys of life, I assure you. A complete pleasure.

Angel I've hurt you. I didn't mean to. I won't allude to it again. Here's my hand.

Arthur (*kisses his hand*) Please.

Buller pokes his head out. Angel sees him and signals him back. He goes back. Hugo pokes his head out from beneath the table. Angel kicks him.

Southerndown (*alone*) Another of them.

Arthur I feel like someone who has died and is rubbing the sleep out of his eyes as he wakes up in heaven. Your eyes are glittering like water in a well after a stone has been thrown in. Your hand. There's oil here. Let me lick it. (*Licks his hand.*) You are above me. Like the sun shining over an abyss. You. Let me kiss your feet.

Kneels. Angel stands.

Destroy me, then. Finish me. If you want to.

Angel You love me. (*to Frederick*) Bring coffee. Cognac.

Arthur Where shall we drink it?

Angel Let's go to my room.

Buller pokes his head out. Tries to signal to Southerndown to shoot Arthur. But Southerndown points gun at Buller. Angel sees Southerndown.

Your father.

Southerndown (*points the gun at Arthur*) Arthur. (*He comes down.*)

Arthur Papa.

Southerndown Parliament has been dissolved.

Arthur Papa.

Angel What should I do?

Southerndown Go to the office. Tell them I sent you. Tell them I will be there soon. (*Pointing revolver at him, takes him out of the door.*)

Buller makes a dash for it.

Angel You can't go that way.

Buller Let me through.

Hugo looks out. Lord Henry crosses the room to another hiding place.

Angel You'll run straight into him.

Buller He'll put a bullet through me.

Angel Quick, he's coming.

Buller Christ. (*He tries to get under the table.*)

Hugo No room. Sorry.

Buller All I wanted was fifty quid.

Buller hides where Lord Henry was. Re-enter Southerndown. He goes to where he thinks Buller is.

Southerndown Where is he?

Angel He's gone.

Southerndown Where's he gone?

Angel He's an acrobat.

Southerndown Is he, be damned. I can't have been expected to know that. Now you. Now you. Animal. You animal. You want to kill me with your endless depravity.

Angel You taught me how to do it.

Southerndown This is my fate, then, is it? Either to drown in your sewage or to be hanged for the pleasure of murdering you?

Angel Kill me then, if you must do it.

Southerndown I've left everything to you and all I asked was the courtesy one could expect from a weekend guest. Your credit has run out. You backstreet whore.

Angel My security is good for a few years yet.

Southerndown You're like a fatal disease I've contracted. And I've been hoping all this time for a cure. And I've found it. Here it is. But it's for you to take.

Handing him the revolver. Angel plays with it.

Angel I can't fire it.

Southerndown Can't you indeed? Pray let me instruct you. (*Takes the revolver back.*) How beautiful you still are to me. From beyond the sunset. I would like to curl up against you, feel your body cupped into mine for the last time and then kill you.

Angel Put the revolver down. Put it down. Forgive me.

Southerndown It's the morphine. All this. It must be. I forgave you long ago. I must kill you or see my son drown in his own blood when I have killed him.

Angel You love me too much to do it.

Southerndown Do I? I suppose I do. Yet I must kill you.

Angel Or punish me then. Or beat me then. Belt me till I bleed. I won't scream or cry out. I'll bite my handkerchief. (*Takes out his handkerchief and bites on it.*) Or let's go to the opera. Don't kill me. Let me go. Please don't kill me. Don't. I want to piss.

Southerndown It's hardly worth it now. Here, I'll show you how to use it. Do you see? (*Shows him the workings of the revolver.*) Do you see?

Angel No.

Angel shoots at the ceiling. Buller runs out from his hiding place.

Southerndown Who's that?

Angel A bird flying from its nest.

Southerndown Who else is here? (*He finds Lord Henry.*) Where did you come from? Down the chimney?

Lord Henry Don't let him kill me.

Southerndown Have you come to lunch?

Lord Henry No. No.

Southerndown Yes. Yes. Stay to lunch. All of you stay to lunch. Where's the groom? Let him come to lunch. (*He pushes Lord Henry out of the door.*)

Angel Come, let's go out. Let's go for a drive.

Southerndown Are you going to shoot me then? It would be the happiest moment of my life. Do it.

Angel Well, let's agree to part, then. Let's do that.

Southerndown We part? How can you be so utterly foolish. How could we part? Part so that I could see someone else find his pleasure where I once fell into hell. . . Facing suicide with you still in my sight. We are part of one another, you and I. I can see your next victim lying on your bed. He's longing for you. Isn't he? Give me the revolver.

Angel No.

Southerndown Kiss me. Kiss me. (*turning Angel's hand on himself*) Come on, use it. You can use it. You can handle it. Squeeze it softly. Do it. Do it. Feel it. Can you feel it? Feel it.

Angel I must piss.

Southerndown Do it.

Angel Shall I? Shall I? Shall I do it? Shall I? I'll do it for you, shall I? No. (*Pushes Southerndown away.*)

Southerndown injects himself with morphine.

If men have killed themselves because of me, does that mean I am then valueless? You have always known from the beginning what you were doing when I didn't know, or I have known it for some of the time – what I was doing. But you always. You took my childhood and my youth as if they were yours to do with. And I have taken your old age. Was it a fair exchange? I have never wanted to be taken for anything but what I am. You want me to put a bullet in my heart. But I won't. I may not be seven any more. Nor sixteen. But I'm not yet twenty. I won't do it. I can't do it.

Southerndown On your knees then, murderer. You murderer. Ask God to give you the strength.

During the struggle Hugo jumps up from under the table.

Angel No. No. Help. Help.

Southerndown turns as Hugo runs out, presenting his back to Angel who shoots him five times. Southerndown falls into Hugo's arms.

Southerndown (*as he falls to the floor*) And you're another of them, are you?

Angel Dear God.

Southerndown Out of my sight. Arthur.

Angel The only man I have ever loved.

Southerndown Water.

Angel Get him some water.

Arthur enters.

Arthur Father. Father.

Angel I shot him. Give him this.

Hugo It wasn't his fault. It wasn't.

Southerndown (*to Arthur*) He's yours now. Take him.

Arthur Come, let's get you to bed.

Southerndown No, leave me. I'm thirsty.

Angel gives him champagne.

Champagne. You don't change, I see. Thank you. (*to Arthur*) You'll be the next.

Lord Henry comes in.

There's another of them. Only he's a fool. Fool.

Angel He's dead.

Arthur Don't move from this room.

Lord Henry I thought it was you who had been shot.

Arthur Get the police.

Angel Don't, Arthur, please.

Arthur Get them.

Angel Please, Arthur. I'll do what you want. Whatever you want. Don't do this, please. I beg of you. Look at me, Arthur. Look at me. Arthur. I beg you. I beg you. Arthur.

Doorbell.

Arthur That will be the police.

Hugo This means I'll be expelled.

FIVE

London. The drawing room as in Scene Four, but almost bare. Angel's picture on the floor turned to the wall. Gunshot.

Tableau: the moment of Angel's shooting of Southerndown. Everyone involved frozen as they were then. Slavin walks through them and speaks to the audience.

Slavin You'll remember where we were. Well now then. There was Angel's arrest then.

Tableau: Angel being handcuffed by the police.

And of course the boy.

Tableau: Hugo arrested in flight.

And after the usual charges and the magistrate and the putting up of the bail and the waiting and the newspapers. Leopold Southerndown's newspapers. The trial.

Tableau: Angel in the dock.

And Arthur's plea for clemency.

Tableau: Arthur in an attitude of appeal.

And defending his father's killer. The charges of murder were dropped and charges of manslaughter replaced them. And Angel was sentenced.

Tableau: Angel under sentence.

For ten years.

Tableau: Angel being taken down to the cells.

And then Lord Henry.

Tableau: Lord Henry tries to pull Angel away from his captors.

Lord Henry.

Tableau: Lord Henry alone and dejected.

Lord Henry, who had financed the whole defence. Strewth. Paid for the whole lot, he did. Paid for the lawyers, the solicitors, the barristers. Paid for it all. And that was not all he did. That was not all.

Tableau: Lord Henry seated with a shawl around him. Near Arthur, pensive. Buller dressed as a servant.

You'll see.

Tableau relaxes into action.

Buller What's keeping the old man then, eh? Why's he keeping us hanging about, then? We got to get off.

Lord Henry Please. Please.

Buller What beats me is how you think he can possibly have been changed for the better by it all.

Lord Henry He is more refined and beautiful now than I have ever seen him before.

Buller Well, I don't know that I can take your word for it as far as looks go, if cholera has done for him what it's done for you. Look what it's done for you and look at me. All this has put me right out of condition.

Lord Henry What puts some people in the grave has restored him like a resurrection.

Buller Well, that's all fine and dandy. But I've had enough of this. I'm not going with him tonight. I've decided he and the old man'll have to manage without me.

Lord Henry Are you going to let him travel alone? I thought Mr Southerndown had arranged things with you. Is there something wrong with the arrangement? Is it financial? Can I change your mind?

Buller The old man'll be with him. He'll be all right. It's sorted.

Lord Henry Mr Southerndown. The travel arrangements have been altered.

Arthur What's that? I beg your pardon. I haven't been listening. (*Makes a note.*) I've been working at an idea in which someone has been sentenced to penal servitude and wondering if it was a suitable subject for a play nowadays. What do you think?

Lord Henry The travel arrangements are altered. They're to go without protection.

Arthur Lord Henry. Forgive me. I don't wish to appear discouraging but I'm not at all certain that your plans for his escape are, well, feasible, anyway. Although I can't find words to express my admiration for all that you have done. Your selflessness. The sacrifices you have made. Indeed your extraordinary enterprise. I have no idea, Lord Henry, and I mean no offence. Well, I have no idea, well to be blunt, how wealthy you are. But the expenses you must have incurred in the case of this enterprise must have, how shall I put it, disorganised your finances. May I offer you the loan of, well, would ten thousand pounds be useful at all? I can make it available to you in cash. It would be no problem.

Lord Henry He has been so brave. You know. All the times we were in the hospital ward together. And so kind to me. So full of tender words. And full of promises for the future.

Buller For one thing, I've got to wait here until the costumes are ready for the new act. I'll get another boat all right. He'll be all right with the old man. I wouldn't have got involved in this if he hadn't done me a few favours and I didn't fancy him before and you hadn't taken me on as his protector. We'll get an act together in Paris. They'll appreciate me in Paris. When I've got fit again. They're more broad-minded abroad anyway. We'll work something up together – you'll see. Here they don't know talent when they see it. I got done for indecency not two years ago. Give me a fifty-bob fine.

Arthur I find it much the same with my work. When I gave up first the art theatre and then the popular theatre after my father's death, I felt myself moved towards a more serious theatre. So I wrote a play about what happened. A play dealing with the death of a man like my father and the person who had done it and how it had come about, and so forth. But they wouldn't license it. It was thought to be improper. Some people read it in Gordon Square.

Lord Henry Sh. Here he is.

Slavin (*off*) Yes, here I am. Here I am.

Enter Slavin.

Slavin I've been all over the place this morning. Selling this and that. Bits and pieces. Sorting things out. Tidying up loose ends. Disposing of my assets. Fixing the papers, getting the passports sorted.

Buller I've got a good hotel for you in Paris. The people who run it come from Bermondsey.

Lord Henry Help me up. I beg you.

Buller You'll be safe from the police here. Safe as houses.

Slavin Where will you be, then?

Lord Henry He wants you to go with him alone. Just the two of you. Without his protection.

Slavin What, you scared, eh? Scared of the cholera and scared of the law. Eh? What's put the wind up you?

Buller Nothing has. I ain't scared. I've got to get the props for my new act sorted out, haven't I? I told 'em. I'll have to come on later.

Arthur Please take this money, Lord Henry. Please do. There's two thousand pounds here I cashed especially.

Lord Henry That's kind of you. But no, I thank you.

Arthur Please. I beg you. Take it.

Lord Henry Please let us go now.

Slavin Patience, my dear Lord Henry. It's no distance to the hospital. You'll be there in no time. I'll be back, with him in tow in five minutes, just you see.

Arthur You bringing him here?

Slavin I am certainly bringing him here. Are you scared too? What's the matter with you all?

Arthur No. I'm not frightened of anything. A sort of apprehension, I suppose.

Slavin Come, Lord Henry. Off we go. Off we go.

Lord Henry and Slavin go out. Arthur locks the door.

Buller Why did you want to give money to that madman? That hopeless excuse for a man.

Arthur What, pray, has that to do with you?

Buller Because of the pittance you pay me. Even though I had to bribe every nurse in the isolation hospital and the young doctors and the porters. And then you offer him all that cash. I had to spend three months in that hospital getting information. Squaring things. Sorting things out. Now I'm too fat for work and too caught up in all this for the authorities but to watch me – and so

I became your servant. And I'm to go to Paris, ain't I, to look after him? Work up the act. What more can I do for you all, eh? And what for?

Arthur Lord Henry has paid you handsomely for your services and covered every expense which you have incurred. And according to my estimate, apart from what you get from me, he also provides you with a monthly allowance of ten pounds. So I really do find it hard to believe that you have done anything out of love and concern for the man we're waiting for so anxiously. I do, however, think it probable that you have exploited Lord Henry shamelessly and taken part in this enterprise only for your own advancement. You'd have ended up in the gutter else, I dare say. Drunk and penniless.

Buller And what about you, eh? Then what about you? What would you be if you hadn't sold your father's fish-and-chip papers, from what I heard, for a million pounds. A million pounds. What would you do if you had to do a day's work, eh? What would you do? All you've done while he's been inside is write something no decent person wants to see, about a bum boy and morphine addict. Which no one'll put on because what the public wants is more in my line of things, ain't it?

Door knock.

Who's that?

Arthur It's him. I haven't seen him for a year.

Buller No, it can't be him. Well open the door then, for Christ's sake. What's the matter with you?

Arthur You hide yourself while I see who it is.

Buller hides. Arthur goes to the door. Hugo comes in.

And who are you, may I ask? You. It's you. What do you want? Why are you here? What have you come here for?

Hugo I escaped from the reformatory this morning. I've travelled all this way. I've come straight here.

Arthur What do you want here?

Hugo Please. I've come to help. I want to help him. I've worked up a plan to help him to escape.

Arthur What are you talking about? What kind of plan? What do you want?

Hugo Please help me. Can anyone hear us? Please, I beg you. You can't be so indifferent to his plight. It was your evidence that saved him from the gallows.

Arthur I know who you are now. You said my father tried to make him kill himself.

Hugo He did. He did. But no one would believe me.

Buller comes out with a tray of coffee.

Buller Would the young gentleman take his coffee in the drawing room or on the terrace?

Hugo What's that fellow doing here? He came out of the same door then. That's the same door.

Arthur I've taken him into my service. He's quite useful. He can throw people out.

Hugo I'm a fool to be here. I'm a fool.

Buller Yes, we know each other, this young gentleman and me. Don't we, eh? What you doing here? Don't you know he's dead, your sweetheart? He's dead.

Hugo Did they hang him after all then, did they? It's not true. How do you know? How do you know? You don't know.

Buller Read this then. Where is it? Read this then. (*Shows him a newspaper.*) 'Mr Leopold Southerndown's killer struck down with cholera.'

Hugo 'The killer of Mr Leopold Southerndown has contracted cholera in prison.' It doesn't say he's dead.

Buller Cholera. He's dead all right. Buried three weeks ago in the cemetery not a little way from here. By the rubbish dump. Little crosses with no name. You'll recognise it, it's got no grass growing. Go and pay your respects, then go back to the schoolroom, or I'll hand you over to the law. I'll follow you.

Hugo It's true. Is he dead, then?

Arthur Yes. I thank God, he's dead. Please leave us now. I'm unwell.

Hugo What point is there now? I have no future now. What's the point of anything. I wanted to save him. I would have, too. Made him happy. Well, I'll go to the devil another way.

Buller No, get out. Go on. Off you go.

Arthur Yes. If you would go.

Hugo I've been a fool.

Buller Off you go.

Hugo exits.

I'm surprised you didn't offer him cash payment as well.

Arthur Spare me your humour. That boy has more honour in him than you in your great body.

Buller What's that?

Arthur Is that him? Here he is. Here he is.

Angel enters dressed in Lord Henry's clothes and wearing his shawl. He is walking with difficulty, supported by Slavin.

Slavin Gee up. Come up, my little Angel. We've got to cross the Channel tonight.

Buller Hell and damnation. Look at him. Look at him.

Angel Slower please. I can't go as fast as you.

Buller Where did you get the nerve to break out looking like that? Like a starved wolf, you look.

Slavin Shut your mouth, you.

Buller I'm not having anything to do with this. How's he going to make it to Paris? Look at him. Look at him. What do you expect me to do with him? I'm going to turn you in, the lot of you.

Arthur I must ask you to be quiet. I must ask you to show some understanding. Angel.

Buller Don't talk to me about understanding. Look what I've done for him. Ruined my career. Look at me. Look how fat I am. Fit for a clown. I'm going to turn you in. The lot of you. (*He goes.*)

Slavin He won't go to the law. I know him. He wouldn't risk it. He'll be back. Where else he got to go?

Arthur Here's some coffee. Shall I pour some for you?

Slavin Hurry up then. I've still got to book our berths.

Arthur Here we are. (*dispensing coffee*)

Slavin (*after drinking his coffee*) Right. I'll be off then. I'm scuttling all over the place. Got to sort out some business. I'll get the tickets and be back for you. You all right?

Angel I'm all right.

Slavin Mr Southerndown, your most humble. Enjoy yourselves, my children. Drink your coffee. (*Sings.*)

Oh I'd like to go again
To Paris on the Seine,
'Cause Paris is a proper pantomime.
And if they'd only take the 'Ackney Road

And plant it over there
I'd like to live in Paris all the time.

Honi soi. (*Leaves.*)

Angel Free. Oh God. Am I?

Arthur Would you like a drink? A brandy with your coffee?

Angel I can't believe how big this room is. I haven't been in a room for two years. Look at the curtains. Where's my picture?

Arthur Are you still so vain?

Angel Yes. It's frightening when you haven't seen yourself for months. I found an old piece of tin in prison and cleaned it up as best as I could. It wasn't very flattering. But it was reassuring to see that I was still there.

Arthur Here it is. (*showing the picture*) It was turned to the wall. Lord Henry wanted it in his house, but it seemed more prudent to keep it here.

Angel Haven't you looked at it at all while I've been away? And now Lord Henry is taking my place in the prison hospital.

Arthur I don't understand how it happened. How was it all arranged?

Angel Oh he arranged it all very carefully.

Arthur How can you be so cold about it?

Angel I don't know. I admire him and his courage. I'll tell you. There was an outbreak of cholera in Liverpool this summer and Lord Henry saw this as the way to get me out. He worked as an auxiliary nurse. Through his university settlement, you know. And good works among the poor. They could hardly turn him down. Well, nothing daunted, Lord Henry took infected clothing from a man who had died. He was given the things to put in the furnace. But instead he put them on. And then he travelled back to visit me, wearing them under his street clothes, and we exchanged some of the dead man's clothing. He was already coming down with cholera.

Arthur And you came down with it too?

Angel And we both found ourselves in the isolation hospital. There was no question of my staying in the prison for fear of infecting others. So we were together in the same ward. He was discharged yesterday. And today he came back on the pretence of having lost his wristwatch and we exchanged clothes. And I walked out. It was easy. And now he is serving the sentence for having murdered your father.

Arthur You still bear comparison to your portrait.

Angel Older. Thinner.

Arthur You look better than you did when you came in.

Angel Come here. Aren't you going to kiss me?

Arthur Shall I?

Angel Are you afraid?

Arthur Your eyes are glittering. Glittering.

Angel Come here.

Arthur Your mouth is thinner.

Angel Am I repulsive, then?

Arthur Oh, now I shall write a poem about your eyes and your mouth.

Angel These awful clothes.

Arthur They make you look more striking.

Angel Look at these terrible shoes.

Arthur Please. Let us be grateful for what we've got.

Angel I can't now. I will. What shall I do about Lord Henry? At my feet begging me to punish him. What shall I do about him?

Arthur Please.

Angel No. Not yet. I shot your father in this room, remember.

Arthur I know but that doesn't stop me loving you. Kiss me. Kiss me.

Angel Hold your head back. (*He kisses him.*)

Arthur You still know how to control me. You're the most dangerous man who ever brought anyone to ruin. But your eyes say something else.

Angel Come with me tonight to Paris. We can be together there. I missed you. If you come with me we'll be together.

Arthur I can feel you under all this. Let me. See you. Please. These awful clothes. Please. I can feel you. The shape of you. Let me feel you.

Angel sags. Arthur supports him.

Please let me feel you. I'm making love to a sick man. I can feel how frail you are.

Angel Will you come with me?

Arthur This is driving me mad. What am I doing to you?

Angel Will you?

Arthur But Buller and the old man are going with you.

Angel We'll get another berth. We shouldn't. This is where your father bled to death.

Arthur Sh. Sh.

SIX

Paris. A white drawing room. Eighteenth-century furniture. Angel's portrait set in a sumptuous frame. Doors at the back through which we can see a gaming table and Turkish furniture and rugs. Angel, Lord Henry, Arthur, the Marchese di Casti Piani, Baron St Eglise, Weil, Phillipeau, August, Baptiste, Hippolyte, surrounding Buller, who is making a toast.

Buller Gentlemen, gentlemen. Thank you. Please charge your glasses. And join me in wishing our host good wishes on his birthday. Damn it.

They all toast Angel.

Arthur (*to Buller*) Well done. Well done, old man.

Buller I'm sweating like a pig

Baptiste (*to Buller*) They tell me that you're the strongest man in the world.

Buller And so I am. So I am. My strength is at your disposal.

Hippolyte I prefer marksmen myself. To strong-men. There is a man at the casino who shoots from the hip.

Marchese (*to St Eglise*) Tell me, old man. Where did you find him? How old is he? He's enchanting.

St Eglise Isn't he? This is his first time out.

August Are you talking about me?

Marchese I was hoping that you were having a good time.

August I am. Thank you.

Baptiste Champagne. (*Takes August away.*)

Phillipeau Pretty mouth.

Marchese Pretty figure.

St Eglise Now. Now. Let us remember ourselves, shall we? He's too young for you.

Marchese They're never too young for me, my dear St Eglise. How much?

St Eglise He's not for sale.

Marchese Uncut diamonds.

St Eglise You're not to be trusted.

Hippolyte Are we going to play?

Baptiste Of course. Let's go in.

Hippolyte Are we playing, Lord Henry?

Lord Henry May I join you presently?

Marchese Can I play with you? Shall we split the stake? You always have such a lucky hand.

Baptiste We'll go in to hell together.

They link arms, Marchese, Baptiste and Hippolyte, and go into the gaming room.

St Eglise (*to Weil*) How are the Jungfrau shares holding up, Weil?

Weil (*to Phillipeau*) He's talking of the new cable railway in the Alps. It's amazing. That's why they're doing so well. Well, I still have four hundred but I'm keeping them for my own use. There's a fortune to be made in them.

Phillipeau I have some. A few. I'd like to accumulate more. Do you think . . .

Weil We'll see what we can do.

St Eglise My astrologer told me to buy. I've put everything into them. If they fail it will be your fault. Your fault, Weil.

Weil They'll be fine. They'll be fine.

Arthur Yes. They're sound. Sound. I paid through the nose for mine. I put everything I had left into them. They've shot up today so I could make a killing. But I think I'll hold on to them. Do you think?

Weil Certainly. Certainly.

St Eglise Good. Good. Let's try our luck in the gaming room. Baccarat, I think. See if we're lucky there.

They go into the gaming room. Buller scribbles a note to Angel and hands it to him.

Buller (*to Lord Henry*) And how is Lord Henry this evening? Are you having a pleasant evening?

Lord Henry Leave me alone. Please.

Enter Marchese.

Marchese I would like a word with you.

Angel If you like.

Buller Then I'll join them at the table. (*Exit.*)

Marchese (*to Lord Henry*) You go too.

Angel What do you want? Have I offended you again?

Marchese Did you hear me?

Lord Henry leaves.

I have a proposition to make to you.

Angel How much do you want?

Marchese You have nothing left to give me.

Angel What makes you think that?

Marchese You're high and dry – you and your writer friend.

Angel If you want me you've no need to descend to threats.

Marchese I've told you already, how many times, that you are not my type. I haven't taken your money because I loved you. I loved you because you had money. You're getting old, but you must realise that. You've seen the competition. Not that you haven't got your qualities. But all you do now is ruin a man's nerves. Still, you're highly qualified for something I have in mind for you.

Angel Are you going to find me a job?

Marchese I told you I was an employment agent.

Angel I thought you were a police spy.

Marchese You can't make a living from that. I once helped a young man in need to find work in Valparaiso but he proved ungrateful and his father had me jailed for my troubles. But the authorities noticed my talent for intrigue and discretion and I did a deal. They give me a stipend of sorts. But it's only subsistence, so I resumed my former profession and I've shipped many a good-looking young fellow abroad to find work suited to his many natural talents.

Angel Life in such an establishment won't suit me. I haven't the talent for it. You can't imagine I could go with just anyone. Can you realise that I have an appetite for that kind of thing. That I can go with anyone.

Marchese In the Theopholous Oikonomopolous establishment in Cairo the clientele is hardly made up of anyone. Most of them come from the English aristocracy. But then there are the Turkish pashas and the Russian diplomats, the Indian princes, and the Arab sheiks. Then there are German industrialists. That kind of thing. You've all the social talents required. You'll live in apartments looking over the El Azhar mosque. You'll dress as you please without any worry as to cost. Eat well. Drink better. All the champagne you need. Your clients will be rich men. And up to a point you'll have your freedom. And if you really don't like a client there are ways out, up to a point.

Angel Do you expect me to believe you when you say your Egyptian friend will pay you thousands of francs for someone he doesn't know from Adam?

Marchese I took the liberty of sending him some of your pictures.

Angel The pictures I gave you.

Marchese (*pointing to Angel's portrait*) He'll hang that one over his front door. And there's another advantage to this opportunity. You'll be safe from those who have an interest in your whereabouts – with Oikonomopolous in Cairo. Certainly safer than you are here now.

Angel You must know I could never find myself in any such place, no matter how amusing you made it sound.

Marchese Shall I whistle up the policeman, shall I?

Angel I can give you three thousand francs.

Marchese In Jungfrau shares. That's what your financial position is. The public prosecutor pays in French francs and Oikonomopolous pays in gold. I never deal in shares. You could be in Cairo in a fortnight if you leave tonight. Here things are so precarious for you. Beats me how you haven't been picked up already. I found out about you quickly enough. But I have a natural talent for that. Still, I don't know how one of my colleagues hasn't got on to you yet. I suppose it's only a matter of time. The train leaves at half past midnight. We have to come to terms by eleven or I'll call the police.

Angel Are you serious about this?

Marchese My concern is only for your safety.

Angel I'll go anywhere with you. But I can't sell myself. It would be worse than prison. Have you no feelings for me?

Marchese Not feelings enough.

Angel I can't sell the only thing I can call my own. I'll give you everything we have.

Marchese I've had everything you've got in cash.

Angel I'll get Arthur to sell the shares.

Marchese No time. If we haven't left by eleven I'll have the pack of you deported in the morning. If we're going I must tell Hippolyte. Excuse me.

Arthur comes in from the gaming room.

Arthur I've hit a winning streak, Angel. Lord Henry is losing his shirt and Weil is betting in Jungfrau shares. Phillipeau isn't doing so badly. Aren't you coming in? (*Exits.*)

Angel Me in a brothel.

Angel reads Buller's note. Re-enter Arthur.

Arthur Won't you play?

Angel Why not? Why not? Get me a drink.

Arthur (*as they go*) I got *The Times* today. Hugo Anstruther has killed himself.

Angel stops. Arthur exits. Lord Henry comes in. Angel makes to go.

Lord Henry Am I so offensive to you?

Angel Good heavens, no. I have no time for you just now, that's all.

Lord Henry You never have time.

Angel No, I never do.

Lord Henry You've taken everything I have. I have given everything to you. I have nothing left. No life. Not a penny. You could at least try to be civil with me.

Angel And aren't I civil? What am I, then?

Lord Henry How can you be like this? What has happened to you? You have become quite quite quite hard. Have you forgotten our passionate exchanges when we were together in the hospital? You weren't so hard then. When I was ready to die for you.

Angel You gave me cholera. Have you forgotten that? It was your idea to give me cholera. That had a meaning, didn't it? What if I had died? Would that perhaps have suited you just as well? Really. Why are you so insistent in pursuing a fantasy that can't be realised? I said things then because of what the situation was then. Things have gone on.

Lord Henry It was deliberate. You knew what you were saying. Did you mean none of it? Was it all deceit?

Angel If you say so. In what way was it all deceit? Tell me. You have to be in this relation to me. You have to be. I have told you from the start that there is no way for you and me. Anyway. You have an admirer of your own now. Pick up with him.

Lord Henry I don't understand a word of what you're saying.

Angel Buller. Buller. Haven't you noticed? He's told me he's mad about you.

Lord Henry I don't envy you. I don't envy you at all. I only want you. I don't envy your terrible capacity for tormenting the weak nor your more terrible instinct for enslaving yourself to creatures of the night.

Angel Who do you mean in particular?

Lord Henry The Marchese. Who has vice emblazoned on his forehead like a sign.

Angel Be quiet before I kick you senseless. He loves me. When I look at him I realise how loathsome you are. If you don't want Buller why don't you try one of them in there? There are boys in there who do it for ready cash. If you have any left. Or shall I lend you some? Look at him. He'll do it for a glass of wine and a plate of oysters.

Lord Henry Do you think one day there will be a rebellion by people like me against people like you?

Angel Do you think one day there'll be a rebellion of people like me against people like you? You have a warm heart, Henry. I have something else. You had money, Henry. I had something else. Imagine having neither. There'd be cause for rebellion.

Enter Arthur, Buller, St Eglise, Weil, Baptiste, Hippolyte. Lord Henry goes out.

What has happened?

Arthur Nothing. I'm making money is what has happened. Come to supper.

Hippolyte Don't boast of winning at the tables. It's unlucky.

They exit. Buller keeps Angel back.

Buller Did you get my note?

Angel What I could understand of it. Go to the police if you must. Do you think I'm frightened of blackmail? I no longer have that kind of money.

Buller Don't lie to me, you lying bitch. You've still got twenty thousand in Jungfrau shares. Your fool of a writer friend has been boasting about it all night.

Angel Then go to him with your demands.

Buller It would take me two days to get him to grasp what I was talking about. And then I'd have to put up with his drivel about its relevance to art and what it brought to bear on what he's working on at the moment. I need cash.

Angel Why?

Buller I'm getting married, that's why. And don't laugh. I have had enough of this. I've met someone who's seen the man in me.

Angel Plenty of us have seen that.

Buller I mean someone who sees something in me. You'll think that's funny. You will. Your sort.

Angel Marry who you like. What do I care if you get married? You've been married before. But why have you been paying court to Henry Wantage?

Buller Because the man's an aristocrat. I know how useful such people can be. There's more than your sort. I'm after a bit of class. I'm not going to be a freak show again for anyone. Not used by anyone like you.

Angel You've got a little wife.

Buller Will you give me the money? I need it quick.

Angel I haven't got it and I don't give in to blackmail. It's Arthur's money.

Buller Then get him to sell up. He'll give you his last penny. Better get him to sell before he gambles it all away. He'll ruin himself, he's not careful.

Angel Always because of marriage. Marriage.

Buller You're not so smart. All you think about is him who's got hold of you. I know you. What does poor Arthur think of that?

Angel Do you want me to get him to show you out?

Buller Have it whichever way you like: if you haven't got the money for me by tomorrow it'll be the end of all this. I'll get some supper. (*Exit.*)

Angel I'm going to die of this.

Enter St Eglise.

St Eglise I'm looking for my young friend. Have you seen him? He's not at supper.

Angel No. No.

St Eglise Perhaps he's through here.

Going to the gaming room. Enter Weil.

Weil Have you . . .?

Angel I think he's through there.

Enter Phillipeau.

Phillipeau Oh it's you. No. I . . .

Weil Through here.

Re-enter St Eglise.

St Eglise He's not there. Have you seen my young friend, either of you?

Phillipeau I haven't.

Weil Nor I. Perhaps he's at supper.

St Eglise No. Strange. Strange. (*Exit St Eglise.*)

Weil Poor old thing.

Phillipeau All of us. Aren't you going to have some supper?

Weil Go on without me.

Phillipeau Ha. Ha.

Weil No. No.

Angel and Phillipeau exit.

Poor old fools, all of us.

Enter Bob, wearing livery and holding a telegram.

Bob Are you Monsieur Weil, sir? They said I'd find you here.

Weil I am indeed.

Bob (*handing him the telegram*) For you, sir.

Weil (*reading*) 'Shares in the Jungfrau railway fallen to . . . ' Crashed. Well. Well. That's the way of things.

Bob Is that all, sir?

Weil Wait a minute. (*Tips him.*)

Bob Thank you, sir.

Weil What do they call you?

Bob My name's Lucien, sir, but they call me Bob.

Weil How old are you?

Bob Fifteen.

Weil Fifteen.

Weil exits. Enter August.

Bob Who are you, then. Eh?

August I'm hiding from them all. Have you seen St Eglise?

Bob No. They're all in there.

August I don't like it here. I wish I hadn't come.

Bob Come with me. Come downstairs. Come on.

August No.

Bob Yes. Come on. Come. No one'll find us down there. I'll show you. (*Kisses him.*)

St Eglise enters.

St Eglise What's this? What's this, then?

Re-enter Weil, Phillipeau and Lord Henry.

August I'm going. I'm going.

St Eglise I found him with a servant. You may laugh. Oh dear.

Weil You'd better sit down, I think.

St Eglise No. Darling. Baby. (*following August out*)

The others go out, laughing.

Lord Henry Can't we play baccarat?

Bob whispers to Angel. Lord Henry goes.

Angel Show him in.

Bob opens the door to Slavin.

Slavin Where did you get him?

Angel From the circus.

Slavin What do you pay him?

Angel Ask him if you're so interested. Thank you. That will be all.

Exit Bob.

Slavin I need some money, my dear.

Angel Do you?

Slavin I've taken an apartment for a lady friend and I'm short of the necessary.

Angel So you've got a lady friend, have you?

Slavin Yes. She's from Italy. She says she was married to the King of Naples, so she says. Something of a beauty in her time, if you can believe it.

Angel And you need the money badly.

Slavin She does – for the rent. Poor old girl. A lot to her, a trifle to you.

Angel Oh, God almighty. (*Laughs and breaks down.*)

Slavin There. There. Angel. What's this? I don't need it that bad. You ought to get some early nights, that's your trouble. That's right, you cry. I've seen you like this before, haven't I, eh? You could cry then, couldn't you? Bawl and shout, couldn't you, dear? Only then you didn't have shoes or such fine clothes, did you?

Angel Take me with you. Take me out of here, please.

Slavin I'll take you with me. We'll take a cab. But first tell me what it is, then. What's made you like this?

Angel They're going to hand me over to the police.

Slavin Who's going to hand you over to the police?

Angel The acrobat.

Slavin I'll see to him.

Angel Yes. Please. Please. Do for him. Do for him.

Slavin If he comes near me, that'll be the end of him. If he came to my lodgings, that would be the thing. My window opens onto the river. Only how can we get him there?

Angel Where do you live?

Slavin 376. Near the old Hippodrome, you know.

Angel I'll get him there. I'll get him there. Send me the rings he wears in his ears. I'd know then. You can take them off before you dispose of him. He don't notice when he's drunk.

Slavin And then?

Angel I'll give you the money. I'll get it. But are you sure?

Slavin Have I ever broken my word to you, ever?

Angel Off you go then. He'll be there. What is it?

Slavin How beautiful you still are. How you smell. How you smell. Let me. Let me. (*Kisses him.*) There we are. Payment. I could ask for more. You'd have to pay.

Exit. Enter Buller.

Angel I think I have found a way out of our difficulty.

Buller Oh, have you then?

Angel Lord Henry is in a bad way. I'm afraid he may do something to himself and you may be the cause.

Buller What does he want?

Angel For you to take him away with you. He'll lend me two thousand pounds to save me from the police and if you'll take him with you I'll deposit the same amount in your name in any bank you name.

Buller And if I don't?

Angel Then you must turn me in. Arthur and I are destitute now, we are. Shall I call Lord Henry?

Buller I can't. My only interest in him is in connection with the aristocracy. He's taught me a few tricks of the trade. I'll give him that. No, I can't.

Angel He's waiting. What shall I say?

Buller My respects, but I'm not that hard up.

Angel I'll tell him then.

Buller No. Hang on. Hang on. I'll get two thousand pounds out of this, will I?

Angel Ask him yourself.

Buller I'm going into the dining room for a bowl of caviar and to get drunk first. (*He exits.*)

Angel calls Lord Henry. He enters.

Angel Henry. You have an opportunity to save me once more if you thought you could.

Lord Henry Have I? And how is that?

Angel By going to a house with Buller. He's threatened to denounce me to the police if you won't oblige him. You will oblige?

Lord Henry I couldn't. I couldn't. He'd be so brutal. I couldn't bear it. I couldn't. I can't.

Angel And what will happen to us all then, if he does as he says? There's a policeman on the corner.

Lord Henry I've got just enough for us to go steerage to America. You'd be safe enough there.

Angel No, you'll do this for me, won't you? America, I think not. Do you? You must tell him you can't do without him. Won't. Flatter him. You'll have to pay for the cab, by the way, here's the address. 376 rue Clairmont. They are expecting you.

Lord Henry Is this a test, is it?

Angel It is. It is. Please, Henry. It's a test.

Lord Henry Angel, you have so often deceived me, why should I believe you now?

Angel Because you do. Don't you? Do this for me. It's all vanity with him. And it flatters you in a way. I shall wait for you.

Lord Henry I cannot reconcile myself with your belief there is no God in heaven. And yet perhaps you're right and there's nothing in it. Let him come.

Angel Have you got the address?

Lord Henry Number 376. Yes.

Angel I'll wait for you. (*calling Buller*) Buller, darling.

Enter Buller.

Buller Excuse me, my mouth's full. Lord Henry.

Lord Henry Mr Buller. I beg you. I beg you. Mr Buller. I beg you.

Buller Yes. OK. You'll do. *À la lanterne.*

They both exit.

Angel Now for the other one. Bob. Bob.

Enter Bob.

Take off your livery.

Bob What sir?

Angel Change clothes with me. Where shall we go?

Bob Come this way.

Weil, Phillipeau, Arthur, August, St Eglise, Baptiste and Hippolyte rush in.

Phillipeau The scoundrel won't give me a chance to recoup.

Weil Your stake is worthless.

Phillipeau I have offered you my Jungfrau shares, sir.

Baptiste What is it?

Hippolyte Weil's taken all his money off him. And thrown in his hand.

Weil Who says that? I said I'll only play for cash. I'm not in the banking house now. And tomorrow, if he offered that trash to me in my office, it would be worth nothing.

Hippolyte What are these shares worth? What did you say?

Weil Yesterday they were worth so much it doesn't matter. Today they're worth nothing at all. Tomorrow, they'll do to line drawers.

Baptiste How has this happened?

Weil I've lost enough. Tomorrow I shall find I have lost everything. I'll start recovering from bankruptcy for the thirty-sixth time.

Arthur Is it true? The Jungfrau shares have fallen? We're ruined.

St Eglise Is this true, the Jungfrau shares have fallen?

Weil Fallen further than you ever thought. You poor old thing.

St Eglise Oh my God. My fortune. (*Collapses.*)

August Dear God.

Arthur and August minister to St Eglise.

Baptiste Dear God.

Hippolyte Let us go, it's getting unpleasant here. Jew. Can't be trusted, you see.

They exit, leaving Arthur, August, St Eglise and Weil.

Arthur Get him a drink.

August Yes. (*Gets him a drink.*)

Arthur You'll feel better now.

Weil I'm sorry, old chap. But that's playing the market. (*Exits.*)

August brings a drink.

August Come on now, old thing.

Angel enters wearing livery.

Angel Have you any cash, Arthur?

Arthur Are you mad? Didn't you hear?

Angel Well then, in two minutes they will be here. We'll be sold. We could have got a cab. Stay if you want to.

Arthur No. We'd better go, I think.

August Come on, old chap.

St Eglise What shall I do?

August Come on. Come on.

Police whistle. Police chase involving all those who have recently left. They arrest Bob.

Policeman Got you.

Marchese You have arrested the wrong man.

SEVEN

London. An attic room divided to provide accommodation for Angel, Arthur and Slavin. There is a curtain leading to Angel's quarters, a makeshift partition making a small dwelling for Slavin, and the principle space where Arthur is lying on a mattress covered with a blanket. Angel is walking about trying to keep warm. Slavin is seated, drinking from an old cup with a jug beside him.

Arthur Listen to the rain.

Angel Feel the cold.

Slavin Have a drop of this, then, why don't you. No? It won't warm you up but it'll make you feel better. No? Gin takes people in different ways. Makes some people very sorry for themselves. Not me. Not me. Pint of gin, I got it downstairs. She've got a nice little gin shop. Down there. Nice fire. She's an enterprising woman. She likes me so she must be enterprising. She got a notice up: 'Drunk a penny, dead drunk for tuppence.' She's a proper businesswoman and knows how to make a thing attractive. I'm going down later when I've got through this. Only I ain't got no money. She'll let me have a warm.

Angel (*looking into a bowl which is catching water from the ceiling*) This bowl is full. What shall I do?

Slavin Chuck it out the window.

Angel does.

Angel I think the rain's stopped.

Slavin Well, now's the time, if you're going to do it. The clerks in the city will still be going home. You'll miss out, you wait much longer. What's stopping you?

Angel No.

Arthur No. I don't want you to.

Angel Oh, don't you? You can afford principles now, can you?

Arthur Don't, Angel. I'm ill.

Angel If I had decent clothes, I'd go up west.

Slavin No. You're better home here. They won't shop you over here. They might rob you. But they won't shop you. Up west they'll rob you and shop you. They're more morally progressive.

Angel I wish I was dead.

Arthur Let's just lie here and let's try to sleep. Let's not be angry any more. And let's hope we never wake up.

Angel Shut up, Arthur. Don't philosophise now, for Jesus Christ's sake.

They hear the sound of a band playing 'God Rest Ye Merry Gentlemen'.

Arthur Is it Christmas?

Slavin It's good to be home at Christmas.

Angel Why don't you get up and try to find work?

Arthur Because I'm ill.

Slavin He's not well.

Angel Let me get in with you. I'm so cold. I got to get warm somehow.

Angel gets under the blanket with Arthur.

Give me a drink.

Slavin Certainly. Certainly.

Arthur and Angel both have a drink.

It's a cure-all. It'll cheer you up and keep his fever down.

Angel It's the quickest way out of here, anyway. Though Arthur's poems would do the trick just as well.

Slavin Yes. It's a universal benefit. From the cradle to the grave. The old girl's got a handle on social policy.

Arthur I wish we were in Paris dining at Maxim's.

Slavin A slice of Christmas pudding'd do for me. I think she'll keep me some – her downstairs.

Arthur I've been dreaming of the perfect cigarette.

Angel Shut up. Shut up.

Arthur I'm ill.

Angel I know you're ill. Don't go on about it. What can I do?

Arthur And you made me ill. I got this from you.

Angel I'm not ill. I'm just freezing cold.

Arthur You got infected by your Parisian pimp.

Angel Don't blame me. You've got nothing from me, ever. Ever. I saw you with who you got it from. And I thought you believed in faith, fidelity, whatever you like to call it. I'm going out.

Arthur No, stay here. I've tried to get a job. I thought I had a perfect system with numbers. But I don't have the cash. I've tried it with rich women. But my clothes were too shabby. And they want a presentable escort.

Slavin I'd have thought you'd have done well with women. You've got a bit of tone.

Angel He'd bore them by talking about art.

Slavin No, women like you to talk. They like a bit of conversation. Women – they're not so crude as men in many ways. Many ways. A woman likes a laugh. Likes a bit of attention. Likes you to like 'em. I like women. She likes to hear your opinions. No – Arthur was unlucky there.

Angel What are we going to do?

Slavin I've given my advice. I've given my advice.

Arthur I don't want you to.

Angel I shall have to.

Arthur I forbid you to.

Angel Lie down, Arthur. I'm going out. Give me my shoes. Put some paper in them.

Slavin does so.

We haven't got a mirror.

Slavin You look all right. Come here. You look a picture. Listen to me. Don't be frightened. It's always alarming the first time and a little bit exciting, eh? But bring 'em back here. We can keep an eye open for you here. Here, eat one of these. (*giving him a sweet*) Take the smell of gin off your breath.

Arthur I want none of the money.

Angel You'll want it when I get it. (*Angel exits.*)

Slavin We'll go there – he brings anybody back. If he brings anybody back.

Arthur I've known him since we were children. It's as if we were brothers. I remember Dr Goulderie calling to see how my mother was. He was about fifteen. He couldn't take his eyes off him, the good doctor. Angel bought him my first book of poems. He's always been like a bright intelligent superior child. When he was a child he was always interested in my work. Listened to me play on the piano. Liked me to explain things. I watched him go from my father to Goulderie, to the artist, to my father, who was always possessive of him, and who he always betrayed – eventually with me. After he shot him. Who knows how the world works. There was always a closeness between us then. I didn't understand – that's why he had such power over me.

Slavin Sh. Hang on. *(listening)*

Arthur What?

Slavin Hang . . . Yes . . .

Arthur I can't bear it. I'll throw him out.

Slavin You haven't got the strength for such a thing. Come on, up you get. Let's get you in there. Quiet now.

Arthur I can't bear it. I don't want to hear.

Slavin You've heard it before.

They hide behind the partition. Enter Angel with Tomkins.

Angel It's not much.

Tomkins puts his fingers to his mouth.

It's cold. There's no fire.

Tomkins puts his hand over Angel's mouth.

What do you mean?

Tomkins puts his hand over Angel's mouth and a finger to his own lips.

I don't know what you mean. You'd better go, I think. You're all right. No one can hear us.

We can see Arthur and Slavin. Tomkins still indicates silence.

I've never done this. I've never been with anyone I haven't been introduced to or whose name I didn't know. Do you believe me? No, I bet you don't. I don't know what to say.

Tomkins makes another silencing motion.

Yes. It's never interested me. Things that must be quite exciting, I should think. It's true. I missed out on a lot. What do you like? Do you take it, all that?

Tomkins comes towards Angel.

What?

Tomkins tries to kiss him.

No. Don't kiss me. You're not supposed to kiss. No, I can't be like that.

Kisses him.

I hope you've got some money.

Tomkins hands him money. Angel inspects it. Tomkins takes it back. He holds Angel's mouth shut as a signal to be quiet.

All right.

Takes the lamp and leads him behind the curtain.

Arthur What's happened?

Slavin Sh.

Arthur You can't hear anything from here.

Slavin I've heard it too many times.

Arthur I've got to listen.

Slavin goes through his pockets. Arthur listens at the curtain.

Slavin Nothing but a pair of gloves. What's this? (*Reads a pamphlet.*) 'Exhortations to pious men and those with the intention of becoming so.' Very helpful. Two-and-sixpence. Come on, let's go back. Come on.

They go behind the partition. Angel and Tomkins come out.

Angel Well then. Do you want to do it again?

Tomkins holds Angel's mouth shut. He puts his coat on, gives Angel the pamphlet. Refuses Angel's offer to take him to the door. Arthur and Slavin come out.

Arthur How much did he give you?

Angel Here it is. Take it. Go on. I'm going out again.

Slavin Sh. He's coming back.

Arthur He's coming for his prayer book.

Angel It isn't him. It's someone else. Who is it?

Slavin Some acquaintance of his who has recommended us to him.

Laughs. Enter Lord Henry, poorly dressed and carrying a rolled-up canvas.

Lord Henry If I've come at an inconvenient time, I'll go. But I haven't spoken to anyone for ten days now. I think I ought to tell you that I couldn't get any money. My brother didn't reply.

Slavin So now you'd like to get your legs under our table, is that it, my lord?

Angel I'm going out.

Lord Henry I haven't come entirely empty-handed. Look: on my way here I was offered ten shillings for it in a junk shop. But I couldn't part with it.

Slavin What is it, then?

Angel Show us.

Arthur takes the canvas and unrolls it.

Arthur Look, it's Angel's portrait.

Angel And you've brought it here, did you, you . . . (*screaming*) Get rid of it. Get rid of it. I don't want to see it.

Arthur What's wrong with you? Look at it. Just to look at it again makes me understand why what's happened has happened. Look at him. Look. Let anyone who looks at that tell me what he would have done.

Slavin Yes, he's a good-looking boy. We must find a nail for it. It will impress the customers.

Arthur There's one over here.

Slavin How did you acquire it?

Lord Henry That night in Paris. I cut it out of the wall.

Slavin Pity it's so damaged. You should have been more careful with it. You'll need a nail at the bottom, too.

Arthur I know what I'm doing. (*Nails the picture to the wall with his boot.*) There.

Slavin It gives the place an air of luxury already.

Arthur looks at it.

Arthur Look. Look.

Slavin Yes. Yes.

Lord Henry Who painted it, did you say?

Arthur Didn't you know him?

Lord Henry Only that he cut his throat and that you despised him. He was very talented.

Angel I'm going out again.

Arthur (*still looking*) In spite of everything, he's still the same. The same look in the eyes. But you've aged, Angel. I hadn't noticed.

Slavin The bloom gone. Ah yes. But you can still say . . . that's the thing about a painting – you can still say that's what I used to look like. No one you pick up tonight will have any idea of our glory days, eh? They won't believe it.

Arthur One doesn't notice the change when you're with someone every day.

Slavin Still, down there he's still worth a dozen of them. Aren't you? Anyway, what matters out there are qualities of the heart. You look for the eyes which are least likely to rob you.

Angel makes to go.

Arthur You're not going down there again. Not while I've got a breath in me.

Lord Henry Where are you going?

Arthur He's going to pick someone up and bring them up here. He's had one already.

Lord Henry I'll come with you, Angel. I'll come with you.

Slavin Here, not on his patch.

Lord Henry I'll be near. I'll look after you.

Angel You're all killing me.

Angel exits, followed by Lord Henry.

Arthur This is hopeless. Hopeless.

Slavin We should have stopped that Lord Henry fellow. He'll frighten 'em off. Look of him'd be enough to put anyone off his stroke. Still, you've got to give it to him. If he hadn't brought the big fellow to my place in Paris, we'd still have him hanging around today.

Arthur My life. It's been utterly useless. Utterly. Utterly. I'm useless.

Slavin The lamp's going out. There's no oil either. It's getting dark.

Arthur My life. Where is it? Where has it gone? He's taken my life. (*Listens.*)

Slavin Hey. Hey. Yes. Yes. We're in luck. Come on.

They go behind the partition. Enter Angel with Euba. The first words heard outside the door.

Euba It's dark. Where's the light?

Angel Come on. Come on. It's all right.

Euba Why is it so dark?

Angel The lamp has gone out. Come on. Come. It's all right.

Euba And it's cold.

Angel Do you want a drink?

Euba Yes, give me a drink.

Angel gives him some gin.

Good.

Slavin (*from behind the partition*) Blimey, it's a Shwarzer. That's a turn up. Still. What's up with you, Arthur? Did you think this was really the occupation of passionate refinement like yours? Do you think they don't do it or something? Or do you think it's a result of oppression? Only natural in people like you. Sex isn't prejudiced, Arthur. It's the true colonist. It pitches its tent in all of us. And we all have our different tasks to perform. Now, me, I'm different to you. But I suspect, Arthur, things might have been different for you if it hadn't been for Angel. You'd have fell for some girl in the chorus as your way out. I only did it when it was sometimes a necessity. Well, it's all a necessity, ain't it? We're in Whitechapel, Arthur. The hub of the Empire. We're not in Kensington Square.

Angel More? No. You're beautiful, aren't you?

Euba goes to kiss Angel.

Hang on, have you got any money?

Euba I've got a gold sovereign.

Angel Let's see it.

Euba I'll give it to you.

Angel I must see it.

Euba You'll see it.

Angel No – now.

Euba shows him the sovereign. He kisses but doesn't give him the money.

Euba I never pay before. You'll get it later. You will.

Grabs him. Angel moves away.

Angel Stop it. Get off. Stop it.

Euba You'll get it, I swear.

Angel Get off.

Enter Arthur.

Arthur Leave him alone.

Euba Who are you? Why you got him here? (*Hits Arthur savagely on the head with a cosh.*) That's right, boy.

Sleep. (*to Angel*) Why did you do that? I would have paid you. (*Goes.*)

Slavin comes out.

Angel Arthur. Look here. Look at him. You see to him. I'm going out. I'm going out again. (*Angel exits.*)

Slavin He can't take it. He'll never make a living out of love because love is his life. Come on, Arthur. Blood! Arthur. Oh dear. Well, you can't stay here. I'll put you in there, otherwise you'll put the customers off. Come on, up you get. No. He's gone. Well. Come on. (*He drags him behind the partition.*) No. Leave him in peace, eh. I'd better be leaving then. I think I'll go downstairs, see if she's got a bit of Christmas pudding for me.

On his way out he meets Lord Henry.

You going to make your quarters here, then? Just see none of the valuables are pinched, OK?

Lord Henry It's dark.

Slavin Yes. Arthur's in there. He's retired for the evening. I wouldn't disturb him. If anyone wants me, I'm downstairs having a drink with a friend. (*to the audience*) I'm going now, you'll pick up the rest. There's not a lot I can do.

Lord Henry I'll watch him do it with strangers as I've watched him with all the others. It's my punishment. Only someone who is not human like I am, not human, can watch how much they don't understand themselves, all these people. That everything they do is senseless and everything they say is false. Today one thing, tomorrow another, according to what they've eaten, drunk or made love or perhaps none of these things. The children are intelligent but they grow into animals. And no one knows what he's doing. When they're hungry, they don't have time to be unhappy, and when they're full, they make the world an atrocity, and then they act entirely by whim. I wonder if anyone has ever been made happy by love. That's what my fate is – not to know. I'm not human. I thank God for that. But I seem to have human capacity. I'd better hang myself. If I was drowning in my own blood I don't think he'd care even then. He has always hated me and I don't know why. Why are men so terrible to men? I've been useful to him. There is that. I could jump off the bridge. The water under the bridge is colder than his heart. I could dream until I drowned. I could dream he was kissing me, as I often dream it. But I always wake again. Ah, yes. The Thames for all its filth is far too clean for me.

He tries to hang himself. The chair gives way but the rope breaks.

I must still bear this life. Oh God, whisper in his ear. Tell him to love me. Love me, please. Love me. Listen to him. Let me be happy just once. Just once. My angel, my star, my love. Pity me. Pity me. Pity me.

Enter Angel with Jack.

Jack Who's that?

Angel It's no one, it's my brother. He's demented. He's ill. Take no notice of him.

Lord Henry Is that you?

Angel Yes. Be quiet.

Jack You've got a pretty mouth on you.

Angel So they tell me. I haven't had any complaints.

Jack No. How much do you want? I haven't got a lot.

Angel Are you going to stay the night?

Jack Why do you ask that? I can't. I got to get back.

Angel You can go home in the morning. Say you missed the omnibus. Stayed with a friend.

Jack How much do you want?

Angel I don't want a lot. What have you got?

Jack No. I'm off. I'm off.

Angel No, please stay. Please. Please. Please.

Jack What do you want me to stay all night for? What you up to, eh? What you going to do when I'm asleep?

Angel Nothing. Don't be afraid.

Jack I'm not afraid.

Angel Don't go, please.

Jack How much do you want, then?

Angel Half of what we said in the street.

Jack Too much. You haven't been doing this long, have you?

Angel The first time tonight.

Lord Henry Angel.

Angel Get out.

Jack He's not your brother, is he? What you got here. He's in love with you, isn't he? Poor creature. (*stroking Lord Henry's head*) Go on. Go on.

Angel Why are you looking at me like that?

Jack I'm looking at you. That's all. You'll be better stripped, eh? I thought that in the street. And your mouth's pretty. I've only got this. (*Takes a coin out.*)

Angel It doesn't matter. Give it to me.

Jack You'll have to split it. I'll need my fare in the morning.

Angel I haven't got any money.

Jack Turn your pockets out.

Angel I've got this. (*Shows his empty hand.*) That's all I've got.

Jack Give it back.

Angel I'll get change in the morning.

Jack No, give it here. Come on.

Angel All right. Come on. I'll light the lamp.

Jack We don't need light. The moonlight'll be enough.

Angel I like you. I do.

They go behind the curtain.

Lord Henry I must go home. I mustn't stay here. I can't. They'll forgive me. I'll finish my degree. I'll do what they say.

Angel (*off*) No, stop. Don't. You're hurting.

Jack You want me to.

Angel No.

Jack Yes.

Angel, partly dressed, comes right out followed by Jack. Lord Henry aims his revolver at Jack. Jack stabs him in the stomach.

(*to Lord Henry*) You be quiet now. (*to Angel*) Now then, what's your pretty mouth for?

There's a very bitter struggle during which Angel tries to bottle Jack. Eventually Jack controls him with his knife.

Angel No. Please. No. Please. No.

Jack Shut it. Shut up. Shut up.

Jack pushes Angel over the table and fucks him violently, threatening him all the time with the knife.

Angel No. No. No. No.

Jack Yes. Yes. Yes.

Angel continues to say 'No' until Jack forces him to say 'Yes' with the knife. Angel eventually cries out 'No.' Jack cuts his throat. He throws Angel onto the floor.

(*recovering*) Yeah. That was good. That was good. (*Washes his hands in the basin, which has been collecting water.*) No towel. (*He uses Lord Henry's scarf. To Lord Henry*) Don't be frightened. I'm not interested in you. You won't be long yet anyway. (*He goes.*)

Lord Henry Where are you? Where are you? My dearest. Let me see you. Angel, my angel. I'll stay with you through eternity. Oh God, help me.

The End.

THE LOOK ACROSS THE EYES

For Bernard and Paul

Characters

Laurence, in his thirties

May, late forties

Jimmy, late forties

Harry, late forties

Young Laurence, sixteen

Christopher, eleven

David, eighteen

The play takes place in May and Harry's house in Cardiff, mainly in the late 1940s

ONE

Laurence Jimmy Murphy was sitting hunched over the fire with the poker in his hand and a cup of tea near him handy in the grate. His sister, May Harrington, was ironing at the corner of the table. She used a flat-iron and she had folded a blanket, scorched and holed from use, into a square to protect the table.

May Stop poking the fire, Jimmy, for goodness' sake.

Jimmy You wanna put some coal on.

Harry Bring a few lumps.

Jimmy Haven't you got a bucket?

Harry Bring it on a shovel for now.

Laurence Jimmy picked up the shovel and went through the back kitchen outside to the coalhouse where, using a hammer, he broke a slab of coal into pieces, which he brought back in, piled on the shovel. He built the fire up.

Jimmy That'll need some small coal in a minute.

Laurence He went again to the back kitchen, this time to wash his hands and to dry them on the towel put out by May earlier. When he had finished he took a packet of sandwiches from the inside pocket of his overcoat hanging from a nail in the back door. He came back into the living room and took the sandwiches out of their brown paper-bag, which he folded carefully and put on the mantelpiece for May to use later. He reached into the inside pocket of his jacket, searching for a soiled envelope where he had put a pound note. He put it on the mantelpiece next to the paper bag. He sat down and began to toast the sandwiches on a copper toasting fork which May's eldest son, David, had made for her in work.

Jimmy She makes you sandwiches then.

Harry No, I bought them.

May For goodness sake, Jimmy, I'd make you a couple of sandwiches.

Jimmy Nah.

Laurence Jimmy had recently taken up lodgings in a boarding house near the docks run by a woman of whom May did not approve. For some years he had lived with an elderly cousin of theirs, where he had been comfortable and well cared for, but advancing years and the death of her husband had forced the old lady to give up her little house and move in with her daughter. May wasn't happy with the present arrangements. Jimmy had no experience of looking after himself. It wasn't expected of him. For ten years after their mother's death, until her marriage, May had kept house for him in town, where they had been born. They were the youngest of ten children with barely a year between them and although May was the younger of the two, it had never appeared to be so to anyone else.

May Do you want any dinner? There's enough.

Jimmy No.

May Are you sure, Jimmy? You're getting as thin as a rake. Look at you.

Laurence She stopped ironing and went over to him.

May Let me look at you.

Jimmy Get off.

May Hold still. Let me look at you.

Laurence She inspected him as she would one of her children.

May Look at your neck. You could do with a good wash and all. Look at the inside of your collar.

Jimmy Gor blimey. Mind your own business. It's my working shirt.

Laurence May left him and went back to the ironing.

May And don't let my fire burn up, there's a fuel shortage.

Jimmy You wanna get a bucket.

May Kiss my . . .

Laurence Jimmy picked up the shovel and went outside to do as he was told. May tested the iron by holding it near her cheek, only to find that the heat was gone out of it. She put it upright on the table and stood for a while, supporting her back with her right hand. She went into the back kitchen to change irons. She wanted to finish one more shirt before her husband and sons came in to dinner. The back kitchen still had a range, which she no longer used for cooking but which was sufficiently heated by the fire in the other room to boil a kettle or heat her flat irons or air the clothes on a wooden airer, hoisted and lowered by means of a pulley fastened to a cleat on the side of the dresser.

She turned from the old range to the gas cooker on which she was making the dinner. Sunday's lamb had lasted them two days and this morning she had used the bone to make a thick soup with potatoes and onions and pearl barley. It was simmering now on the stove in a big pan. She stirred it and tasted it and when she was satisfied she looked into the saucepan next to it, where were steaming dumplings, which she had made from suet and flour. This was a favourite meal with them and since they would eat their bread dry with the soup there would be no grumbling about margarine from the boys today. Jimmy came in with the small coal. May turned from the cooker and, protecting her hand with a piece of flannel and the end of her apron, she picked up the hot iron and went into the other room, where Jimmy was putting the small coal on the fire. May went on with the ironing. Jimmy began to eat one of his sandwiches.

May You'd better move in with us, I think.

Jimmy I'd watch it.

Laurence She spat lightly on the iron, which sizzled loudly, and having measured the heat, she began to iron the shirt, carefully.

Jimmy Blimey, it's hot in here.

May Well, take your coat off.

Jimmy Nah.

May You've gone a contrary bugger, our Jimmy.

Jimmy I'll be going in a minute. You've gone a terrible woman for swearing.

May It's you, God forgive me. You've got me heart scalded.

Jimmy You never hear me swear.

Laurence She never did.

Jimmy Not like him.

Laurence Jimmy nodded his head towards the house next door.

Jimmy He's got a mouth on him.

May Who?

Jimmy Next door, Tommy Ryan.

May Is he home?

Jimmy Yes, I just saw him out there.

May Isn't he working?

Jimmy He was working this morning. He was picked out all right. Must have been a soft job.

Laurence Jimmy and Tommy Ryan had stood in the pen with the other dockers early that morning under the scrutiny of the docks manager. Jimmy hadn't been picked to work again. He had taken his book to be stamped in the office and then cycled over to May. Whether it was his poor sight, or past militancy, or religion, or whatever it was that worked against him, he did not know. It was something.

Jimmy Well, they was never any good.

May Who?

Jimmy Them.

May Who?

Jimmy Tommy Ryan, all of them.

May What are you talking about?

Jimmy Him next door. They used to live in Mary Ann Street. That was a rough house.

May Don't talk daft, Jimmy, he comes from right down by Adeline Street. Lived down the bottom from Harry.

Jimmy They never did.

May They did. The ones you mean were cousins of his.

Jimmy I went to school with one of them. He was in my class.

May I know. I know.

Jimmy Well, how could you know better than me?

May Because you was bloody backward then and you're bloody backward now.

Jimmy Well that's nice. (*He chuckles.*)
Well, we'll wait till Harry comes in and see who's right.

May Shut up will you, for God's sake. I'm sick of your voice.

Jimmy We'll wait till Harry comes. He'll know. Where is he?

May I give him a tanner for a bet.

Jimmy Has he had any compo through?

May No.

Jimmy He'll never get any. It's a waste of time with them people.

Laurence Harry had contracted a skin disease in his youth. For years it had been in remission but during the war, soon after he was conscripted, it had flared up again when May had lost her baby. It was so bad now that he couldn't work.

May I don't know what she sees in him.

Jimmy Who?

May Her next door.

Jimmy Oh yeah.

May She thinks he's Clark Gable.

Jimmy Does she?

Laurence She stopped ironing for a moment.

May It's the rent man today.

Jimmy You plays a different tune now.

May Yerra, you mean old get. Keep it. His hands are in a shocking state again. Nothing'll shift it.

Jimmy I don't know why he give up the dock. God, he was a blue-eye down there. I've been down there since I was fourteen. I've never had a quarter of the jobs he used to get.

May Aye, well, what we all should have done and it wouldn't matter where he was now, would it? And his skin was ruined from working as a lagger in the channel dry dock. He was years in the dry dock right after he left school.

Jimmy You can't see them admitting to that. Has the ship's owners' doctor been?

May They sent someone here last week. He came in a little cream sports car, with the hood down. It's going to drag on and on.

Jimmy I can never see it coming off. He never had any right to a book anyway.

May Where?

Jimmy On the docks.

May He did you know. Bloody cheek.

Jimmy He did not.

May He bloody did. His father was an iron ore man.

Jimmy Get out.

May Look, see this.

Laurence She brandished the iron at him. He chuckled again and got up to make ready to leave. May finished ironing the shirt. She folded it and put it with the others ready to be aired, on the deep window-ledge behind her. She would do what little remained tomorrow or at the end of the week. She folded the blanket and put it away in the cupboard and then she took the iron into the kitchen.

Jimmy Where's my clips?

Laurence May came back in and began to lay the table for dinner.

May Well, where did you put them?

Laurence She left the table and went over to the fireplace.

May Here they are. They were on the mantelpiece. If they were a dog they'd bite you.

Laurence She found the pound Jimmy had put out earlier. She kissed it.

Jimmy That's all you think about is money.

Laurence Jimmy put his clips on.

May On your way, brother. I'll give it to you on Friday.

Laurence She put the pound in the rent book. The back door opened. May's second son, Laurence, came in from school.

Jimmy Aye, aye.

Laurence Jimmy went out. Laurence said nothing.

May What's the matter with you?

Young Laurence Nothing's the matter with me.

May Something's the matter with you.

Laurence Laurence had failed in one subject to get his school certificate. May and Harry had insisted on his staying on at school for another year to resit his exams. He didn't want to. He didn't want to.

Young Laurence What's for dinner?

May Hang on, hang on, take your blazer off. Sit down.

Laurence Laurence took his blazer off and put it on the back of the chair. He sat down. May went into the kitchen and brought him his soup.

Young Laurence Aren't there any doughboys?

May Wait a minute, wait a minute.

Laurence She went back into the kitchen to fetch the dumplings. She gave him two.

Young Laurence Great.

May Yes. You've cheered up now, see.

Young Laurence Yes.

May What d'you do in school?

Laurence Laurence didn't answer. Jimmy came back in.

Jimmy Where's Harry's pump? I got a flat tyre.

May Out there.

Laurence Jimmy went out grumbling to himself as David and Christopher, May's other two sons, came in. David and Jimmy had seen each other that morning in the docks. David was an apprentice welder. Christopher, the youngest, had recently passed the scholarship and was in the same school as Laurence. David had given him a lift home on the back of his bike.

Christopher Hello, Mam. What's for dinner?

May You'll see. It's your favourite. You don't look too bright either. What's the matter with the pair of you?

David I'm all right. I don't know about him.

Christopher And I'm all right too.

May I know you're all right. Come on then, sit down.

David I'd better wash my hands first.

Laurence He went into the kitchen. May followed him. Christopher sat at the table next to Laurence.

May (*to David*) What's the matter?

Laurence David dried his hands.

David I'm all right, Mam.

May I don't know.

David I'm all right, honest.

Laurence He went back in and sat down. May ladled soup into two plates, added two dumplings to each of them and brought them in.

Christopher Can't I have a big plate?

May No, I'm keeping the other big plate for your father. That'll do you.

Laurence Oh, Mam.

May Come on now, there's plenty. Come on now.

Laurence Jimmy came in again.

Jimmy It's no good, I must have a puncture. I'll have to take Harry's bike. He won't mind.

May No. Now go on. Go on.

Jimmy Gor blimey.

May Yes, I know. I'll see you tomorrow.

Laurence Jimmy went out.

Christopher Have you made enough doughboys for afters?

May You haven't finished your dinner yet.

Laurence She had made enough doughboys for afters, and when they had finished the soup she cleared the plates and brought them each a doughboy on a plate with jam to sweeten it.

Young Laurence Yeah.

David Thanks.

Christopher Great.

May I'll make tea when your father comes in.

Laurence When they had finished eating, Christopher went out to play and Laurence went upstairs to read. David sat by the fire.

David That was lovely, Mam.

May Did you like it?

David Lovely.

Laurence May cleared the table.

David I'll do that.

May No, I'll do it, you sit down, you must be tired.

David I am.

Laurence Harry came in as May was setting a place for him.

Harry I see Jim got my bike.

May He's got a slow puncture.

Harry He didn't see me.

May How did you do on the horses?

Harry Hopeless. Hello, son.

May Are you telling me the truth?

Harry Of course I am.

May Look at me. You bloody big liar.

Laurence She hit him. He laughed.

Harry Mine came up.

May What was the odds?

Harry Five-to-two. There's your tanner. I bought five Park Drive, OK?

Laurence He gave her a kiss and her sixpence.

May Give old cheerful Charlie one, for Christ's sake.

Harry Cor blimey.

Laurence He tossed David a cigarette.

David Thanks.

Laurence He lit his cigarette from the fire.

May Don't do that.

Laurence Harry lit his cigarette from David's and then handed it back.

May And before you sit down to dinner, go and do your hands. Come on.

Harry I reckon I'm doing them too much.

May I don't know. Here they are, ironed and aired.

Laurence She gave him clean, rolled-up bandages for his hands. She had washed them that morning.

Harry Ta.

Laurence With his cigarette in his mouth he began to unknot the bandages at his wrist.

May Shall I do them?

Harry I'll manage.

May Listen what a flutter does for him. You're a different fella, isn't it terrible? That's the devil in you.

Harry Aye.

Laurence Harry went upstairs to their bedroom, where the cream was for his hands. May turned to David.

May Don't go to sleep, David, come on. You'll have to go back to work soon. Come on.

David All right.

May Come on.

David In a minute.

May David.

Laurence David didn't respond. May stood looking at him. Then she turned and called to Harry upstairs.

May Aye, Harry.

Harry Yes?

May I think our Jim'll have to move in with us.

Laurence She waited.

May Did you hear?

Harry Yes.

Laurence Harry came in, having put on the clean bandages.

Harry Tie these for me, will you?

Laurence May tied the bandages carefully. Harry sat down at the table.

May He looks awful uncared for.

Harry Where we going to put him?

May Well, Jimmy can have Christopher's bedroom, or he can go in with the boys.

David Christ.

Harry Well, please yourself.

May Anyway, it'll be a help.

Harry Yeah.

May Well, how do you think the rent is going to be paid today?

Harry I haven't said anything.

May You never do. All right, we'll let the poor bugger stick where he is.

Harry Please yourself. It's nothing to do with me. Any dinner, Mother?

May Look I've told you often enough, don't talk to me in that bloody stupid way.

Harry All right. All right. All right.

May Do you know, I'll knife you before we're much older.

Harry You've been going to do that ever since we met, my dear. You got a big mouth.

May Yerra, you're as common as they come.

David Shut up.

May What did you say?

David I'm going back to work.

May You haven't had a cup of tea yet.

David That's OK.

Laurence He kissed his mother and went out. May went into the kitchen to get Harry's dinner. She brought it back and set the plate down before him.

Harry What's the matter with David?

May Don't ask me now. I expect we'll hear it all Friday when he brings his pay packet in. He doesn't want to finish his time.

Harry Well, that's stupid talk, isn't it?

May Well, don't talk to him in a tone of voice like that. You've got no manner of talking.

Harry Don't worry, my dear, I shan't say a word.

May Yerra, you're an ignorant bloody get, you are.

Laurence Laurence came down.

Young Laurence I'm going back to school.

May You're early.

Young Laurence Yeah.

May Will you take Christopher with you?

Young Laurence No I won't. He's big enough.

May Well call him in when you go.

Laurence Laurence put on his blazer, picked up his books and kissed his mother before going back to school. He went through the back door.

Young Laurence Christopher!

May I don't know what's the matter with the pair of them.

Harry Well, I think we should have taken him away and put him to a trade.

May It's only the one subject. It's only French. He's champion at everything else. He've got to have a language.

Harry Don't they teach another language?

May No. Or, well . . . not in his class.

Laurence Christopher ran in.

May Go and wash.

Christopher Mam.

May Go and wash.

Laurence He went into the kitchen and washed his hands and face. He came back in.

May Come here. Look at you.

Laurence She cleaned his mouth with the end of her apron.

Christopher Don't.

May There we are. Go on. Go on.

Laurence Christopher kissed his mother and ran out.

Harry He's no bother.

May No, he's no bother.

Laurence Harry pushed his plate away.

Harry Mother, that was great.

TWO

Laurence Later that night Harry was sitting by the fireplace in his pyjamas. The fire had long since gone out. His hands prevented him from clearing the ashes or laying the fire. Perhaps David would do it in the morning. He was the first up. May came in wearing her nightdress with a cardigan over it. She was barefoot.

May What's the matter, can't you sleep?

Laurence He shook his head.

May Your nerves bad?

Harry Shocking.

May Oh, Harry.

Harry Now leave me alone, there's a good girl.

May You're a silly man. You're very silly to be like this. Come back to bed.

Harry Go on, I'll be up.

Laurence He had been like this now for nearly four years, ever since he had been invalided out of the army because of his hands, and on compassionate grounds because she had lost the baby. She went back to the war in her mind.

May They should never have called a man your age up.

Harry Don't be silly, May.

May Well, what bloody use were you going to be to them. It half-killed me at home here. And if I hadn't lost the baby, they'd never have let you out and then you'd have been over there.

Harry That's no way to look at it.

May We don't know what would have happened. You might have been killed. You might have. Then you wouldn't have come home. How do you think I felt?

Harry Don't keep on.

May Feel.

Harry Shut up will you. It's got nothing to do with it. It was my hands.

May I will not shut up. I don't think it was really so bad. I really don't. To me it's not those things that harden you. It's wicked to let the death of children harden you when you've got other children. There's so much more preventable to make you hard. Look at it that way.

Harry You don't know what it's like being on the touchline of these things.

May No? But I do, you know. Carrying a baby. Whether you really want it or not, but you think, well, it's God's will and you can't but look forward I should think, not if it's your twentieth. And then there's nothing and no explanation given. You don't feel in the thick of things. Let me tell you. Look at you. You're like six penn'orth of bad ha'pennies. I felt. You can't imagine it. Oh, it's a terrible feeling.

Laurence Harry remembered the night he came home from the army and how long it had taken to cross the country.

Harry God, it was pouring down. And the blackout, and no trains. It was comical it was so depressing.

Laurence They both laughed.

May Listen.

Laurence They both looked up.

May He've got out of the boys' bed now, and he's got into ours again.

Laurence Christopher travelled from bed to bed like this most nights.

May Go up and tell him to go back.

Harry He'll wake the bloody house up. Leave him. Leave him.

Laurence When he was fifteen, Harry's oldest sister Violet had lost her first child at birth. It was during the First War, in the winter of 1917, and her husband Tom was at the front. He'd gone in to see her as soon as he was allowed. Popped his head round the door and said.

Harry Hello, Vi.

Laurence She turned to look at him, smiling because she was so fond of him, but he was struck by her eyes, which were not smiling. How are you? he'd said, not knowing what else to say. I'm all right, love, how are you? Vi had said.

He looked into May's eyes now. They were different from Vi's, less simple, more acute. Less soft, less pitiable, less disconsolate, more bright, more forgiving, more clever, more kind, more arresting, more unnerving, more inconsolable. His boys had this look across their eyes. So had Jimmy, although his eyes were failing.

Years later, ten years, fifteen, Harry would come into this room. This room where they were sitting now silent. He would come in to find Jimmy sitting by the fire reading a folded newspaper, lengthwise, near his eyes.

Harry What are you reading with no light on for, Jimmy? You haven't got no sight as it is. You're getting childish, Jimmy. Who did your sandwiches?

Jimmy I did. I was going to the match. They kept me waiting over an hour.

Harry Have you had any dinner?

Jimmy Nah.

Harry I expect Laurence put something ready for you out there.

Jimmy I dunno.

Harry Did you get your money?

Jimmy Aye. You had a bet?

Harry No.

Jimmy That'll be the day.

Harry I had a two bob double.

Jimmy What?

Harry The favourite, the first race, and I had a tip for the four o'clock.

Jimmy You always back the blinkin' favourite.

Harry Look, I've had a bet on every dinnertime for over going on sixty-odd years.

Jimmy They come up?

Harry One of them did.

Jimmy Which one?

Harry The favourite.

Jimmy Mug's game.

Harry Aye, I must be a mug to be still going out to work at my age.

Jimmy You must be doing all right on it.

Harry Look at you. You wanna get some exercise. I haven't turned into a bloody old-age pensioner like you. I saw someone helping you across the road last night.

Jimmy Couldn't have been me.

Harry You couldn't see me, though.

Jimmy I must have been helping them.

Harry Well, it was the blind leading the blind then.

Laurence His hands would be cured by then. David would have finished his trade by then, he would be married with children of his own by then, with a house and a mortgage. I would fail my exam again, but my grammar school education would have got me a job in the council offices, I would still be living at home. Christopher would have gone to university and be living away and would rarely come home. I would have come in from work. Hello, unc, I would have said.

Jimmy What? Oh aye. You all right?

Laurence Had your tea?

Jimmy What?

Laurence Had your tea? I put it up for you.

Jimmy Nah. I'm all right.

Laurence I'll get it for you, shall I?

Jimmy Aye, all right.

Laurence Where's Dad?

I would have got him his tea. May would be dead by then. Things would be different by then. May would be dead by then. But now Harry and May were sitting with each other in the night, and they had no understanding that after this things would change between them and that she would lose strength and that he would get better.

May Come on. Let's go up.

Harry All right.

Laurence They went upstairs and got into bed and went to sleep with their youngest boy between them.

THREE

Laurence The next day, Jimmy was sitting by the fire, the paper close to his eyes. May poured him a cup of tea.

May Your sight's getting worse, Jimmy. Why don't you get glasses?

Jimmy Nah.

May Oh well.

Jimmy I've brought Harry's bike back. I'll have to mend my puncture. I wonder if David have got a patch.

May His puncture kit's out there. You'd better ask him though.

Jimmy Aye.

May You eaten today?

Jimmy Aye, aye.

Laurence Jimmy looked tired, she thought.

May What work you been on?

Jimmy I been working on the Glasgow.

May Oh dear.

Laurence The Glasgow was a coaster which came into Cardiff every two weeks. On alternate weeks it went over to Dublin. It was the most hated boat on the dock. The cargo was always unwieldy and couldn't be moved by crane. It always took a long time to unload and so it was poorly paid. Today it had brought loose timber, none of it lashed.

May Oh dear.

Laurence She gave him his tea. Jimmy put the cup in the grate.

Jimmy I'd better move in with you I think.

May I'd watch it.

Laurence Said May. How they loved each other.

LOVELY EVENING

For Rose

Characters

Harry

Laurence

Jimmy

Neighbour

Marion

Waiter

The play takes place in Cardiff
in the early 1950s

ONE

Harry Lovely evening. I say, lovely evening.

Laurence It was. It was a lovely evening. It had been a lovely day and now it was a lovely evening. And there were children outside playing in the street and there were swallows flying low over the roofs and in the distance the sound of an ice-cream van and in the park they would be playing bowls and baseball. No, they wouldn't be playing baseball. If there was a baseball match my father would have said. But there might be a couple of people playing tennis in the old tennis courts and the swimming baths would still be open and there would certainly be kids on the swings and kids playing in the empty band-stand. And all over the city I dare say there would be people like my father and my uncle getting ready to go out because it was such a lovely evening. Not that the weather really had much to do with why either of them was going out. It was Wednesday and my father went to Benediction on Wednesdays and then to a meeting of one of his sodalities and after that for a pint. My uncle went out every evening whatever the weather was like. Rain, hail or sleet, he still went out. It would take something to keep him in. But still it was a lovely evening and it made the going out easy.

Harry Get cold later, mind, I should think. You going out later, Laurence?

Laurence I certainly was going out.
I don't know, Dad. I might later. I don't know.

Harry You going out I'd wear a jacket. I wouldn't go out in my shirt sleeves.

Laurence I certainly wouldn't go out in my shirtsleeves.

I was going to wear my new gaberdine trousers and my sports coat and a white shirt open over the collar of my jacket.

My father had his foot on the side of a chair and was brushing his shoe. My uncle was peering into the mirror over the fireplace, fastening his collar.

Jimmy Where's my stud? Where's my back stud? You had my back stud, Harry?

Harry I don't know where your stud is. I don't wear unattached collars.

Jimmy Where'd I put that, now? Gor blimey. Seen my stud, Laurence?

Laurence Let's see. Here it is.

It was on the mantelpiece, lying at the foot of the statue of Our Lady of Lourdes. At least he hadn't cut himself shaving.

Jimmy Thank you.

Harry There we are. You want these, Jimmy?

Jimmy Aye. Gimme the soft brush. I don't need polish.

Harry Make sure you put it out there after. Where you going anyway?

Jimmy What you want to know where I'm going?

Laurence Every evening he went out and every evening my father asked him where he was going. Just as my mother had always done. And every evening he didn't say. It was as if they were keeping faith with her by this ritual. She certainly would have asked him where he was going. And he certainly wouldn't have told her.

It was the same with my brothers and me when they were still at home. She'd quiz them. All of us. Me. 'Where you going, Laurence?' she would say. 'Out.' 'Where out?' 'Out.' 'Where?' 'Out, Mam. I'm going out.' She always knew where my father was going and if she didn't he'd tell if asked. But she usually knew where he was going. As we did tonight.

Harry There's Confession tonight, Laurence.

Jimmy Yes.

Laurence I wish I'd been to Confession. Only without having to go. But how could I say, 'I'm sorry for what I've done, but I'm afraid I know I'm going to do it again'? I wished he hadn't brought it up. I wish he'd go out so I could forget about it.

Harry Ttt. Well I'm off. Lock the back door if you're going out. You going out?

Laurence I don't know.

Harry Have you got your key, Jimmy?

Jimmy Aye.

Harry And put the shoe brush out there. Tara. Tara. I won't be late.

Jimmy There we are. I want a raincoat, Laurence?

Laurence No, it's not going to rain.

Jimmy Right. Do you want this?

Laurence Aye. I might. Give it to me.

Jimmy OK. There we are. Tara.

Laurence Tara.

When he had gone I too prepared to go out. First I cleaned my shoes, then I went upstairs to wash and change, and when I came down I checked my hair carefully in the mirror, then took a clean handkerchief from the pile on the window-ledge, locked the back door, got my raincoat and went out.

Woman's Voice All going out tonight, Laurence?

Laurence Aye.

Woman's Voice It's a lovely evening.

Laurence I walked down to Willows Avenue and got the bus into town.

TWO

Marion What have you brought a raincoat for?

Laurence It might rain.

Marion It won't rain.

Laurence Won't it?

Marion Silly.

Laurence Not so silly. I might need it.

Marion What for?

Laurence You never know.

Marion I've only brought a cardigan in case.

Laurence Well, I've only brought a raincoat in case.

We had met in the little park opposite the museum planted to commemorate the Welsh National Eisteddfod which had been held in Cardiff in nineteen-whenever, 1920-something. The garden was pretty in a tight and tidy sort of a way. In the centre was a circle of red granite stones like a miniature Stonehenge, recalling the

Eisteddfod's druidical past. And nearby stood a statue of Lord Ninian Crichton Stuart who fell at the Battle of Loos and who had been Cardiff's M.P. Aristocratic, Scottish, Tory, Catholic. And nearby too, and more appropriate, was a statue of John Cory, coal owner and philanthropist.

Marion What did you want to meet here for? I've never been here before.

Laurence I dunno. A change. Different, more private. You must have been here before.

Marion I haven't.

Laurence You must have walked through it when you've been to the museum.

Marion Not that I remember.

Laurence Do you want to sit down?

Marion No. I want to look first. It's pretty, isn't it? Look at that statue first. What's it say?

Laurence Lord Ninian Edward Crichton Stuart. M.P. for Cardiff, Cowbridge and Llantrisant. Lieutenant-Colonel, Sixth Battalion, Welch Regiment. 15th May 1883. Fell in France at the Battle of Loos fighting bravely for his country, 2nd October 1915.

Marion Ninian. There's a name. Ninian.

Laurence Ninian didn't seem an odd name to me. Ninian. I was in school with an Aelred, an Ambrose and five Michael Collinses.

Marion These must be old, these stones. Here.

Laurence Nah. They're mocky.

Marion They're not. They're real. They're real stones.

Laurence But they're not old.

Marion Why are they in a circle? What are they for? What are they meant to be?

Laurence They're meant to be an ancient place of worship, of sacrifice.

Marion Are they? Oo.

Laurence Yeah. That's where they would have sacrificed virgins at dawn. In there.

Marion Oh no.

Laurence Yeah. They would have. Would you have liked to be sacrificed at dawn?

Marion No, I wouldn't.

Laurence Would you like me to sacrifice you in them stones?

Marion No. Now. There's people.

Laurence You would. You'd love it.

Marion Now I'm warning you.

Laurence What?

Marion You know.

Laurence Know what?

Marion You know.

Laurence No. What?

Marion Stop it.

Laurence What?

Marion Laurence.

Laurence Why won't you let me?

Marion I'm not going to let you do anything here.

Laurence I know. But why won't you ever?

Marion Now don't start all that. You go far enough as it is.

Laurence You'd like it.

Marion Well whether I would or not, you're not going to find out.

Laurence If you liked me you would.

Marion If you liked me you wouldn't ask. And what would you think of me if I did?

Laurence I'd think you were a real woman.

Marion Oh aye. You'd think I was common. That's what you'd think.

Laurence I wouldn't. I wouldn't.

Marion No. I don't think you would. But there we are.

Laurence I'd be careful.

Marion You're not going to get a chance to be careful. Are you going to sulk?

Laurence No.

Marion You are. I'm going if you're going to be like this again.

Laurence I'm sorry. I'm sorry.

Marion Come on. Let's sit down. There have to be limits, Laurence.

Laurence Don't there?

Marion What's that supposed to mean?

Laurence Nothing.

Marion You think I'm stupid.

Laurence I don't. I think you're far from stupid.

Marion You see. You're a pig, you are.

Laurence All right. Calm down. Calm down. I know. I know.

Marion What's the matter with you, eh?

Laurence Nothing.

Marion There is.

Laurence Oh, I'm fed up.

Marion Are you?

Laurence Yeah.

Marion What with? With me?

Laurence Not with you. Don't be silly. Not with you.

Marion What with?

Laurence I don't know. Work. Yeah. I'm fed up with it. I don't want to be clerking for the council. The money's rubbish anyway. I'm packing it in. I am.

Marion Don't be silly. It's a good job. The hours are good.

Laurence Is it? Are they?

Marion What else are you going to do?

Laurence I don't know.

Marion Go to sea?

Laurence Oh. Aye.
You don't like it there, do you?

Marion It's all right. Yes. I do. Yeah.

Laurence Well, I don't. What do you want to do?

Marion Well, let's sit here for a bit now we're here.

Laurence Do you want to go to the pictures?

Marion No, I don't want to go to the pictures. Not on a lovely evening like this, I don't.

Laurence Well, what do you want to do then?

Marion I don't know. What's the hurry? What do you want to do?

Laurence Ah well.

Marion Don't start again.

Laurence Let's go for a drink.

Marion What?

Laurence Yeah. Come on.

Marion No.

Laurence Why not?

Marion I'm not going into a public house.

Laurence Why?

Marion Because I'm not. I wouldn't mind sitting outside somewhere.

Laurence Where?

Marion We could get a bus somewhere.

Laurence Ah. No. What's the difference between having half a shandy sitting outside the Carpenter's Arms on Rummy Hill and having half a shandy in Hallinan's? What's the difference?

Marion All the difference. It's nice out there. It's in the country.

Laurence Rummy Hill the country! Anyway, I don't want to go all the way back out there. We're in town now.

Marion We'll go for a coffee later.

Laurence Great.

Marion My mother wants to know when you're coming to tea again.

Laurence Oh dear. Does she?

Marion Don't be like that.

Laurence Like what?

Marion You know. She likes you.

Laurence Does she? I don't think she does.

Marion How do you make that out? She says you're a nice boy. But she says this is all hole-and-corner and you're not serious.

Laurence And she doesn't think I'm good enough for you.

Marion What makes you say that?

Laurence Of course she didn't think I was good enough for her. Fair dos. She was her mother. What else was she supposed to think? What would my mother have thought of her? Aye. Yeah. Well, she would have liked her. She would have thought she was a nice girl. She would have liked her because she was pretty and sweet and affectionate and no contender. 'Why can't you go out with a nice girl like that?' she would have said. Until you did. It was a matter of principle. She thought my father was a stranger enough in our lives without girls. 'He's going out with some girl,' she would say. How my brother David managed it to the altar, I don't know. Christopher had gone to university and never brought a girl home. Serious. Why did she want to bring serious into it? Why did she want me to go there to tea? I didn't want to go there to tea. All that. I didn't want to take two buses up the Heath. It was like a foreign country. I couldn't manage it. Any of it. The salad cream. The lincrusta. The red-hot pokers. The fourteen-inch television. The chair-back covers. The dining suite. The Festival of Britain curtains in the front room. In the lounge. It was all . . . I couldn't manage it. The china statue of the lady in the long dress holding her skirt out stranding on the window-ledge facing the street. It was too strange. Especially the statue of the lady in the long dress. There were many statues like that in the windows of houses like that. Boys holding bunches of grapes. Coy little girls. And other ladies in long dresses dancing or with their skirts ruffled in the wind, holding Afghan hounds on leads. My mother had a particular dislike for them. She was quite violent in her dislike. I think she saw them as graven images and in retaliation she put a chipped plaster statue of the Sacred Heart in our front-room window like a sign of faith or a statement of content over form. When it came to religious objects, taste was beside the point. And beauty was in short supply in the Catholic Truth Society. But in other matters, had she the cash she would have been for the modern, not the contemporary. And apart from the sparkling windows and the standard of housekeeping, she would have found it all as alien as I did.

Marion Will you?

Laurence Don't go on. Eh? Do you want to go for a walk?

Marion All right. Where shall we go?

Laurence Do you want to go into the castle grounds?

Marion OK.

THREE

Laurence She put her arm in mine and we walked out of the gardens and made our way to the great park of Cardiff Castle, past the Museum and City Hall, past Lord Tredegar on his horse, past Lloyd George brandishing his fist, and past, below us, the Marquess of Bute, Lord Ninian's father, standing in his own little garden. We went through East Gate, past the stables and the tennis courts, past the high walls of the castle gardens, over which we could see the derelict Norman keep on its mound, above the moat which was full of water lilies and beyond that we could see the clock tower, the centrepiece of this last eccentric throw of Victorian Gothic built by Lord Ninian's father who had been, my father said, as rich as any oil sheik and who had ruled over the growth of the city like a prince and whose name was everywhere recorded. And whose family had now retreated from the city and South Wales, realising its assets over the years and finally disposing of the castle and its grounds by way of a gift to the people and retreated to Scotland, declining from sultanate riches into mere wealth. In the freedom of the park she took my hand as if making a claim and a promise. I slipped my finger through hers so as to close the deal, whatever that was. We walked alongside the feeder canal, the black water diverted from the Taff above Black Weir flowing through the park and underground now most of its way, through town to fill the old docks. We stopped by a folly built like a pagoda with a bridge over the water.

Marion I don't like it, do you?

Laurence I don't know. It's all right.

Marion I don't like it.

Laurence I watched her looking at it, in her cotton dress and white sandals.
  I was serious.

Marion Don't.

Laurence Come on.

Marion No. Look. People.

Laurence Please.

Marion Don't, you're hurting me.

Laurence Sorry. Sorry.

Marion I should think so.

Laurence Please.

Marion You're hurting me.

Laurence Am I?

Marion Yes.

Laurence Am I?

Marion Stop it.

Laurence Oh.

Marion Come here.

Laurence She took my hand and led me to the grove of shrubs, rhododendrons, masses of them, masses, all in bloom, all coloured red, in the middle of the park.

Marion They won't last much longer. Look.

Laurence She picked up a bright red petal from the ground.

Marion Here.

Laurence Red.
Please.

Marion No. There are people.

Laurence There aren't.

Marion I can hear them.

Laurence Come, let's go into the trees.

Marion Shall we?

Laurence Yes.

Marion I might ruin my dress.

Laurence Why do you think I brought a raincoat?

FOUR

Marion Am I all right?

Laurence Yes. What do you mean?

Marion Is my skirt marked?

Laurence Turn round.
No, you're fine. I told you I'd need my raincoat.

Marion Where's my compact? Oh. Here it is. Look at you.

Laurence What's the matter? What you laughing at?

Marion You've got lipstick all over your face. Give me your handkerchief.

Laurence No.

Marion Come on.

Laurence Look, you don't want it.

Marion Oo. Sticky.

Laurence I told you. Give it to me. Give me your mirror. Blimey.

Marion Yes.

Laurence Lend me your comb. God, I'm gorgeous.

Marion Give it back.

Laurence Come on then.

Marion Hang on. Do I look all right?

Laurence We walked back through the park near the trees.

Marion You're quiet.

Laurence I'm all right.

Marion Why are you laughing?

Laurence Nothing.

I was thinking of the first time I'd been to Confession after going out with a girl and having impurity to confess. And how I'd gone into the confessional not knowing how to tell my awful sin. 'Pray, father. Give me your blessing for I have sinned,' I said. 'Hello, Laurence. How's your mother?' he replied. I was too shocked to make a break so I stayed and lied by omission, confessing such venial sins that I wondered why he wasn't on to me. I'd never been able to confess anything like it since and I was case-hardened now in the knowledge that I was certainly facing damnation if I didn't rectify matters. What if I dropped dead? Sacrilege was a terrible sin.

We turned left out of the West Gate and went to look at the long wall over the top of which at intervals were stone animals with yellow glass eyes, seeming to swarm over it.

Marion I don't like them.

Laurence I do.

Marion What's that?

Laurence A lynx. It's going to get you.

Marion Don't.

Laurence Look at the hyaena.

Marion No. Come on. Let's go for a coffee.

Laurence We walked back along Castle Street and crossed over to go into the Cadena.

FIVE

Waiter Can I help you, sir?

Laurence Two coffees, please.

Waiter That's two coffees. Anything else?

Laurence Anything else?

Marion No thank you.

Waiter That's two coffees, then.

Laurence Yes.

Marion It's warm in here. It was beginning to get quite chilly.

Laurence What you doing tomorrow?

Marion Gonna wash my hair. You?

Laurence I dunno. Nothing. Shall I see you dinner time?

Marion Yes.

Laurence In the canteen?

Marion I'm bringing sandwiches if it's like today.

Laurence Sandwiches? No.

Marion If it's nice, yes.

Laurence Coming to the Kennard Saturday?

Marion Oh. No, I want to go to the City Hall.

Laurence Oh. Blimey.

Marion Well, it's nicer.

Laurence And it's dearer.

Marion Come on. Yeah?

Laurence All right.

Marion Here we are. Two coffees.

Laurence Thank you.

Marion All right?

Laurence Yes. Thank you.

Marion I could do with this.

Laurence Me and all.

Marion Listen, Laurence. What am I going to tell my mother?

Laurence Oh. Don't.

Marion Why won't you?

Laurence I will. I will.

Marion When though?

Laurence Oh, come on. Leave it for tonight. OK? Drink your coffee.

Marion You're selfish, you are. You are. You're selfish.

Laurence Drink your coffee.

We drank our coffee and when we had finished, I asked for the bill.

Waiter Thank you, sir.

Marion Let me pay for mine.

Laurence No. Don't be daft. What shall I leave for the tip?

Marion I don't know.

Laurence That'll have to do. Come on.

We walked out and along Castle Street to Duke Street, and across to the bus stops outside Marments.

Marion I must put my cardigan on. It's quite cold.

Laurence Yeah.

Marion And look how dark it's got. Here's your bus.

Laurence No. I'll wait with you.

Marion You don't have to.

Laurence Yes. What you doing Sunday?

Marion I don't know. Why?

Laurence I just wanted to know.

Marion Do you want to go somewhere?

Laurence No. I just wanted to know.

Marion Why you being so mysterious?

Laurence I'm not.

Marion You are.

Laurence Come on. Here's your trolley.

Marion Tell me.

Laurence Come on. Get on.

Marion Gimme a kiss then.

Laurence Come on. See you tomorrow.

Marion Goodnight.

SIX

Laurence It was quite dark when I got home. The street was empty. The sounds of the evening had gone. The children long since called in.

Woman's Voice Chilly now, Laurence.

Laurence Yes.

Woman's Voice Your father's in.

Laurence Goodnight.
I let myself in through the front door.
Aye. Aye.

Harry Is that you, son?

Laurence Yes. Jimmy not in?

Harry He won't be long now, I know him.

Laurence I went to the mirror to check if there was any lipstick on my collar. There wasn't any lipstick on my collar. Why was I checking for lipstick which I knew wasn't there? It's not as if my father would notice, or say if he did. I felt for my handkerchief in my pocket. Why was I doing this? Why was I feeling guilty about feeling guilty? Pray, father, give me your blessing and get off my back. There are other things to worry about without this worrying me. Churchill is Prime Minister. People are going to the Museum to look at the Queen's Coronation dress. My uncle is still singing the praises of Eamonn de Valera. My father listens to *Down Your Way*. The BBC is run by people who think the druids went to chapel. My girlfriend likes Dickie Valentine and I hate my job. And my mother's dead. And we can't get over it and she's not here to say, 'What's on your handkerchief? Ttt. I don't know. You be careful.' I am careful. That's all I am is careful. And I can't make retribution and I can't wear this shirt again, can I?

Harry What say?

Laurence What do you think?

Harry What, son?

Laurence Will I get away with wearing this shirt in the morning?

Harry Aye. Course you will.

Laurence No. I'd better iron a clean one.

Harry Aye. I saw David.

Laurence What was he doing over here?

Harry She was down her mother's.

Laurence He all right?

Harry He looks thin. He's working too hard. He worked a doubler. He asked if we'd heard from Christopher.

Laurence What you say?

Harry I said we'd had a card.

Laurence Yeah. A month ago. It's cold in here. Do you want me to put a match to the fire?

Harry No. I only just laid it for the morning.

Laurence We mightn't need it in the morning.

Harry No, leave it. Aye, aye. Here he is.

Jimmy Aye. Aye.

Harry You're late. Where you been till this time?

Jimmy What do you want to know where I've been?

Laurence And so it went again. But my father wasn't the skilled interrogator that my mother had been. Not that she would have got anything out of him. But the questioning would have been more thorough.

Do you want a cup of tea?

Harry I won't have one. He'll have one though.

Laurence Will you?

Jimmy What?

Laurence Will you have a cup of tea, unc?

Jimmy Aye. I don't mind, if you're making one.

Laurence I'd better do the sandwiches.

Harry I'll do mine.

Laurence What do you want?

Harry What have you got?

Laurence Cheese, cooked ham, tomatoes. The usual wide selection.

Harry I'll have ham, Laurence.

Laurence What'll you have, unc?

Harry He'll have what you give him.

Laurence I'll put the kettle on.

Harry Aye, Laurence. Put some pickle on mine.

Laurence I made their sandwiches. Ham for one, cheese for the other. And when I had finished I wrapped them in greaseproof paper and put them in paper bags and stowed them in their working jackets hanging on the back door. Then I made the tea.
Here you are.

Jimmy Thank you, Laurence.

Laurence You sure?

Harry Quite sure, son? Thank you.

Laurence What are you doing Sunday?

Harry What do you mean?

Laurence You going out Sunday afternoon?

Harry No. No. Why?

Laurence Nothing. I might ask someone over.

Harry I could go out.

Laurence No. No. I didn't mean that. I mean is it all right?

Harry What do you mean? Of course it's all right. He'll be in, mind.

Laurence That's all right.

Jimmy What's that?

Harry He's got a visitor coming Sunday.

Jimmy Oh aye.

Laurence You going to be in?

Jimmy I dunno.

Harry Of course he's going to be in.

Laurence What would she make of this shabby room? Of them? Of me and them? What would we have for tea? Would I get salad cream?

Harry Well, I'm off. You want the clock, Jimmy?

Jimmy Aye.

Harry Don't forget to wind it.

Jimmy I won't forget. Blimey.

Harry Goodnight. God bless.

Laurence Goodnight. I'd better iron my shirt.

Jimmy This time?

Laurence Aye.

Jimmy So you got a friend coming Sunday, then?

Laurence Aye.

Jimmy Do you want us to look tidy?

Laurence No. You're all right.

Jimmy Right then, I'm off. I'd better wash this.

Laurence Leave it. I'll wash it now.

Jimmy Where's the clock?

Laurence Will you call me before you get out?

Jimmy Aye. Goodnight.

Laurence Goonight.

Jimmy It was a lovely day.

Laurence Aye.

Jimmy I wonder what it will be like tomorrow?

Laurence Aye. Goodnight.

He went up to bed. I plugged the iron in. I took his cup and went into the kitchen and when I had washed it I put it away and emptied the teapot and made things ready for the morning. I went back into the living room and took a shirt from the pile of clean laundry on the window ledge and began to iron it. Yeah. It was a lovely day and it had been a lovely evening. Hadn't it?